The Art Museums of New England

The Art Museums of New England

Massachusetts

S. Lane Faison, Jr.

David R. Godine · Publisher · Boston

This edition first published in 1982 by
David R. Godine, Publisher, Inc.
306 Dartmouth Street
Boston, Massachusetts 02116

Library of Congress Cataloging in Publication Data
Faison, Samson Lane, 1907-
    The art museums of New England.

    (Godine guides ; 3)
    First ed. (1958) published under title: A guide to the art museums of New
England.
    Includes index.
    1. Art museums—New England—Guide-books.
2. Art—New England—Guide-books. I. Title.
N510.5.N4F2 1982   708.14   80-83952
ISBN 0-87923-372-9
ISBN 0-87923-373-7 (pbk.)

This is a revised and expanded version of Mr. Faison's *Guide to the Art
Museums of New England*, published in 1958 by Harcourt, Brace & Co.

Manufactured in the United States of America

Gratefully dedicated to the directors and staff members of the institutions here surveyed, and to hospitable friends along the road

Contents

How to Use This Book

The survey of museum collections is arranged south to north by states, Connecticut to Maine, and alphabetically by towns within each state. It comes in two forms: a complete hardcover volume that covers all six states and three individual softcover volumes, one for Connecticut and Rhode Island, the second for Massachusetts, and the third for New Hampshire, Vermont, and Maine. Each of the four volumes has an index. The complete hardcover volume is paged consecutively; the separate paperback volumes are paged consecutively as the complete volume is paged: Connecticut and Rhode Island from page 1 to page 111, Massachusetts from page 113 to page 358, and the northern three states from page 359 to page 463.

The map that introduces each state is dotted to indicate proper locations. Each location refers to an adjacent identification list in alphabetical order, which will allow you to turn to the appropriate entry in the main text. In planning a tour these maps should be helpful.

A major feature of the book is a network of cross references to examples in other museums related to the work under discussion. Each reference is therefore followed by a number in parentheses, indicating first the state where the item appears, then the item number. For example, the Degas pastel at the Hill-Stead Museum in Farmington, Conn. (CT 3) is placed in a larger critical and historical context by reference to other works of Degas in the museums of Boston (MA 81), Northampton (MA 179), and Providence (RI 18).

Rather than appending a bibliography, which in a book of this kind would be either too long or much too short to be useful, I have included occasional references to books and articles in the text itself. These are for the general, but curious, reader. The scholar will understand their introductory purpose, and pass on.

Preface

This work surveys, critically and historically, some 550 works of art selected from the *permanent* collections of over one hundred art museums, historical societies, and libraries open to the public in the six New England states.

While the text is directed to the general reader, I have reason to believe that the scholar, too, will be surprised to learn what artistic riches exist in out-of-the-way places. Over twenty years ago, when I first undertook such a survey, I had little idea that sixty institutions would fall within its scope. Since then, many of those originally covered have doubled in size, twenty-four new ones have been established, and eighteen others have subsequently developed collections worthy of inclusion or were originally omitted through oversight.

My earlier book, published in 1958 by Harcourt, Brace and Company under the title *A Guide to the Art Museums of New England*, went out of print within six years. So it has remained, but in the meantime I have filed away corrections and additions in the hope that an updated version would someday be forthcoming. This happy event took place when David Godine, in search of an author for such a book, discovered mine in limbo. He had recently published *New England Gardens Open to the Public*, by Rolce Redard Payne, as the second in a projected series of all–New England handbooks (the first, *The Boston Basin Bicycle Book*, was published in 1975). The present book now becomes the third; it is to be followed by a comparable volume, *A Guide to Historic Houses of New England Open to the Public*, by Margaret Supplee Smith and R. Jackson Smith.

The word "guide" has been eliminated in the new title because it suggests a purely descriptive compilation à la Baedeker, whereas I propose an excursion into art criticism and art history based on the vast treasure available to the public in New England. Some of the present text repeats selections and comments in the older one. While masterpieces of art are not quite so dependable as the heavenly bodies, and in the interim connoisseurship has reduced the magnitude of a few of them, for the most part the original text has been greatly expanded rather than cut. Everywhere it has been corrected, refined, or reoriented as the case seemed to demand.

Twenty-odd years ago I did not suspect that even if the Boston Museum of Fine Arts were eliminated, the whole range of world art—from antiquity to the present, and from Western art to Far Eastern, Pre-Columbian, and so-called primitive art—would still be abundantly represented in fine original examples in New England's museums. Today, if we leave out of account the world's great metropolitan centers, it is fair to say that no region of comparable size anywhere can boast such a concentration of art museums as New England. Yet the area of the six New England states is about the size of Oklahoma and less than a third of that of France, and under one-sixth of France's size if we subtract the museumless expanses of hinterland Maine. Even more extraordinary is the concentration in Massachusetts alone—an area just half the size of Denmark. Almost half the museums and nearly three-fifths of the works of art surveyed here are in the Bay State.

Arranged south to north state by state, this is not a book to be read in the usual sequence. The informed student of art will find what is wanted by consulting the table of contents or the index; these will lead to quick answers as to what is to be seen in any given institution, or which of them have significant examples (cited in these pages) of the work of a given artist or of types of art, such as African, Chinese, or Pre-Columbian. The general reader who wishes to get an overview of the development of art history might well start with the section on the Boston Museum of Fine Arts. This provides a kind of miniature survey of Western art, and it contains the book's most significant coverage of Far Eastern art. Less comprehensive surveys will be found in the sections on other leading museums. The fullest discussion of primitive art is contained in the entry on the Peabody Museum at Harvard University.

In a selective project of this sort, injustices inevitably occur. For omissions and misplaced emphases I can only ask the reader's indulgence. Some explanation, however, is necessary for the treatment of historical societies and libraries. As the number of these in New England is very large, it was possible to include only those that own works of art of consequence, or more modest ones that interestingly supplement the discussion of works commented on elsewhere. The exclusion of such an institution is in no way to be taken as a judgment of its intrinsic eminence.

The total of some 550 works illustrated and discussed is a compromise between the claims of broad coverage and portable size. *Portable*: a book to be carried with you into the museum and, it is hoped, read in the presence of the original works of art. *Coverage*: this or any other total could easily have been devoted to the Boston Museum of Fine Arts alone. While it was obvious from the start that B M F A should receive more emphasis than any other, it became equally obvious that to allow the total for all the museums of Boston and Cambridge to exceed a quarter of the selections for the whole book would mean eliminating many small museums elsewhere. (As it has worked out, Boston and Cambridge are represented by 128 works, or about 23 percent of the whole.) Smaller places contain works that are worth a pilgrimage; and the experience of traveling to see a fine object becomes part of the experience the object itself can provide. I do not mean that you will come upon a Chartres Cathedral or an Arena Chapel in rural New England, but who could wish that these shrines were in Paris or Florence? In somewhat the same way a watercolor, a precious ivory, or a superb impression of a Rembrandt etching, suddenly come upon in a small museum, or a modest painting by a hitherto unfamiliar artist, can have a greater effect than if the same work were seen—or very possibly missed —in a major institution.

The reader will discover, with a few exceptions in the case of prints, that furniture, photographs, and prints are not discussed in these pages.

The same holds true, again with a few exceptions, for the decorative arts in general. This policy was dictated by limitations of space and by the theory that all these arts are "multiples," in the broad sense that identical or nearly identical examples are usually to be found in several institutions. Where it is appropriate, however, reference is made to important collections of decorative arts, furniture, photographs, and prints.

Visitors are warned not to expect that my selections (often made from works in storage) will always be on display, museum by museum, to welcome them. Shortage of exhibition space often dictates a policy of rotation, and temporary shows can mean that whole galleries have to be cleared and their contents stored. Loans to other museums can account for other absentees, yet there is an extra dividend of pleasure in finding a work in unexpected surroundings and new contexts.

Within the limits defined above, each entry attempts a selection of what is outstanding in the museum under discussion. On many occasions you will naturally question why certain works were not included. There are many answers, and I will leave to your judgment which of the following are appropriate: (1) limitations of space in the book; (2) discussion of a generally similar work in some other museum; (3) too many works by the same artist to warrant inclusion of yet another one; (4) poor condition of the work in question; (5) attribution of the work to the given artist doubtful; or, finally, (6) my opinion of it less enthusiastic than yours.

Two pairs of terms frequently appearing in these pages seem to require explanation. By *classical*, I mean pertaining to the art of Greece and Rome. By *classic*, I mean characterized by such restraint, high idealism, and formal discipline as is found in Greek art of the fifth century B.C., in Chinese art of the T'ang dynasty, in Gothic sculpture of the thirteenth century, in the painting of Raphael and Titian and Poussin, and in the nineteenth-century painting of Corot, Cézanne (especially in the 1880s), and Seurat. I hope I have used these terms consistently.

The second pair of terms is *size* and *scale*. By *size*, I mean physical dimensions. By *scale*, I mean the size that the work *seems to suggest*, irrespective of its actual measurements. In this connection, Viollet-le-Duc pointed out in his *Dictionnaire Raisonné de l'Architecture* that although Notre Dame in Paris is approximately the same height as the Arc de Triomphe, the former is scaled to human beings and does not dwarf the neighboring houses; whereas the latter—scaled, we might say, to Napoleon's ambition—is restrained by no such modesty. Contrariwise, a self-portrait in the Louvre by the fifteenth-century French painter Jean Fouquet, painted in gold enamel on a black ground, seems to expand to life size even though this little roundel measures only 3 inches in diameter. It was once attached to the frame of a small two-paneled altarpiece.

Before acknowledging my indebtedness to many kindly persons, I am happy to add a concluding word about the present state of admission fees to art museums in New England and elsewhere in the United States. Many make no charge whatever. When fees are imposed they are modest indeed as compared with the cost of concert or theater tickets, or with golf or ski-tow charges. Free or not, museums often provide a prominently displayed opportunity for the visitor to make a contribution. The need for such support is both real and pressing.

In each of the institutions discussed in these pages, staff members have been generous in providing information, advising me in my choice of works, and in supplying photographs. Many friends along the road have housed and entertained my wife and me, and made our more than four thousand miles of New England travel the more enjoyable. A list of all these benevolent people would inevitably be so long as to defeat its purpose. The book itself is therefore dedicated to them *en masse*. In so doing we hope they will understand that no such screen of collective anonymity clouds our grateful memories of kindnesses received.

Vivian Patterson, a graduate student in the Williams College / Clark Art Institute Master of Arts Program in the History of Art, has been enormously helpful as my research assistant and amanuensis-without-portfolio. The sections on the two museums in Williamstown are in large part her work.

It has been a continuing delight to work with David Godine, my publisher, and William B. Goodman, his editorial director. Their enthusiastic collaboration in my task is warmly appreciated.

The original text and thereby the present one owe much to the cultivated mind and eye of my friend, the late Professor John McAndrew, a former director of the Wellesley College Museum. For scholarly assistance in Rhode Island, I am indebted to my friend Winslow Ames, a distinguished collector and art historian. I must especially thank Cornelius Vermeule, Curator of Classical Art at the Boston Museum of Fine Arts, for extensive and sustained support, not only within and beyond the confines of the museum itself, but also beyond his professional field.

Colleagues in the Williams College Department of Art have given generously of their time and expert knowledge and have saved me many a slip. If flaws remain despite all the assistance outlined above, or if my critical estimates sometimes seem eccentric, the *culpa* is *mea*.

Finally, there is the problem of thanking my wife adequately for her participation in this venture. In truth she is all but the joint author of this book. It is *not* true that without her it would have been written sooner—as occasional dedications have slyly suggested.

S. Lane Faison, Jr.
Director Emeritus
Williams College Museum of Art

Williamstown, Mass.
October 15, 1981

Massachusetts

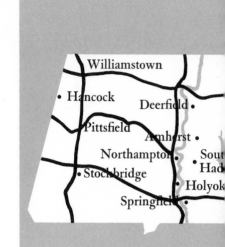

Massachusetts

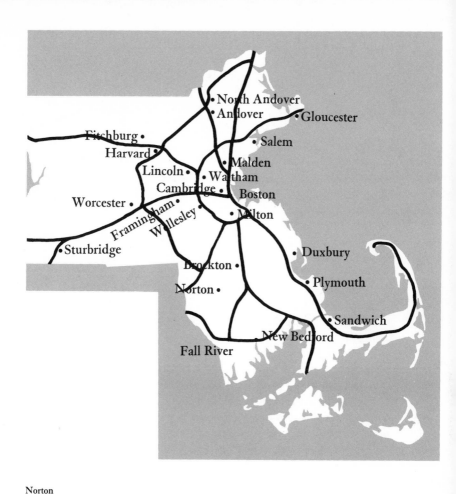

Mead Art Building, Amherst College

Location: Routes 9 and 116
Hours: Mon.-Sat. 9-5, Sun. 11:30-5; closed August and summer weekends
Admission: Free. Ⓗ

The building was erected in 1949 from funds bequeathed by William R. Mead, an alumnus and member of the firm of McKim, Mead & White. Its symmetrical plan is in the tradition of that great Beaux-Arts triumvirate. Interior rearrangements have increased the exhibition space, which was originally concentrated in the main entrance gallery so that students on their way to art courses would pass through it. This plan was linked to a policy of frequent rotation of the exhibits, and since the collection has grown rapidly through the years a great proportion of it is stored in well-appointed areas on two lower floors. For works not on view, apply to members of the staff.

A special gallery contains Assyrian reliefs from the palace of Ashurnazirpal at Nineveh (ninth century B.C.). Approximately the size and shape of one of the smaller rooms of the palace, it has been decorated to suggest the opulence of that ancient court. These reliefs and the similar ones at Bowdoin, Dartmouth, Middlebury, and Williams colleges, at the University of Vermont, and at Yale were presented in the 1850s by alumni of the respective institutions who were missionaries in the Middle East. The stones were cut for shipment across the desert by camelback, and across the seas by sailing vessel. Amherst owns six of these reliefs. One of the largest, nearly 8 feet high, represents King Ashurnazirpal himself. A smaller one depicts a *Winged Bird-Headed Deity*[1] who fertilizes the sacred date palm (highly stylized) with a pinecone dipped in pollen from a square pail. The cuneiform inscriptions cut across the surface of the larger reliefs are repetitious in their celebration of the king's exploits. Close study of the reliefs themselves will reveal differences of workmanship—not surprising in view of the immense number of such slabs that once decorated the palace. The British Museum has the greatest number of them, but no less than seventy-three are in the United States. For further information, see the excellent brochure published by Dartmouth College, which, like Amherst, owns six examples (J. B. Stearns and D. P. Hansen, *The Assyrian Reliefs at Dartmouth*; Hanover: Dartmouth, 1953).

A second permanent installation in the Mead Art Building is the banqueting hall from Rotherwas House (1611), an outstanding example of Elizabethan decoration. It is fully paneled in walnut, and its richly polychromèd oak mantelpiece shows Virtues supporting the crest of the original owner, Roger Bodenham of Herefordshire. This Baroque accent gives the hall a Jacobean flavor, but Elizabethan and Jacobean styles merged so thoroughly that a composite term, "Jacobethan," is gaining acceptance. Normally used as a student reading room, on special occasions this hall is furnished with pieces from the college's collection, supplementing the wall cupboards and chests that are permanent fixtures of the room. The molded plaster ceiling is, of course, a modern reproduction, but the chandelier is a fine example from the period.

European and American furniture at Amherst, especially of the eighteenth century, can be termed, without exaggeration, magnificent. The collection is also rich in porcelains, silver, and textiles, and in small bronzes. An array of miniatures features work by Edward G. Malbone (1777–1807), the leading American practitioner in this field. It also includes the only known portrait of Patrick Henry. In the Far Eastern section, Chinese art and Moghul painting are strongly represented, as are drawings and prints, including Japanese color woodblock impressions. The example of Rembrandt's smaller etching of *Christ Preaching* is rightly prized.

Early on, Amherst received many gifts of ancient classical art, and later acquisitions have developed the collection into one of considerable importance. In the fall of 1979 a catalogue was published, including special essays on the three objects we are about to discuss. A marble *Cycladic Figure* from Neolithic times yields to the larger one at Boston (MA 56) in size, but at a height of nearly 2 feet it nevertheless ranks as the largest known example of its particular kind. Even in this distant era the individuality of the artist asserted itself. The Boston example, by comparison, is sveltely elongated with the arms tightly crossed against the lower thorax; the Amherst one is squatter in proportion, its stubby arms barely meeting at the front, the hips much more swollen. A date of c. 2700 B.C. is suggested.

A small bronze handle from an *oenochoe* (wine pitcher) ornamented with a fierce Gorgon's head is a great rarity in Archaic Greek art, especially because this monster sprouts horns. It comes from Magna Graecia, the Greek colony in south Italy. Its beautiful green patina is, of course, the work of ages in an underground deposit.

Most impressive of all is an *Attic Grave Stele*[2] in Pentelic marble 4 feet high, dating from about 340 B.C. In his article on this fine piece,

Cornelius Vermeule hails it as a precious relic from Athens "in the twilight years of the city's glory." The invasions of Philip of Macedon were soon to come. The relief represents a large amphora (for the shape compare M A 288), but with greatly elongated neck and handles of the type known as *loutrophoros-amphora*, used on ceremonial occasions to memorialize young men in their prime. (A differently shaped vessel was used for young women.) Above this vase is a floral offering flanked by two "tear bottles." Expertly carved in very low relief on the body of the amphora are four mourning figures. The stele presumably stood in the family "plot" of a cemetery.

The Amherst collection of Greek ceramic vases is noteworthy for its range and its quality.

Medieval art includes a sixth-century pavement mosaic from Syria, depicting animals and birds; Coptic textile fragments; and a fragment of a sixth-century sarcophagus. A crude but strong echo of a Roman Corinthian capital, from the ninth-century Rhineland, foreshadowing the achievement of the great twelfth-century Romanesque sculptors, is seen here in an example hardly surpassed by any in the United States today. This limestone *Double Capital*,[3] 15 inches high, comes from the Toulouse area in southwestern France. Comparable ones are in the Toulouse Museum. Note the refinement of the carving of the winged birds, joined at the head (replacing, as it were, the Corinthian rosette in this position). The abacus has a decorative meander of acanthus leaves (flattened reminders, only, of their once luxuriant growth on Roman examples). Monastic cloister arcades supported on paired columns, of which there are many examples, required such capitals as this. The theme of interlaced birds and animals derives from the arts of the barbarian invaders (echoed in the Merovingian buckle at Worcester, M A 292), and ultimately from the ancient art of China.

Purchase in 1941, at the important Brummer sale, of a life-size Catalonian fresco of *St. Sylvester*,[4] from the Cathedral of La Seo de Virge, was a major addition in the Gothic field. Its thirteenth-century date is indeed Gothic, but conservative Spain continued to maintain its Byzantine and Romanesque traditions, as may be seen in the rigid

3

4

frontality, the flattened and angular hand, and the staring eyes. Comparison with Boston's great twelfth-century apse (MA 61), also from Catalonia, will show how little of the style of the thirteenth-century French Gothic cathedrals penetrated south of the Pyrenees. This remarkable fresco is yet another illustration of the statement of Henri Focillon that the development of art is not always in chronological order.

The gift in 1961 of twelve Italian Renaissance paintings filled an important gap in the museum's coverage of Western art. Of these *The Madonna and Child with St. Ambrose*, by the Bergamask-Venetian Girolamo da Santa Croce, is perhaps the finest. An earlier gift from Professor Charles H. Morgan, former director of the museum, a *Holy Family* by the early sixteenth-century Florentine Domenico Puligo, is a good example of Raphaelesque art just beginning to turn toward Mannerism. Puligo was a close follower of Andrea del Sarto.

Baroque painting is superlatively represented by *Charity*,[5] an oil sketch by Peter Paul Rubens (1577–1640). Freely brushed on a wood panel 14 inches high, it is in the master's developed late style, about a year or two after his design for the Whitehall ceiling in London (CT 52). The astonishing degree of Rubens's transformation of High Renaissance symmetry, pyramidal composition, and linear clarity can be quickly measured by comparison with the Puligo *Holy Family* just mentioned. The sketch was made for an additional tapestry in a celebrated series he had designed for the royal court at Madrid in 1625–28. The series represented the Triumph of the Church and the Eucharist.

Indications of the impact of Rubens and of Bernini, his counterpart in seventeenth-century sculpture, can be seen in a marvelous little gilt-bronze *Seated Hercules*, 6 inches high and probably by a French artist. As in the contrast between Rubens and Domenico Puligo, its Baroque fluidity can be set against the elegant frontality and grace of a small gilt-bronze *Crucifix*, from the atelier of France's major sixteenth-century sculptor, Jean Goujon.

To facilitate his enormous output, Rubens employed a small army of students and assistants, some of whom, like Anthony Van Dyck, went on to major careers of their own. He also employed collaborators of established reputation to whom he could entrust the execution of landscape backgrounds, floral elements, still lifes, and the like. One of these

5

was his contemporary Frans Snyders (1579–1657), the showiest exponent of still life and animal painting of the whole Baroque era. Amherst's acquisition of a *Still Life*,[6] oil on panel measuring 55½ by 78½ inches, brought to America an outstanding example of Snyders's specialty. Glowing in vibrant color, its forms crisscrossed in serpentine profusion and energized by the figure at the right and by the hounds at the base, it affords a release of tensions by a view of the sky through a not quite absolutely geometric window grille. Observe this window carefully. An extra small diagonal is surely there to complete the all-important thrust of the dead peacock. Long before current inflation, the flaming red crustacean at the right was already known as "the fifty-dollar lobster." Of special local appeal is the fact that the picture came from the collection of the first Earl Amherst.

In his book *The Art Collection of Amherst College*, published in 1972 on the occasion of the college's sesquicentennial anniversary, Charles H. Morgan lists the extraordinary heirlooms of the Amherst family that the college has acquired: letters, documents, and maps relating to the French and Indian Wars, a Worcester dessert service of 123 pieces (early nineteenth century, belonging to the first earl, who also owned the great Snyders *Still Life*), a handsome tureen, and no fewer than twelve family portraits, including those of Sir Jeffery himself by Reynolds and Gainsborough. Subsequently a third, by Blackburn (see ME 11), was added by gift. Morgan's statement that "there is no comparable collection of English family treasures in the United States" appears to be no exaggeration.

Although the metric rhythm of "Jeffery, Lord Amherst" would be ruinous if applied to the first line of the college's great song, that in fact was his correct title—as were Jeffery, Baron Amherst, and Sir Jeffery Amherst, and General Jeffery Amherst. He lived from 1717 to 1797, and not the least of his achievements was to become the eponym of a Massachusetts town and a Massachusetts college. The first earl was his nephew; *our* Jeffery had refused that title.

The fine Blackburn and Gainsborough portraits, painted in 1760 and c. 1785 respectively, are not housed in the museum (and it will probably be difficult to see them), but the version painted in 1765 by Sir Joshua Reynolds (1723–92)[7] not only is one of the museum's

6

7

major treasures, but must rank as one of Reynolds's masterpieces. No
other example in New England, at least, comes close to it in subtlety of
color and expressive content. At the generous size of 49 by 24 inches,
it shows the brilliant general in full armor at the age of forty-eight after
his many victories over the French in North America (Louisburg, 1758;
Ticonderoga, 1759; Montreal, 1760). He was governor of Virginia
from 1759 to 1768. The portrait itself became famous through en-
gravings, but these give no idea of the beauty and ease of the brushwork, nor of the glinting silver-grays of the armor, the strange pallor
of the face, and, most memorable of all, the lavenderish pink of the
wide sash. The insigne of the Knight of Bath gave Reynolds another
opportunity to indulge his love of painting for painting's sake—something that is less apparent when he browned up his palette in emulation
of Old Master works darkened by time.

Amherst has other important British portraits, including one of *Vice
Admiral John Amherst*, a rare early work by the landscapist Richard
Wilson, painted in 1749; but we pass on to a dashing oil sketch of
Charles Baring Wall[8] by Sir Thomas Lawrence (1769–1830), third
president of the Royal Academy and the most fashionable European
artist of the early nineteenth century. This is a study for a family
portrait in one of the great English residences. As in Yale's portrait of
Admiral Sir John Markham (CT 56), Lawrence dazzles us with textures
sparkling as they catch the light. The rapidly brushed passages in black
and white beneath the youth's chin imply an Old World confidence and
ease altogether foreign to the plain and hard-won competence of American Colonial painting.

Most of Amherst's important collection of American portraits came
as the gift of Herbert L. Pratt, donor of the Rotherwas banqueting hall.
While those of George Washington by Charles Willson Peale and his
son Rembrandt, and the Blackstone pair by Copley, are standard fare,
the *Portrait of James Peale*[9] painted in 1789 by his brother Charles
Willson Peale (1741–1827) has the unfussy observant look of Copley
at his best, as in Bowdoin's *Thomas Flucker* (ME 12). In the presence
of qualities like these one can hardly complain at the lack of Gilbert
Stuart's brilliant, but acquired, European stylishness, or of Sir Thomas
Lawrence's indigenous flair.

8

9

An excellent coverage of nineteenth-century American landscape painting begins with a splendid example by Asher Durand (1796–1886), *In the Woods*. Durand was a pioneer in what came to be known as the Hudson River School. Its landscapes were approved by William Cullen Bryant and even apostrophized in his poetry. But the great prize here is a pair—we might almost say a diptych—by Thomas Cole (1801–48), English-born but entirely American as to career. *Past*[10] and *Present*[11] were painted in 1838. We have discussed an Italian extravaganza of Cole's at Hartford (CT 26), but in *Past* and *Present* he introduces the idea of a time sequence already initiated in a more ambitious series, *The Course of Empire*, a quartet now in the New York Historical Society. Cole, Bryant, and Durand maintained a close friendship. At Cole's death, Bryant read a long eulogy and Durand painted his most famous picture, *Kindred Spirits* (New York Public Library), showing Cole and Bryant on Table Rock, overhanging a gorge in the Catskills.

In his writings about American scenery, Cole expressed the feeling that it lacked "historical and legendary associations," and that it was "not so much of the past as of the present and future." Thus, in the Amherst pictures, he turned to the Romantic appeal of the Middle Ages. *Past* evokes the pageantry of a medieval tournament before the walls of a great castle; but *Present* shows the same castle as a glamorous ruin in the poetry of a fading light. Amherst also owns oil sketches for both pictures.

For study of the work of George Bellows (1882–1925) Amherst can offer his papers (in the college library), a large selection of his drawings and prints, and a bewitching portrait of his daughter, *Anne in Black Velvet*,[12] painted in 1917. The subject was a favorite one for him; a portrait of her four years later, in a purple wrap, is at Andover.

10

11

Bellows waxed melodramatic in prizefights and street scenes, but in the portraits of his family he eschewed all such protestations. If his observation is less searching than that of a Copley or an Eakins, it is in the same honest vein. The color is wonderfully fresh, especially here in its contrast with a black that glistens like Velázquez's. Further discussion of Bellows is included in the sections on Rockland (ME 32), Duxbury (MA 150), and Springfield (MA 221).

Nineteenth-century sculpture at Amherst includes bronzes by Barye (a fine *Jaguar*), Saint-Gaudens (small replica of the Springfield *Puritan* and the tondo *Portrait of R. L. Stevenson*); genre plaster groups by John Rogers; and Rodin's early bronze head, *Man with a Broken Nose*. Post-1900 sculpture is on the conservative side, with bronzes by Kolbe and Despiau lingering in the memory. But a truly modern note is struck by *Stringed Figure*,[13] in gold-patinated bronze by Henry Moore (born 1898). It is in his most abstract period, restricted to the years 1937-39. Reminiscing a quarter-century later about his "string sculptures," Moore recalled a visit to the Science Museum in London's South Kensington, where he was enthralled by mathematical models with strings attached "to show what the form between would be." So he decided to make some—as it turned out, many. "They were fun," he discovered, "but too much in the nature of experiments to be really satisfactory. That's a different thing from expressing some deep human experience one might have had. When the war came I gave up this type of thing. Others, like Gabo and Barbara Hepworth, have gone on doing it. It becomes a matter of ingenuity rather than a fundamental human experience" (Philip James, editor, *Henry Moore on Sculpture*; London: Macdonald, 1966).

Among Moore's works of this kind, the Amherst piece is exceptional in retaining much of the master's profundity. Reclining in its boat-shaped container, the "figure" is partially defined by the tautly stretched strings, which indeed help to show "what the form between would be." But the main purpose of their startling introduction into sculpture is to create tension and energize the heavily static forms beneath. Roughened surfaces suggest weathering, as if this object had descended from a timeless past. While it lacks the grand conception of Yale's *Draped Seated*

13

12

Woman of 1959 (CT 69), even at its modest size it obliquely suggests that conception.

Not everyone will agree with Moore that Gabo and Barbara Hepworth (born 1903) were merely ingenious in their string sculptures. One of Hepworth's studies for such a piece, executed in oil and pencil on a gesso board, can be seen at Amherst. Cleanly designed and light as air, it has a poetry of its own.

University Gallery,
University of Massachusetts

Location: Route 116, north of the town
Hours: Tues.-Fri. 11-4:30, Sat.-Sun. 1:30-4:30; closed Mon., holidays, and during academic recesses
Admission: Free. Ⓗ

The gallery forms part of the impressive Fine Arts Center of the performing arts. Active in temporary exhibitions of very recent American arts, the gallery has developed an extensive permanent collection in this field of works of art on paper: drawings, prints, and photographs. It also owns one of Joseph Cornell's magical boxes.

Addison Gallery of American Art, Phillips Academy

Location: On Route 28
Hours: Tues.-Sat. 10-5, Sun. 2:30-5; closed Mon. and holidays
Admission: Free. Ⓗ by arrangement

Housed in a dignified building of 1931 with a highly imaginative new wing by Benjamin Thompson, a collection that includes the very finest paintings of Homer, Eakins, Inness, and Hopper makes the Addison Gallery one of the leading museums of American art in New England. The whole development of American painting from the eighteenth century to the present, and to a lesser degree that of sculpture and the decorative arts, can be studied here in superb examples. The collections of drawings (including many cartoons), prints, and photographs are extensive, as are those of silver, pewter, glass, and furniture. A series of ship models illustrates American maritime history in the era of sail.

Andover maintains an active program of temporary exhibitions, including student work, and it has an enviable reputation for developing shows of an educational nature. During the 1970s the gallery was the center of a foundation-supported program of studies in art as therapy.

Because of our extensive coverage of Colonial and Early Republican art in other museums, selections here are limited to the nineteenth and twentieth centuries; but the visitor will not be disappointed in the representation of the distinguished tradition that gave later American art its momentum and confidence.

I am happy to seize the advantage whenever it presents itself to bring home the point that art is not restricted to painting, nor to what is glibly called fine arts. Some "fine" art is very bad indeed; and humble items often surpass it in quality. Avoiding invidious comparisons, I invite the visitor to inspect a large *Firehouse Sign* from Portsmouth, N.H.[14] The designer is unknown, as is the carver, who may have been the same person. I present this object as good sculpture, in somewhat the same spirit as one might call a Greek vase sculpture on the basis of its shape. This is not to imply that the Kearsarge sign is on the same artistic level, but only that its maker was highly skilled. We are told that 1870, when General Grant was President (and when "3 Kearsarge 3" was organized), was a bad time for the arts in America. How much later than 1870 this sign was made is not known, but it was certainly well before 1900.

Figured sculpture at Andover includes one of the best-known works of Elie Nadelman (1882–1946), *Seated Woman*,[15] in cherry wood (the

14

chair made of iron) about 3 feet high, dating from 1917. It provided
the cover illustration of the catalogue for a memorial retrospective
offered in 1948 by the Museum of Modern Art, and also shown in
Boston and Baltimore. (If a pair of *Circus Women* is still better
known today, that is for extracurricular reasons: the architect Philip
Johnson had the original group, of papier-mâché 5 feet high, greatly
enlarged to form presences in the foyer of his New York State Theater,
Lincoln Center.)

Born in Warsaw, Nadelman made his reputation in Paris, and after
his triumphant debut in 1917 at a New York gallery became a leading
figure in the New York art world. Lincoln Kirstein, in his essay for the
Museum of Modern Art's catalogue, points out that while Nadelman
absorbed much of European modernism, from the art of Seurat onward,
in America "he provided precedents" for George Bellows, Guy Pène
du Bois, Gaston Lachaise, and the caricaturist John Held, Jr., of *Vanity
Fair.*

We turn now to the gallery's superb array of nineteenth-century
American painting. A fair proportion of the leading figures can be
studied to advantage here, and I regret to pass over fine examples of the
work of such artists as Thomas Doughty, Fitz Hugh Lane, John Quidor
—whose eccentric creations make the pages of Washington Irving
come visually alive—Eastman Johnson, Whistler, and William Harnett
(see MA 220). Masterpieces by George Inness, Thomas Eakins, and
Winslow Homer must now claim our attention.

The White Monk[16] (also called *The Pines and the Olives*), an oil
over 3 by 5 feet, is signed and dated 1873 by George Inness (1825–
94). Comparison with *The Elm* (ME 23) of a decade earlier will
quickly show his rapid advance from Hudson River School derivatives
to something with great originality. Youthful trips to Europe before and
after 1850 had laid the foundations for what was to happen, but it was
an extended stay in Italy from 1871 to 1875, particularly in the environs
of Rome, that profoundly altered his vision. The scene of *The White
Monk* was inspired by the view from the Villa Barberini at Albano.
Beyond the umbrella-frieze of the pines, a brilliant red orange streaks
the horizon against turquoise greens higher up. Feathery olive trees

15

16

cluster mysteriously in the foreground—and then we notice the brooding figure of the white-robed monk, expressively off center and facing the edge of the composition. We have the feeling, as nearly a century later in the horizontal canvases of Jackson Pollock, that the picture extends indefinitely past the frame, both at left and at right. It is this sideways expansion (not to mention the color) that makes Inness's effect so different from the "classical" landscapes of Claude Lorrain, by which he was clearly affected.

Outside Philadelphia, where he lived and worked, and—secondarily —New York, the places to visit for the best view of the art of Thomas Eakins (1844–1916) are Andover and the Yale University Art Gallery. It is difficult to choose, at Andover, among three masterpieces: *Elizabeth at the Piano*[17] (1875), the *Portrait of Professor Henry A. Rowland* (1891), and *Salutat* (1898). In my earlier version of this book I opted for the great portrait, with its elaborate scientific notations ornamenting the frame. In the intervening years my enthusiasm for Eakins's work of the 1870s has continually risen (but not at the expense of the later works), so this time I have selected *Elizabeth*, seated in black Spanish gloom relieved by touches of red, with shafts of light accenting her face, her right hand, and the sheet of music on the piano.

Eakins's all-important four-year exposure to European art and study in Paris under Gérôme (examples of whose work are in the Clark Art Institute, Williamstown, Mass.) ended in the winter of 1869/70 in Spain. In the Prado at Madrid, Velázquez and Ribera were the masters he most loved—not the great Venetians and emphatically not Rubens. Seville, where Eakins decided to stay, was the home of Ribera until that seventeenth-century painter of shadowy mysteries moved on to Spanish-dominated Naples. The impact of the art of Velázquez and Ribera is particularly strong in *Elizabeth at the Piano*. Whether Eakins's near obsession with musical subjects was stimulated by the musical interests of Degas and other Impressionists (he was their slightly younger contemporary) is unclear, and at any rate unlikely. The fact remains that throughout his career Eakins painted pianists (see MA 176), violinists, cellists, guitarists, singers, and at least one music critic (*John Neil Fort*, a portrait in the Williams College Museum of Art). As we have

17

suggested in an example at Yale (CT 76), even his scullers seem to pause between strokes as if enthralled by distant musical strains.

Among Andover's works by Winslow Homer (1836–1910), a difficult choice is made easy because *West Wind*,[18] an oil 30 by 44 inches signed and dated 1891, stands near the top of any list of his later masterpieces. In a major Homer retrospective of 1973 at the Whitney Museum of American Art (also shown at Los Angeles and Chicago), it was accompanied by two other oils from Andover, *Eight Bells* (1886) and *Kissing the Moon* (1904). Sometimes Homer's lonely women against a storm-tossed sea prey too much on our sympathy (will her man come back safely?); but not in *West Wind*. Here the woman's shape, like a Whistler butterfly monogram, is intrinsically expressive. She leans hard against a gale that blows everything along an upward left diagonal. In *Winslow Homer at Prout's Neck* (Boston: Little, Brown, 1966), Philip C. Beam points out that the cliffs are actually sixty feet high and that the near waves can be seen only in a great storm. He also recounts an exchange between Homer and his good friend John La Farge (whose Venetian-oriented art we have discussed at Bowdoin College, ME 16). La Farge criticized Homer for using too much brown, whereupon Homer bet him a hundred dollars that he could paint a picture in browns only and that it would be accepted and admired. Homer won the bet. This marvelous composition seems to have inspired the Clark Institute's *Sleigh Ride* (MA 259), painted about two years later—but in blues that must have pleased his friend.

Near the turn of the century, Maurice Prendergast (1859–1924) painted a magical little watercolor, *Float at Low Tide—Revere Beach*[19] (c. 1896). It sparkled brightly at an exhibition of the artist's watercolors in New England collections (see CT 99). This early work came soon after Prendergast's return to Boston from two years of study in France. The theme, introduced by Boudin (see CT 21), and the design, which echoes the flat patterns of Japanese prints, are reminders of that experience; but the magic is Prendergast's own.

George Bellows and Edward Hopper, both of them born in 1882 and trained by Robert Henri, took their start in the urban world of the so-called Ashcan School—well represented here by John Sloan's

19

18

Sunday Morning—Women Washing Their Hair (painted in 1912 and included in the Armory Show of 1913). Bellows's career was cut short by his death in 1925. The excitement of city life remained with him to the end, but he also found an escape from it in his Maine landscapes and marines (see MA 150) and in his serene family portraits. Andover has a very fine one of his daughter, *Anne in a Purple Wrap*, where she appears growing up, four years later than the example we have discussed at Amherst (MA 12).

Hopper lived—and worked unremittingly—until 1967. His early painting, much of it bequeathed by his widow to the Whitney Museum of American Art, has Henri's *brio*, but gradually a pervasive calm, strongly tinged with loneliness, settled on his spirit. It is often pointed out that as modern "isms" came and went, Hopper plodded his own solitary path. Nevertheless, we see some similarity with the vacant streets and squares of Giorgio di Chirico, painted around 1915, which had their spell on him. By 1928, when he executed *Manhattan Bridge Loop*,[20] Hopper was in full stride. At the impressive size of 3 by 5 feet, it remains one of his finest works, even in the competition of such later ones as *Morning in a City* (MA 278). The emptiness of an early Sunday forenoon is accentuated by the single figure at the far left—a device we have just seen in Inness's *White Monk*. As in that picture, too, the scene appears to stretch beyond its frame at the two sides—in Hopper's composition aided by a wide belt of deep shadow across the whole front, tilted enough to the left to lead us to that little Everyman. The skyline, with its harsh metallic rhythms, is a concentrate of the American metropolis. Note Hopper's discoveries in shape repetition: the iron structures of different sizes and their relationship to the corniced buildings. The more we study this picture the more its selectiveness and design emerge. Its realism is only its skin.

In collecting contemporary American art Andover has been imaginative and daring. Visitors interested in this field should observe the dates of acquisition of many works by artists now on the verge of becoming Old Masters. One of these, Jackson Pollock's *Phosphorescence*, signed and dated 1947, came three years later by gift from the pioneering Mrs. Peggy Guggenheim. Purchases of other artists, in a list too long to detail, include Alexander Calder, Hans Hofmann, Franz Kline, Loren MacIver, George Rickey, Ben Shahn, Bradley Walker Tomlin, and Andrew Wyeth. A museum that can show the early stage of careers like these is automatically important.

20

A superb example of the work of Marsden Hartley (1877–1943) is in a different category. *Summer, Sea, Window, Red Curtain*[21] was painted in the year before he died (but purchased in 1944). We have seen Hartley's extraordinary change from a small 1909 oil at Bates College (ME 18) to the Berlin-inspired *Military* of 1913 at Hartford (CT 30); but without some study of the steps leading to his final transformation we should be totally unprepared for Andover's rich, deep-toned poem about a Maine summer. The composition echoes that of Matisse's window views, but not the scumbled surfaces, the dark reds of the foreground, or the high-keyed blues in the distance. If Matisse sacrificed everything else for a final triumphant statement in pure color and silhouetted shape, Hartley fell in love with the action of stroking oil paint on canvas.

Phosphorescence,[22] by Jackson Pollock (1912–56), signed and dated 1947 at the lower left center, is only five years earlier than the frenetic example we have discussed at Hartford (CT 34). In a career, however, that developed so rapidly, and one cut short in the artist's mid-forties (like George Bellows's), five years can make a great difference. While it is easy to make such a statement from hindsight, in the meteoric rush of some brief lives of genius (shall we adduce those of Watteau and of Mozart?) we sense a race against time. However that may be, *Phosphorescence* appeared when Pollock was just beginning to gain recognition beyond a small fringe of avant-garde, but astute, critics— and of a group of like-minded artists, all of whom were surprised to learn later that they were classed as Action Painters, Abstract Expressionists, or even New York School. Pollock's full-blown statement —in his painting, that is, for he never went in for verbal explanations— came around 1950, in such immense canvases as *Autumn Rhythm* (Metropolitan Museum of Art). The Andover example has a relatively modest size of 44 by 28 inches, it is executed in oil and aluminum paint (the silvery parts), and it is vertically conceived. While the long silvery lines were drawn with a stick or the wrong end of a paintbrush, this is not yet one of Pollock's "drip" paintings. James Thrall Soby, one

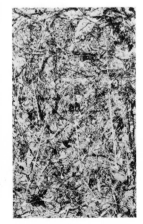

21   22

of the too few critics of modern art who was both sensitive and verbally articulate, liked to recall that Pollock, who enjoyed escaping the New York scene in solitude at the farthest end of Long Island, used to lie in tall grasses to watch the migration patterns of birds. That is surely not the subject of *Phosphorescence*, but it may help to demonstrate that Pollock's abstraction is not without reference to the phenomena of nature.

In a selection of works ranging from prehistory to the present, we must use caution in including artists whose reputation is not already established. The penalty of not doing so is, unfortunately, the omission of some major figure. Nevertheless, in view of the success of the Addison Gallery in guessing "right" about new artists, I reproduce a big oil,[23] 95 inches square, by Deborah Remington (born 1930), whose work is otherwise unknown to me. It was purchased in the year of its execution, 1971. Its title, *Axios*, is not particularly helpful beyond suggesting the symmetry of ancient Greek art. (Quartet opus 59 no. 3, by Beethoven, is not very helpful either.) Titles are necessary for reference, but one of the phenomena of modern art is their appearance after, or during, the completion of a work, not beforehand.

We should not ask, therefore, what *Axios* represents, but what it *is*. It is at least a very handsome ornament, but unfortunately praise on that score is too often regarded as a kiss of death. So what *else* is it? An echo of Euclidean perfection in the timeless beauty of an equilateral triangle? A search for order in a disjointed world? As always, time will tell—I hope, with some confidence—that Andover chose well.

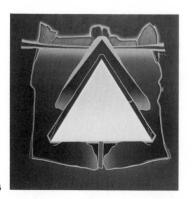

23

A Boston Miscellany

New England's greatest city has two museums of great art and two libraries where art can be found. Accordingly, we devote special sections to the Boston Athenaeum and the Boston Public Library, as well as to the Isabella Stewart Gardner Museum and to that Grand Central Station of art in New England, the Museum of Fine Arts.

Art of quality in the home of the Red Sox is of course not limited to these four institutions. In the following brief account we survey others, open to the public, which the reader should not miss. We are not concerned here with architectural history, that being the province of another volume in the Godine series of New England handbooks. But the contents, or adornment, of such buildings should not be neglected because they fall, as it were, in a no-man's-land between jurisdictions. We cannot include them all, but the reader would be well advised to start at the Boston Park Visitor Center, 15 State Street, opposite the Old State House. It provides information, brochures, and data on tours of the city. Another helpful center is the Society for the Preservation of New England Antiquities, with headquarters in Bulfinch's celebrated First Harrison Gray Otis House at 141 Cambridge Street. The society publishes an illustrated listing of the many historic houses it owns and operates in New England, the great majority of them being in the Boston area.

The Old State House (1712), a gem of Colonial Georgian architecture, now contains the Museum of Boston History, maintained by the Bostonian Society (admission charged). Many of the portraits are of more than historical interest, and the harbor views include notable examples by Fitz Hugh Lane (MA 155) and John White Allen Scott (1815–1907). The commercial signs often display typographical talent, and the maritime exhibits (including scrimshaw) make a small complement to major collections discussed elsewhere in this book. Scrimshaw, by the way, seems to have derived from the French word, *s'escrimer*, to work hard for small results.

Faneuil Hall, close by, has atop its cupola a gilt weather vane in the form of a grasshopper. Such weather vanes (see NH 16) are usually a nineteenth-century phenomenon in America, but this one dates from 1742, when the original building (before its 1806 enlargement by Bulfinch) was completed. The Colonial builders dedicated Faneuil Hall to Liberty and Loyalty—the latter meaning to the British king. In that spirit the weather vane had symbolic ties with the Old Country: "Deacon" Shem Browne copied it from one atop London's Royal Exchange, which in turn reproduced the crest of Sir Thomas Gresham, founder of the Exchange in 1558. The Grasshopper survived Faneuil Hall's tumultuous history—until 1974, when it was stolen, but soon recovered and reinstalled, freshly gilt. If you want to see its considerable beauty, a visit to the Heritage Plantation at Sandwich is suggested: here is displayed, at eye level, a small variant of about 1882, with a lovely green patina, but no golden skin.

The reopening of Quincy Market, beyond Faneuil Hall, as a combined commercial and cultural center has been hailed as one of the great innovations of urban renewal. The joys of this place will become immediately apparent, but it would be easy to overlook the fact that on the fifth floor of the South Market Building the Museum of Fine Arts has opened a downtown extension (open free, Tues.-Sun. 11-6). This venture has met an extraordinarily enthusiastic response; as a result, you might find here, in the changing exhibitions from the museum's permanent collections, something you missed at Huntington Avenue.

At the New State House (new in the sense that Bulfinch's masterpiece of 1789 plan and 1795–98 execution retired the old Georgian one for such use), there are portraits and sculptural memorials in abundance, not infrequently of artistic interest. More certain in that respect, however, is Saint-Gaudens's Shaw Memorial, at the foot of the entrance stairs, across Beacon Street. We discuss the work of this great sculptor in the section on Cornish, New Hampshire.

Across Copley Square from the Boston Public Library is H. H. Richardson's Trinity Church, with more sculpture by Saint-Gaudens, and painting by John La Farge. Farther out Boylston Street is the Institute of Contemporary Art, with its active program of changing exhibitions.

For adults, preferably accompanied by one child or more, there is joy to behold at the old Congress Street Wharf, superbly reconditioned to house the Children's Museum and the Museum of Transportation (admission charged). Who is to say that art is not present in the Elegant Car Gallery, or in the actual performance of children, their imaginations so skillfully enlisted? On the Congress Street bridge, a few yards away, is the Boston Tea Party Ship and Museum, accurately billed as An Adventure in History. That might persuade you to trek northerly to Charlestown to visit the U.S. Frigate *Constitution*, "Old Ironsides" herself.

The Boston Athenaeum

Location: 10½ Beacon Street
Hours: October through May, Mon.-Fri. 9-5:30, Sat. 9-4; closed holidays
Admission: Free

Although this august institution, incorporated in 1807, is owned and maintained by some 1,050 shareholders, visitors in small numbers are welcome to the limit of the available guide service. The address suggests compactness and great antiquity, but the building, designed by Edward C. Cabot in 1846 in Palladian style, is large. Two floors were added in 1913. Cabot was the grandson of Thomas Handasyd Perkins, whom we shall meet shortly, a major donor with his brother James in the era before the Athenaeum moved to its present quarters.

As everyone knows, the Museum of Fine Arts had its origin in the art collections of the Athenaeum, and certain paintings, including Stuart's original oil sketches of George and Martha Washington, passed to the museum on an indefinite loan basis. Protracted discussion of the "gentleman's agreement" by which this was accomplished was resolved in 1980. At three-year intervals these patriotic icons will move between the Museum of Fine Arts and the National Portrait Gallery in Washington.

Much of the art collection, however, remains; and to see it, a tour of these lovely surroundings is, happily, necessary. A beautifully designed illustrated booklet, *Change and Continuity*, published by the Athenaeum in 1976, is warmly recommended. A recent innovation is a series of changing exhibitions of contemporary Boston-area artists in the second-floor gallery.

The very large collection of prints emphasizes eighteenth- and nineteenth-century examples depicting Boston and New England scenes and daily life. These, together with daguerreotypes and photographs, run into the thousands.

I regret to pass over a multitude of white busts of important personages that pop up in alcoves, hover on balustrades, rest on tables, or glower from pedestals. They are somewhat relieved by a squadron of equally spotless Venuses, Medicean and otherwise. Truth to say, the paintings are more distinguished.

Nevertheless, among the busts is a Houdon plaster of George Washington, which came from Monticello. There are other plasters and many versions in marble, but this one is thought to be the "original." It may well be, but that brings up a problem too complicated to go into here. A plaster model of Thomas Ball's equestrian *George Washington* (1858–64) in the Boston Public Gardens presents no such difficulty.

I do not mean to ignore the historical interest of all those busts. An authoritative article on them, by the late director of the Athenaeum, Walter Muir Whitehill, appeared in the June 1973 issue of *Antiques* magazine.

Thomas Sully (1783–1872) suffers from a plethora of canvases of soulful ladies in white playing the harp. That he was a portraitist of great distinction may be seen in a series painted between 1815 and 1830 for, and preserved at, the U.S. Military Academy, West Point. The Athenaeum's *Portrait of Colonel Thomas Handasyd Perkins*,[24] 44 by 58 inches, full-length, and painted 1831/2, is their equal. With his brother James, Thomas established trade centers linking Boston and London with Canton—hence the Oriental ewer in the lower right corner. This portrait made a powerful impression at a major exhibition of the China Trade, held in 1979 at the De Cordova Museum in Lincoln. The colonel was an important patron of many fine artists, including not only Sully but also Washington Allston and Fitz Hugh Lane. Above his long brown coat and gleaming white collar, his commanding face is convincing testimony of his abilities. The pose is comfortably relaxed, and allows full play of a long curve—suggesting Hogarth's "line of beauty"—that extends from his left foot to the extended left arm. A top hat completes the colonel's elegant attire. The Athenaeum's commission for this portrait was to have gone to Gilbert Stuart, but his death in 1828 gave Sully the opportunity to create what many consider his masterpiece. Like Stuart, Sully studied in London, and his art has a European flair often compared with the stylishness of Sir Thomas Lawrence (see CT 56). He was, in fact, English-born, but brought up in the United States.

Chester Harding (1792–1866), whose memorable portrait of Amos Lawrence can be seen at the National Gallery, Washington, and also at the Williams College Museum of Art, is again in top form in the Athenaeum's *Portrait of Hannah Adams*,[25] painted about 1827 in her early seventies. Miss Adams had many distinctions. She was the first American professional woman writer, the first woman to use the Athenaeum, the first person to be buried in Mt. Auburn Cemetery, and the author of *Alphabetical Compendium of the Various Sects* (1784) and of *A Summary History of New England* (1799). A much less spontaneous portrait by Harding, a full-length of Daniel Webster, hangs in the

24

Athenaeum's entrance vestibule near his comparable image of John Marshall.

Among four Gilbert Stuart portraits in the collection, that of William Smith Shaw is perhaps the most accomplished.

European painting is represented, and certainly dominated, by an *Interior of St. Peter's,*[26] over 5 by 7 feet, painted in 1756/7 by Giovanni Paolo Panini (1691–1764). A companion piece, representing a *Roman Picture Gallery*, was sold in 1975 to the Museum of Fine Arts, where there is room for it. It is safe to say that no photograph can catch the spaciousness and at the same time the multifarious details of the vast interior of St. Peter's; and Panini has fortunately peopled it to give what is so easily missed in the actual building: its scale. If the occasion seems more festive than religious, that is altogether in the spirit of the eighteenth century. A less strenuous Panini is discussed in the section on Springfield (MA 214).

25

26

Boston Public Library

Location: Copley Square at Dartmouth Street
Hours: Mon. 1-9, Tues.-Thurs. 9-9, Fri. 9-5; closed holidays (the Print Dept. and the Rare Books and Mss. Dept. close at 5 P.M. Mon-Fri. and are also closed on Sat. and Sun.)
Admission: Free

If this were a book on architecture, I should launch into superlatives over the magnificent design of the original building by Charles Follen McKim (of McKim, Mead & White), erected 1888–92, and over the large addition at the rear, completed in 1972 from designs by Philip Johnson. The latter has become the functioning Public Library, allowing the McKim building to serve as a research library—and, to no inconsiderable degree, a public art museum.

The great facade on Copley Square opposite Trinity Church once had as a near neighbor the Victorian Gothic Museum of Fine Arts (1870), replaced by the Copley-Plaza Hotel after the museum moved in 1909 to its present building on Huntington Avenue. The entrance is embellished by the work of three sculptors of reputation: the three heraldic seals above are by Augustus Saint-Gaudens, the bronze doors by Daniel Chester French, and the large seated bronze figures of Art and Science by Bela L. Pratt. The commission for the figures was originally assigned to Saint-Gaudens, but at his death in 1907 the work had not progressed beyond preliminary models. He did, however, complete one of the four bronze memorials (a medallion portrait of benefactor Robert C. Billings) in the spacious, Renaissance-inspired Court.

As for the Main Staircase, I shall not compete with Henry James's paean: "its amplitude of wing and its splendour of tawny marble, a high and luxurious beauty." Here, framed in yellow Siena marble, specially quarried for the purpose, are murals by the celebrated Pierre Puvis de Chavannes (1824–98). These peaceful, reticent canvases, painted in film of dirt. One must look carefully, and lean on one's knowledge of the setting or its lighting, are thoroughly appropriate but they do not make the impact that is their due. Also they have acquired with time a film of dirt. One must look carefully, and lean on one's knoweldge of the master's great murals in Paris, Lyons, or Amiens, to find in them what the French art historian and critic Henri Focillon rightly saw: "le bleu de la mer, l'azur du ciel—le ciel et la mer des dieux." We have chosen one of the smaller panels, *Physics*,[27] for its greater visibility. Here, as in the others, a lovely play of white drapery about these reborn divinities heightens the purity and serenity of the blues of sky and sea. While the elaborate allegories may be hard for the tough modern mind to digest, the beauty and sureness of the composition carries them. A description of the whole project, by the artist himself, is available at the library (as also for the Abbey and Sargent murals we are soon to discuss). "I have sought," he wrote, "to represent under a symbolic form and in a single view the intellectual treasures collected in this beautiful building." Of *Physics* he wrote, "By the wondrous agency of Electricity, Speech flashes through Space and swift as lightning bears tidings of good and evil."

A very different series of murals, by Edwin Austin Abbey (1852–1911), adorns the Delivery Room (serving the Main Reading Room), to the right of the top of the Main Staircase. An 8-foot frieze representing the *Quest of the Holy Grail* tops a Venetian-style *salone* 64 feet long, wainscoted and timber-ceilinged, where all is deep brown, dark red, and gold. Unlike Puvis de Chavannes, Abbey had control of the décor of the whole room; and his late Victorian version of the Arthurian cycle suits to perfection its equally Victorian mixture of the Middle Ages and the Venetian High Renaissance. Abbey was one of the outstanding illustrators of his day, and from his earliest beginnings in Philadelphia he became obsessed with the romance of English medieval legends. The murals were installed in 1895, and Henry James wrote a fine account of them (available on request). We start with the child Galahad, descended by his mother from Joseph of Arimathea; continue with his going forth with the blessing of Sir Lancelot and Sir Bors; attend his installation in the Seat (or Siege) Perilous at the Arthurian Round Table; attend the benediction by King Arthur of the Knights of the Holy Grail; and follow the story through eleven more scenes to its culmination in the appearance of Joseph of Arimathea with the Holy Grail. We illustrate the third scene, one of the largest, *The Round Table and the Siege Perilous*.[28] Sir Galahad, as always in red, is led in by a figure swathed in white (Joseph of Arimathea), as the great hall with its vast company is suddenly suffused with light. In the robed chair, no man, not even King Arthur, has "sat with safety"; "it awaits only a blameless occupant."

It seems gratuitous to point out the superiority of Puvis de Chavannes as a composer-designer, but Abbey portrays the great theme in all its glamour, and his colors—the deep reds dominating the creamy whites and yellows—have a strong appeal. Apart from such mural achievements, Abbey is best studied at the Yale University Art Gallery, with its large collection of his drawings (some for the Boston murals), sketches, and oils, including a large one devoted to another of Abbey's major concerns, the works of William Shakespeare. The collection came to Yale in 1937.

27

28

A third series of murals, by John Singer Sargent (1856–1925), is reached by narrow stairs from the top landing of the Main Staircase. Here again, the artist had full control of the whole area, but for Sargent it was a long corridor-hall. He began work in his London studio in 1893 and the last canvas was installed in 1919. There are many lunettes, two wall panels over the staircase, and a frieze at either end below elaborate retables. The theme is *Judaism and Christianity*. We reproduce a section of the north frieze, devoted to the Hebraic Prophets, showing *Zephaniah, Joel, the Seated Obadiah, and the White-robed Hosea*.[29] (A full description of the project is available on request.) The lighting here is murky, and the first impression is of glinting gold, in an almost Byzantine splendor. The Prophets, in their splendid contrasts of black and white, are the most memorable figures in this sometimes overelaborate ensemble. A quarter-century ago, E. P. Richardson (*Painting in America*; New York: Crowell, 1956), compared Sargent's achievement favorably with Puvis de Chavannes's and Abbey's: "But for an interior space, conceived as a decorative unity and given a powerful, dramatic atmosphere by means of wall paintings, I find to my surprise that Sargent's much criticized and highly unpopular room must be given honors that our period may be reluctant to grant." Subsequent opinion has generally supported this estimate.

An attractive handbook, published in 1977, gives an excellent summary of the library and its artistic contents. In addition to works already discussed, there are many oil portraits, busts, and other marble sculptures. The Albert H. Wiggins collection of nineteenth- and twentieth-century prints is both vast and important, and the same is true for the photograph collection, of which a mimeographed summary was issued in 1977. Another survey lists the extensive holdings of Boston architectural drawings and photographs. Last, but not least, are the rare books and manuscripts preserved with loving care in a special section of this great treasure house.

29

Isabella Stewart Gardner Museum

Location: 280 The Fenway

Telephone: (617) 734-1359

Hours: September through June: Tues. 1-9:30 P.M., Wed.-Sun. 1-5:30; July and August: Tues.-Sun. 1-5:30. Free concerts September through June, Tues. at 8, Thurs. and Sun. at 4 (phone for information)

Admission: Charged. Ⓗ

The celebrated collection of Isabella Stewart Gardner (1840–1924), incorporated as a museum in 1900, was opened to the public in the year following her death. Housed in her Fenway Court residence, a palace in the Venetian style completed in 1903, it comprises the results of a lifetime of acquiring works of art. Among many expert advisers, Bernard Berenson was most active in Mrs. Gardner's behalf. An endowment provides for flowers in the Great Court, and for regularly scheduled concerts. A brief guide to the collection was published in 1976, and in 1974 the second edition of the catalogue of paintings. Catalogues of Oriental and Islamic art, drawings, sculpture, textiles, and books and manuscripts are also available. The list of publications gives some indication of the range of artistic treasures here to be seen.

While an itinerary from one floor to the next would be convenient to the visitor, a roughly chronological sequence will make much more sense to the reader—who, as visitor, can readily find the objects in the following discussion, as they come into view, by quick reference to the illustrations.

Our first two examples will be found among the many sculptures that adorn the court. The headless *Draped Female Figure*,[30] known as the *Peplophoros* (peplos wearer), is a Graeco-Roman copy of a superb Greek work of about 455–450 B.C. Of Greek marble, probably from the islands, it stands about 5 feet in height. The missing head and neck were carved separately and adjusted to the cavity at the top of the torso.

30

Whether seen from front or back, the figure is almost columnar, with that restrained grace that marks such figures of the same mid-fifth-century period as those of the Temple of Zeus at Olympia, or the famous bronze *Charioteer* of Delphi. The weight shifts as the right knee bends, just enough to define the form of the body beneath these virtual Doric flutings. At once static and energized, this lady, perhaps Persephone, achieves the timelessness of Euclidean geometry; indeed, the purity of geometric form is everywhere apparent, not least in the rectangular shape described by the chiton as it falls from the breasts. What nobility!

Our second selection, in the opposite corner of the court, represents *Odysseus Creeping Forward during the Theft of the Palladium*.[31] Like the *Peplophoros*, it is Graeco-Roman (c. 50 B.C.), but this time in an archaizing style in the manner of Greek art of c. 490 B.C. Neo-Archaic sculpture could achieve grace and refinement (as in the lovely relief discussed at Yale, CT 63), but not here. This figure fitted into the left-hand angle of a pedimental composition, and as such was visible only from the front. The drapery, in almost comical contrast with Odysseus's brutish anatomy, is pure rhythm, swinging the figure along toward its appointed mission. The contoured pose adapts well to the claims of the frontal plane of the pediment, and the design is remarkable for its repeated and interlocked triangles.

A superb *Stained Glass Window*,[32] French Gothic of the thirteenth century, may have come from Soissons. The design and draftsmanship are similar to those of the windows at Chartres, and one would like to believe, as seems possible, that Henry Adams advised its purchase. Like many such windows, its pieces have largely been renewed through the centuries, for the erosive effect of wind and rain is very great. In its original state the window seems to have depicted the martyrdom of Saints Nicaise and Eutropie. There were probably fewer colors and an even greater dominance of reds and blues. The window is best seen in the afternoon light.

A little gold-ground panel, *The Presentation of the Christ-Child in the Temple*[33] by Giotto (1267–1337), will be found on a stand not far from Sargent's strange portrait of Mrs. Gardner. The attribution to the

31

32

founder of Florentine art and herald of the Renaissance is based on style and quality: no document proves that Giotto painted it, and many consider it the work of an able follower. The arrangement is close to one of Giotto's famous frescoes in the Arena Chapel at Padua, and, as in other works by Giotto in egg tempera on panel, the effect strongly suggests the rugged simplicity of his murals. Note the forceful concentration on the Child by slow curves of drapery upward from the left, and the closing of the composition at the right by the slow spiral movement about the solemn apple-green figure of the prophetess. Contrast Giotto's sparing use of ornament with that of the Sienese painter Lippo Memmi in a little *Madonna* of similar date, nearby.

Few intercity rivalries were more intense than that between Florence and Siena, whether on the field of battle or in the production of religious art. The latter is easily seen in a comparison between Giotto—whose *St. Francis Receiving the Stigmata* at the Fogg Art Museum (MA 114) again more likely by a close follower, gives a stronger impression of his power —and the two great founders of Sienese painting, Duccio and Simone Martini. If Giotto's scenes are enacted by simple peasants or villagers of a stamp not unlike Cézanne's *Card Players*, Duccio's and especially Simone's take us to the world of Byzantine icons and the courtly elegance of Gothic Paris. Simone Martini (1285–1344) is unquestionably the author of the five-panel altarpiece representing the *Madonna with Saints Paul, Lucy, Catherine, and John the Baptist*,[34] although his co-worker Lippo Memmi may have assisted. Comparison with the seven-part altarpiece in Williamstown, by a close follower of Duccio (MA 248), will clarify the grace of Simone's aristocratic style; both polyptychs date from the 1320s. At the same time as these airless gold and bronze-toned images were fashioned in Siena, Giotto in Florence was exploring the space and substance of the world we live in.

33

34

A similar tale of two cities (only fifty miles apart) may be carried into the fifteenth century if we confront the exquisite little tempera panel *The Child Jesus Disputing in the Temple*[35] by Giovanni di Paolo (1402?–82) with a fresco fragment representing *Hercules*[36] by Piero della Francesca (c. 1410–92). Though Piero's major work was done at Arezzo and Urbino, he was trained in Florence and his artistic bent was decidedly Florentine. The *Hercules* displays the grave mien and the anatomical knowledge of the Renaissance, together with its disciplined energy. Giovanni di Paolo, on the contrary, deliberately continued to work in the style of Simone and Duccio. If the setting avows the new (Renaissance) architecture, it is only in superficial details. But there is a disturbing new emotionalism, as of a proto–van Gogh. One feels the strain involved in turning the back on one's own time, while yet achieving an original statement.

It is not certain that Paolo Uccello (1397–1475) painted the incisive profile *Portrait of a Young Lady*,[37] for such representations were common in mid-fifteenth-century Florence. Most critics today doubt such an exalted attribution. Like Uccello's work, however, is the sure sense of pattern (possibly reflecting his early training in mosaic and stained glass), as well as the force of the drawing and the observation unaffected by any desire to flatter. It is curious that Uccello, one of the leading exponents of Renaissance perspective and massive form, increasingly

35

36

37

reverted in the latter half of his career to the flat spaces and the heraldic profiles (as here) of Gothic tapestries. This enchanting silhouette may be described as a strict side view of a Renaissance portrait bust, steamrolled into a calligraphic arabesque. The lady's ponytail is fashionable once again.

Among many fine examples of Florentine Renaissance painting, the *Madonna with the Eucharist*[38] by Sandro Botticelli (1444–1510) is the outstanding masterpiece. It once belonged to the Chigi family of Rome, and it was acquired for Mrs. Gardner by Bernard Berenson. An early work with echoes of Botticelli's master, Fra Filippo Lippi, it already conveys the haunting, wistful nostalgia of which that worldly monk had no conception. Seldom was Botticelli's hand surer in the swinging quality of the line, the crisp detail, and the gently pervasive light. The wheat and grapes symbolize, of course, the Bread and the Wine. This meaning helps explain the gently troubled smiles of Angel and Virgin. The picture has suffered damages, for example in the far eye of the Virgin.

Botticelli's *Madonna* dates from the early 1470s, and we turn now to two of his near contemporaries, both non-Florentine, who found new possibilities for expression in the verticality and curvilinear interlacement of late Gothic art. Carlo Crivelli (c. 1430–95), who worked in the area around Venice, was influenced by the great Andrea Mantegna (represented in the museum by a somewhat placid *Holy Conversation*), but eschewed that master's astringent formalism as well as his bold adventures into illusionary space. In Crivelli's *St. George and the Dragon*[39] the vertical format virtually eliminates the possibility of a deeply receding continuum. Instead, we have a tapestrylike fairyland, with warped perspectives in the small, but not far distant, towers and spires. The dragon, the horse's tail, and the little landscape at the right all wind *up*, rather than back. St. George and his horse occupy most of the picture space, and Crivelli has loaded them with embossed and gilded detail. A violence, charmingly unconvincing as befits a fable, takes over; and there are interesting similarities to the forms and facial expressions of Giovanni

38

39

di Paolo's picture, already discussed. It is made very clear that the helpless and diminutive little lady will be rescued.

Even more narrowly vertical is the highly ornamented panel representing *St. Engracia*,[40] by Bartolomé Bermejo, a native of Cordova who was active in Valencia, Barcelona, and in Aragon, where St. Engracia was especially revered. Bermejo's technique is clearly indebted to the great Flemish master, Jan van Eyck. This comes as no surprise, since Flemish painting was greatly prized in fifteenth-century Spain; but in the *St. Engracia* there is none of van Eyck's Luminism. Instead, the harsh, incisive line and the loaded ornamentation have such similarities with the art of Crivelli as to suggest—as indeed happened—that all across northern Italy, southern France, and into Spain the discoveries of the Florentine Renaissance met with grudging acceptance. One of Bermejo's finest works, the *St. Engracia* dates from about 1477. The artist died just before the end of the century, and little is known about his beginnings.

Soon after 1500 in Florence, Renaissance style developed a broader and grander phase under the influence of Leonardo da Vinci and Michelangelo and their prodigious younger rival Raphael (1483–1520), and just at this time the artistic center of gravity moved to Rome. Raphael's own development into a High Renaissance master is marvelously illustrated at the Gardner Museum itself; we need only compare his early little *Pietà* of c. 1504 with his *Portrait of Count Tommaso Inghirami*[41] of about 1513, painted in Rome, where the subject was secretary of the Lateran Council.

In the *Pietà*, part of the predella (or foot-piece) of the large altarpiece of the *Madonna* in the Metropolitan Museum of Art, New York, the twenty-year-old painter has softened the lines, broadened the forms, and filled the scene with luminous atmosphere. In the portrait the scale (not the size) is enormous, in keeping with the new Roman culture dominated by Pope Julius II. The shapes, greatly simplified, and with sparing description of detail, are—so to speak—as globular and capacious as the Roman Pantheon. First of all there is the spherical shape of

40

41

the body, defined by sloping shoulders, inward-curving arms, and fat, cigarlike fingers. The great girth at the waist is ringed by the sash, and echoed at the neck by the collar band. But the purest globe is, of course, the head; and within the head are smaller globes: an earlobe and two bulging eyeballs. Observe these eyes closely. A subtle extra turn of the right one, giving a slightly walleyed effect, splits the focus of the count's gaze. He looks *up*, presumably toward a speaker, but not precisely *at* him. By this small but telling detail, Raphael avoids the illusionary suggestion of a psychological moment and shifts the emphasis beyond the passage of time. He uses it in other portraits as well, and we find it repeatedly employed by such sixteenth-century masters as Bronzino and Holbein, and in the nineteenth century by Ingres. By contrast, seventeenth- and eighteenth-century portraits, with their Baroque concern for catching the moment on the fly, focus the eyes sharply—often on the spectator—as in the portraits of Rubens, Hals, and Rembrandt and in the busts of Bernini and Houdon (see CT 67), and in Impressionist portraits by Renoir.

A quick comparison between the Houdon bust just mentioned and the Gardner Museum's superb bronze *Portrait of Bindo Altoviti*[42] by Benvenuto Cellini (1500–71) will again illustrate this basic difference in intentions. Cellini's detachment, what we may call his psychological distance from his subject, is reinforced by a rigidly vertical axis and by the near frontality of the pose.

As for Hans Holbein the Younger (1497–1543), the Museum offers his portraits of *Sir William* and *Lady Butts*.[43] Holbein was trained by his father in Augsburg in the methods of local late Gothic painting, matured at Basel in German Switzerland, and through the influence of the Dutch humanist Erasmus became court portraitist to Henry VIII of England. That his work resembles as much as it does the portraits that Raphael painted in Rome indicates how rapidly the forms of High Renaissance art spread over Europe. Sir William Butts was court physician to Henry VIII; and he appears as a character in the last act of Shakespeare's play. These portraits date from the end of Holbein's career, when his style became more incisively linear and somewhat

42

43

flattened under the influence of English taste—seen at its extreme a generation later in the wallpaper images of Queen Elizabeth. For the close connection with Raphael, such earlier Holbeins as the *Portrait of Georg Gisze* (Berlin, 1532) are clearer examples. No matter at what time we consider Holbein, however, we always find a Northerner's obsession with detail—for instance, in Lady Butts's collar and the ornament at her breast.

We turn now to Venice, where Gentile Bellini (c. 1429–1507) and his more famous brother Giovanni, the master of Titian, settled and spun out their distinguished careers. In 1479 Gentile was sent as portraitist to the court of Mahomet II in Constantinople. The miniature *Portrait of a Turkish Artist*,[44] in watercolor on parchment, seems to have been made there by Gentile, though it is just possibly the work of an Oriental. An argument against such a theory is provided by an undoubtedly Persian copy in the Freer Gallery in Washington, its mass flattened out as we should expect. Returning to Venice, Gentile peopled his great processional panoramas with turbaned Orientals, and this exoticism continued to mark Venetian painting into the time of Titian.

An insistent tradition tells us that Titian died in 1576 at the age of ninety-nine, but modern scholarship has settled on a birth date close to 1490. The Gardner Museum's *Rape of Europa*[45] is often cited as Titian's masterpiece, and I will make bold to declare it the greatest painting in New England, if not in America. Measuring 6 by 7 feet, it was painted in 1559–62 for King Philip II of Spain. For 150 years it hung in the Royal Palace in Madrid, where it was copied full-size by Rubens, and adapted by Velázquez for the background of *The Spinners* (Prado), before it passed into French royal collections and in 1896, via Bernard Berenson, to Mrs. Gardner. Van Dyck, the chief pupil of Rubens in

44

45

Antwerp, made a watercolor sketch from the Rubens copy, and this too can be seen in Fenway Court. Perhaps this extraordinary "pedigree," with its testimony to the admiration of other great artists, speaks more loudly than a verbal appraisal. I shall point out only two details: the way the rose scarf echoes the action of Europa's head and arm, and the vaporous poetry of the distant landscape, where, on a strand set before mountains reminiscent of Titian's own birthplace in the Dolomites, Europa's friends mourn her strange levitation by Zeus disguised.

Some idea of the revolutionary nature of Titian's career may be gained from comparing *The Rape of Europa* to a small panel by a window, *Christ Bearing the Cross.* Once attributed to Giorgione, it has likewise been ascribed to other pupils of the aged Giovanni Bellini. Whoever painted it, this little picture is a replica of a work by Bellini himself. In his youth Titian also painted in this manner. We may assume a gap of fifty years between the two pictures; and it is doubtful that any more far-reaching change in the history of art occurred in so short a time.

Returning to Sir Anthony Van Dyck (1599–1641) and to England, where he attained Holbein's position nearly a century later, we consider his *Portrait of a Lady with a Rose.*[46] Like Holbein a foreigner, he developed at Antwerp in the studio of Rubens. If Holbein can be said to have created the image of the Tudor courtier, Van Dyck established the Stuart aristocrat in a style still influential on today's enfeebled portraiture of British royalty. Van Dyck's final decade of residence in England gradually drew him away from the robust energy of Rubens's art. The present work, silvery in tone, its refinement—especially in the elongated fingers—carried almost to the point of listlessness, is probably of very late date (compare the full-length example at Yale's British Center, CT 53).

How far Van Dyck deviated from his master may be judged by a comparison of the last picture with the *Portrait of Thomas Howard, Earl of Arundel,*[47] by Peter Paul Rubens (1577–1640). The preparatory drawing is in the Clark Art Institute, Williamstown (MA 264). This superb half-length, in full armor, of the Earl Marshal of England and

46   47

patron of the arts, was almost certainly painted in 1629/30 when Rubens was in London on a diplomatic mission to the court of Charles I. During this time he was also occupied with designing the ceiling for the Banqueting Hall of Whitehall Palace (see CT 52). Darkly glowing in its exceptionally deep coloration, its mysterious and cavernous spaces set off the massive forms with more than a foretaste of Rembrandt, who at this time was still in his early twenties. As Baroque art, it is unusually reserved, but all the elements of this style are nonetheless present. The alert gaze, sharply focused on the spectator, is one of these elements; and it is even more strikingly apparent in the Clark Institute's drawing. We sense a psychological connection between sitter and artist, rather than the aloofness, mentioned above, felt in portraits by Raphael, Bronzino, Holbein, and Ingres. Curiously, Van Dyck's *Portrait of a Lady with a Rose*—by a lift of an eyebrow and a slight turn of her left eye—coyly evades us; among seventeenth-century portraits this is something of an exception. The pale gray-silver tones of the armor in Reynolds's 1765 *Portrait of Jeffery, Lord Amherst* (MA 7) tell us much about changing taste from the Baroque century to the Age of Enlightenment. The same may be said for Rubens's claret reds as against Reynolds's lavenderish pink sash.

Our next three pictures, two Rembrandts and a Vermeer, help give the Dutch Room its name. The *Lady and Gentleman in Black*[48] (1633, a year earlier than the large portraits in the Museum of Fine Arts) and the *Landscape with an Obelisk*[49] (1638) are superb examples of Rembrandt's maturing style between the ages of twenty-seven and thirty-two. Of the other two of his works in this room, *The Storm on the Sea of Galilee* (1633) is unusually coarse and melodramatic, while the *Self-Portrait at Twenty-three* (1629) is already well along the road to his youthful arrival. The famous *Anatomy Lesson of Dr. Tulp* (Amsterdam) came only three years later. At this period Rembrandt was under the strong influence of the Baroque style—more so in his religious works than in his portraits—with its strong contrasts of lighting, and its forms

48

49

receding from the picture surface. Later he muted these dramatic effects and eliminated such sharp edge and detail as we find in the double portrait. (Contrast the Fogg Museum's *Head of Christ*, c. 1648, MA 124.)

A special article by John Walsh, Jr., "Child's Play in Rembrandt's *A Lady and Gentleman in Black*," appears in the museum's annual bulletin for 1976. A recent cleaning and relining had made this picture more wonderful than ever. During that process X-rays showed many small changes made by Rembrandt as the picture progressed, and two major ones. Instead of the chair at the lower left, there was an amorphous black shape, perhaps a cloth; and between the husband and wife there was a young boy, right arm raised and holding a stick, or perhaps a whip. This surprising revelation leads to speculation. Did the child die? Or did Rembrandt (and/or his patrons) decide on a different kind of picture? What was the child (who seems never to have been more than roughly blocked out) doing? Perhaps he was using a whip to spin a top, but unfortunately there is no sign of any top to prove it. The lady originally looked askance at the child, around to her right and somewhat behind; now she gazes past the mysterious, but compositionally indispensable, chair—its rich red cushion accented by a shaft of light in an otherwise black-and-white and deeply shadowed picture. Although nothing happens, the figures are charged with psychological energy. It is not enough to say they are preparing to stroll outdoors. One senses without being able to explain further that Rembrandt, as he did so often, took a thoroughly conventional theme and gave it new significance.

However that may be, Rembrandt has made the two heads stand out from the minutely detailed ruffs by the most subtle modeling; and the same can be said for the modeling of the lady's black skirt. How do you model in pure black on black?

The careful observer will discover Rembrandt's signature and the date, 1633, in a place where it would seem to belong.

Mystery is further heightened in the *Landscape with an Obelisk*, painted in 1638. Rembrandt often drew and made etchings of landscape, stormy or otherwise; but there are less than twenty oils. Note how the forms have become blurred since 1633, how the light is more evenly distributed and its contrasts reduced, how the cool blues, greens, and mauves are played against the earth tones. Mystery and wonder ride triumphant. Why an obelisk set so close to an ordinary rustic mill? To ask the question is almost to answer it: this is no ordinary landscape, but a vision. Once again, Rembrandt has transformed the expected, and in so doing he was unique among his contemporaries. In his provocative and authoritative study, *Rembrandt, Life and Work* (London: Phaidon Press, 1964), Jakob Rosenberg points out that the master's interest in landscape, which began about the time of the Gardner example, ended around 1645. The reason for this leads to "the problem of Rembrandt's humanity." He found that human content was essential to his own self-expression.

Jan Vermeer of Delft (1632–75), a younger contemporary of Rembrandt, was the most gifted of many Dutch interior painters. Of those who were not primarily storytellers, most were attracted by the magic of light caught on surfaces (Ter Borch), or by the poetic silences of a sequence of rooms (de Hooch). Vermeer suspended all these elements in exquisite aesthetic balance, and still found a place for oblique allusion to human interest. *The Concert*[50] is a superb example. His art bespeaks the prosperity of the Dutch republic after the middle of the century. But it stands far above the status of a mere economic document. Leeuwenhoek, inventor of the microscope and also a native of Delft, was one of Vermeer's friends. There is no necessary artistic significance in this, but Vermeer's paintings do have a strikingly vitreous surface. Visitors to the Museum of Fine Arts will recall the original of the van Baburen *Procuress* hanging on the wall at the right in *The Concert*.

Off the main court, in a Spanish gallery especially arranged for it, is *El Jaleo*,[51] by John Singer Sargent (1856–1925). Dramatically lit from below, the flamenco dancer and her musicians seem to be actually performing. All that is lacking is a sound track, punctuated with cries of *jaleo!*—the flamenco equivalent of the bullfight's *olé*. At the Paris Salon of 1882 it was a sensation. Bought by a New York dealer, it was acquired by the Boston collector T. Jefferson Coolidge. After many attempts, Mrs. Gardner persuaded him to part with it; thereupon began a long association between Mrs. Gardner and the artist. Sargent had made many sketches on a trip to Spain, and from these he developed his big composition in his Paris studio. However imposing, *El Jaleo* seems external by comparison with the psychological bite of dance hall scenes by Degas and Toulouse-Lautrec. It is the Salon piece *par excellence*, not a personal revelation. A quick look at the Clark Institute's small *Venetian*

50

51

Interior (MA 260), painted in the same year, will convince you that when Sargent protested less he was indeed a very fine painter. Showy pictures are unfortunately like performances by brilliant piano technicians: the performance can run away with the music.

Unlike most collectors of the Old Masters, Mrs. Gardner had a lively interest in the art of her own time. Several small galleries on the ground floor demonstrate her ability to discover quality in contemporary work. They contain fine Whistlers, and several masterpieces by the French Impressionists. Totally unexpected, however, is an early oil of the best quality by Henri Matisse (1869–1954). There are surprisingly few paintings by this artist in New England, and a large proportion of them are from his rather easy, agreeable phase of about 1920. *The Terrace: St. Tropez*,[52] however, dates from 1904, when his style first crystallized. Though based on Impressionist art and the dotted color spots of Georges Seurat and Paul Signac, its range of color was, and still seems, daring, as does its use of bold patterns. The house shown here belonged to Signac, and Mme. Matisse posed for the figure in Japanese kimono, seated against the wall. Thomas Whittemore, who restored the mosaics of Hagia Sofia, acquired the picture from the artist, and gave it to Mrs. Gardner about 1910.

Mrs. Gardner was seventy then and Bernard Berenson, her onetime protégé and subsequent agent, had just passed the age of forty. How did he compare with her in his response to contemporary art? Note, to begin with, that Berenson was born in the same year as Matisse. In 1958, he published *Essays in Appreciation*, containing estimates of Matisse and Picasso written when he was in his eighties. The tone is infuriatingly condescending, yet it should be pointed out that Berenson recalls writing a letter to the New York *Nation*, about 1910, defending Matisse from an attack by its Paris correspondent. Appealed to by the Steins in Paris to help the struggling Matisse, whom they so greatly admired, Berenson had bought what he calls "a rather rough painting of a forest clearing." The illustration states that it is in the Belgrade Museum, "formerly in the Berenson Collection." The picture is clearly not up to the standard of Mrs. Gardner's example of about the same period, but Berenson chose it and Berenson disposed of it. In 1950 he called on Matisse, then busily engaged on the Vence Chapel. The essay ends with a querulous complaint: Matisse did not "refer in the slightest to what I had done for him forty years ago."

52

Museum of Fine Arts

Location: 465 Huntington Avenue

Hours: Tues. 10-5, Wed. 10-10, Thurs.-Sun. 10-5 (entire museum including West Wing); Thurs.-Fri. 5-10 (West Wing only); closed Mon. and major holidays

Admission: Charged; free Sat. 10-12. Ⓗ

New England's greatest art museum is surpassed in the United States only by the Metropolitan Museum of Art in New York. While other great American museums may surpass it in certain departments, the overall range and depth of the Boston collections continue to keep the Museum of Fine Arts in this exalted rank—a fact the more remarkable in view of the purely private status of the museum. There are nine departments: American decorative arts and sculpture, Asiatic art, classical art, contemporary art, Egyptian art, European decorative arts and sculpture, paintings, prints and drawings, and textiles. In addition, there are major collections of photographs and of musical instruments, and a vast art library.

The Asiatic collections are recognized as the finest in the world in a single institution. The collections of Egyptian and classical art are rivaled in America only by those in New York. The print collection is one of the seven most important in the world. The celebrated collection of paintings is especially strong in French art of the nineteenth century. Near Eastern and medieval and Renaissance decorative arts are superbly represented, and the textile collection (including tapestries and costumes) is world famous. Those of Early American silver (especially Paul Revere), furniture, and painting (over sixty works by John Singleton Copley) are unrivaled; the additional Karolik collection of painting and furniture is especially noteworthy.

It should be clear from the above that any survey of these riches on a scale comparable to our discussion of other New England museums would require a separate volume. My selection of under fifty masterpieces merely skims off some of the cream. It is designed primarily to fill in gaps in this book in an overview of world art from early antiquity to the present. The reader should assume that for most works discussed elsewhere an example of equal or superior quality is in the Museum of Fine Arts. My selections, however, give a fair impression of the range of riches here to be seen, and some inkling of their grandeur. Catalogues both general and particular are of course available; and the museum's illustrated handbook, revised from time to time, is an indispensable supplement to what is discussed in these pages.

The Museum of Fine Arts was the first in the United States to be incorporated (1870). In 1876 it opened to the public in a Victorian Gothic structure on Copley Square. At this time many of the paintings owned by the Boston Athenaeum—including Stuart's oil studies of George and Martha Washington—were transferred here on indefinite

loan. The present building, which opened in 1909, has been greatly
expanded by additions through the years. In the summer of 1981, the
impressive West Wing, designed by I. M. Pei, was opened to the public.
Capped by an Italian-inspired glass-roofed "galleria" over two hundred
feet long, it provides superb space for temporary exhibitions, an auditorium, and services for a fast-growing attendance; and it frees the
original building for more complete display of the permanent collections.
In 1921–25 the upper hall and staircase rotunda at the Huntington Avenue entrance were decorated with allegorical paintings by John Singer
Sargent. In 1979 an imaginative decision was fulfilled by the opening
of the museum at Faneuil Hall Marketplace (open free of charge Tues.-
Sun. 11-6, closed Mon.). This downtown extension, with its entrance
at Number One, Old South Market Building, offers changing selections
from the museum's collections to the millions who visit the historic
market on Boston's waterfront. In this connection, the visitor to the main
museum should not miss Gilbert Stuart's *Portrait of Joseph Quincy*
(1772–1864), founder of the chief structure of the marketplace and later
president of Harvard. The portrait, one of Stuart's most incisive and
painted in 1824, shows the Quincy Market in the background. A visit
is warmly recommended, both for itself and because something you
could not find at Huntington Avenue may well be on view, temporarily,
Avenue may well be on view, temporarily, here.

In the particular field of Old Kingdom Egyptian sculpture the
Museum of Fine Arts is second only to Cairo among museums the
world over. This happy condition is the result of excavations sponsored
since 1905 by the museum and directed by the late George A. Reisener.
The third of the Great Pyramids and its valley temple, at Gizeh, yielded
rich finds, none more remarkable than the schist effigy of its builder,
the *Pharaoh Mycerinus and Queen Chamerernebti*.[53] The rigidly frontal
pose, with the left leg ceremonially advanced, gives a powerful expression of absolutism; the durability of the stone is fully exploited to
accomplish it. Nevertheless, a degree of resilience at the joints and subtle
differences of facial expression indicate the sculptor's own sense of
vitality. The figures emerge as from a stone shroud.

Further evidence for this statement is provided by the unforgettable
Head of Prince Ankh-haf,[54] the son-in-law of Cheops, builder of the

53

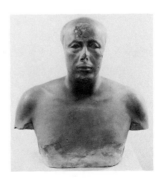

54

Great Pyramid. Found in the chapel of his tomb, this portrait shows how the sculptor, freed from traditional demands for representation of the pharaoh, could explore the individual personality. Here the limestone has been faced with stucco and painted a rich reddish brown. Like much great sculpture, this piece has a quality of compactness; the skin is stretched taut over bone and muscle.

Both of these masterpieces come from the Fourth Dynasty (2723–2563 B.C.), the head of the prince just before 2600, and Mycerinus and his queen—perhaps the first couple in the history of art—within the next quarter century.

After these sublime echoes of Egypt's greatest age, the small wooden model of *Four Offering Bearers*[55] strikes a note of intimacy. They were made some seven hundred years later, in the Middle Kingdom, when the monarchy was again centralized following a long period of political chaos. Though such figures were also carved in the Old Kingdom in the attempt to perpetuate in the tombs all facets of earthly life, here the proportions are markedly slenderer. Refinement attenuates the older strength. If we ponder, however, all that has happened to our Western world since the age of the Gothic cathedrals, we shall soon understand how sluggish was the velocity of change in Egypt.

At a height of 44 inches, the marble *Cycladic Idol*[56] is one of the largest known examples of its kind. Such figures, presumably representing the deceased or a deity of the dead, were produced in quantity in the Cyclades group of the Aegean Islands in the early Bronze Age during the period 2700–2300 B.C., known as Early Cycladic II. Small examples are so numerous that even today islanders use them as dolls. But a figure of the size of the Boston example is exceedingly rare. Compared with the example discussed at Amherst College, it is markedly elegant, and the iron component in the marble gives it an especially lovely rust-red tinge. Such art might easily have inspired Constantin Brancusi in his polished simplifications of natural form, and, through his influence, the sculptures and paintings of Amedeo Modigliani. Certain late abstractions of heads by the Russian-born German Expressionist painter Jawlensky, come even closer to Cycladic heads. Such twentieth-century enthusiasm for Cycladic art signals the waning influence of the high idealism of fifth-century Greek art; at the same time it serves to

55   56

remind us that "primitive" is perhaps a misnomer when used in the English sense and that it should be used to mean "early," as in the Romance languages.

Artistically as well as chronologically, Cycladic art is early Greek art. Note that it is roughly contemporary with Egyptian art of the Fourth Dynasty, and that already it has broken away from its stone shroud to explore tension and resilience in the human figure.

The museum's celebrated little *Snake Goddess*, in ivory and gold, distantly resembles the ceramic examples from the Palace of Knossos, now in the Herakleion Museum. These date from c. 1600 B.C.—some hundred years before the gigantic eruption of the volcano on Santorini Island, sixty miles to the north, produced a tidal wave that destroyed the Cretan fleet—and Knossos itself—and rendered Crete defenseless to the invasion of the Mycenaeans from the Peloponnesus. The Minoan Cretans worked in ivory and in gold, but no other example of work in ivory with gold is known. The unique Boston example has a surprisingly Victorian air.

The collection of Greek and Roman art is unquestionably the finest in New England, but in order to leave room for discussion of the excellent examples at Worcester, Providence, and Brunswick, only a minimum has been selected here. Although Boston's collection of Greek vases is considered the greatest in America, our discussion of this field is centered on examples in the college museums of Bowdoin, Smith, and Mount Holyoke. To sharpen your expectation of highest quality, however, you would do well to examine a black-figure amphora (squatter than the example at Worcester, MA 288) representing the *Departure of a Warrior* as he steps into his two-horse chariot, and two red-figure examples: a small two-handled cup, or skyphos, of the early fifth century, with the transparent "wet" draperies of marble sculpture of the time, that tells the story of Helen of Troy; and a krater by the Pan Painter representing the *Death of Actaeon*, considered to be one of the finest Greek vases in America.

The Greeks have been called a nation of art critics, so completely did their sense of artistic values affect all forms of their life. Even their coins show this predilection. To celebrate a victory of the Greek colonists over the Carthaginians in Sicily in 480 B.C., Gelon, the tyrant of Syracuse, issued a *Ten-drachma Silver Piece*.[57] The side shown here contains the profile of his beautiful wife, Daramete, encircled by four dolphins and the name Syracuse (reading counterclockwise from right center). The Boston example, the prize of its large collection of ancient coins, is the finest known impression of this design, which has been hailed as the most beautiful in the history of coinage. Note how finely the noble head is centered, how the several large and small circles echo

57

the shape of the whole coin, and how deftly the dolphins weave their motion around it. One is grateful that such beauty was pressed into silver, not a baser metal.

The collection of Greek and Roman engraved gems at Boston is likewise outstanding. Indeed, it ranks with that of Vienna, one of the great collections in the world.

Greek gold is another area in which the museum is rich. An earring of the mid-fourth century B.C. representing a *Victory Driving a Two-Horse Chariot*[58] is perhaps the greatest of these Boston treasures. Its large size (2 inches high) suggests that it was ordered as a votive offering to a goddess. Here in miniature we have all the fine workmanship, the elegance, and the sophistication of the marble and bronze sculpture that followed upon the Age of Pericles.

The so-called *Bartlett Head of Aphrodite*,[59] named for a former owner, is a superb example of the refinement that marks fourth-century art. It comes closer than anything in America to the style of Praxiteles and may even have been carved in his lifetime. The celebrated *Hermes with the Infant Dionysus* at Olympia, sometimes considered a work of Praxiteles himself, at other times a copy of a bronze by that master, seems by the standard of the *Bartlett Head* slick and disappointing. Here the grain of the Parian marble and its delicate translucence have been exploited to catch a mood of soft reverie, but without loss of strength. As in the work of Leonardo da Vinci, whose *Mona Lisa* this *Aphrodite* foreshadows, and in the highly sensuous art of Correggio, there is a feeling of exaltation, of something beyond the limits of mortal beauty.

The difference between Greek and Roman ideals—that is, apart from Roman imitations of Greek art (see CT 63)—can be seen by contrasting this lovely head with a terra-cotta *Portrait Head* dating from the last century of the Roman republic. This tired Roman might be called an ancient existentialist. Be he senator, banker, or jurist, nothing godly resides in him; yet he has developed, through force of character, his own system of values. The realism is so penetrating that we must suppose the use of a life mask; yet the sculptor truly possessed life-giving powers, for nothing, not even a death mask, is quite so dead as a life mask.

More creative, in the sense of psychological interpretation, is the recently acquired *Portrait Bust of Elagabalus*,[60] Syrian high priest and Roman emperor from the age of thirteen in A.D. 218 to his murder four years later. Cornelius Vermeule, the Curator of Classical Art, has written a fascinating account of this work in *Iconographical Studies*, published by the museum in 1980. Elagabalus was the youth's priestly name, after

58

59

his favorite Syrian deity, and he was falsely reputed to be the son of the Emperor Caracalla; as emperor he took the name of Marcus Aurelius Antoninus, but he became known even in his lifetime as the False Antoninus. In his brief imperial adolescence, he cut a wide swath of bizarre sexual adventures. In this portrait he resembles nothing so much as the street-wise Roman boys painted by Caravaggio. The arrangement of the drapery is standard in busts of this time; it is only in the face that the artist sought individual expression. Such work gives pause to the easy theory that Roman sculpture went progressively downhill after the Age of Augustus.

After the fall of Rome, the arts were patronized primarily by the Church, and with the rise of Romanesque art in the eleventh and twelfth centuries architecture dominated the forms of sculpture and painting to a marked degree. Carved Romanesque capitals abound in our museums, but Boston is still unique in America for owning the wall paintings of an entire apse, though they were acquired some sixty years ago. These paintings from Santa Maria de Mur[61] in Catalonia, northeast Spain, date from the mid-twelfth century. The style derives from Byzantine art, but it is more vehement in its rustic way. Christ in a glory is surrounded by the symbols of the four Evangelists with the twelve Apostles ranged below, while the story of the Nativity (damaged) occupies the lowest register. The white ground acts as a foil for a forceful play of line and sharp angle.

As for Byzantine art proper, the museum owns two frescoed heads from the same series as the example at the Williams College Museum of Art (MA 270). These are exhibited in the medieval galleries. The date is probably seventeenth century, but one six hundred years earlier has also been proposed. Evolution in Byzantine form is not its most interesting aspect.

The *Baptism of Christ*,[62] in gilt copper over a foot high, is an unusually important example of French medieval metalwork. Though it was made in Limoges as late as 1200–1250, its lean forms still echo those of Byzantine art. Like the Catalan frescoes, it has a quality of rustic vigor. The rounded sculptural modeling, however, is related to the Gothic sculpture of that time. The stylized water is gouged out from

60

61

the copper plate and filled with gray enamel by a process called champlevé.

The *Virgin and Child on a Crescent Moon*,[63] lower Austrian, c. 1450–60, in polychromed and gilt poplar wood 70 inches high, superbly represents the deep undercutting and angular tension of late Gothic art. It once formed the center of an elaborate altarpiece for a church near Linz on the Danube. Figure and crown are carved of one piece. Less intimate than the smaller example of c. 1430 in the Busch-Reisinger Museum (MA 99), it has a more majestic air. Both should be contrasted with Boston's statue of *St. John Evangelist*, also of polychromed poplar, Tuscan work of the fourteenth century, which preserves the more static and monumental character of thirteenth-century cathedral sculpture. (The legs and feet of the *Evangelist*—seemingly out of proportion—are modern.)

Dating from about 1400 is a rare wool-and-linen tapestry 16 feet long representing *Wild Men, Animals, and Moors*.[64] German work marked by considerable violence, it may have come from Strasbourg on the upper Rhine, since the coats of arms are those of two families from that city. Its labyrinthine patterns are as abstract as its colors, in which deep reds and cream tones predominate. The meaning is difficult to interpret, but it appears to reflect the strange admixture, current at the time, of love and the macabre. Here the "wild men"—ordinarily but not always symbols of evil—attack the fortress of love defended by black Moors, struggle with animals, and bear gifts to a wild woman and her child. Gertrude Townsend, the museum's former curator of textiles, devoted a long article to this tapestry in the museum's *Bulletin* for spring 1958. Relevant background for the emotional character of such

62
        63

64

work is contained in J. Huizinga's classic study, *The Waning of the Middle Ages* (London: Edward Arnold & Co., 1924), in the first chapter, entitled "The Violent Tenor of Life."

A many-crocketed retable from Aragon,[65] in northern Spain, painted by Martín de Soria in the late fifteenth century, tempera on panel and measuring nearly 14 feet in height, combines Italianate forms (and a hesitant use of Italian perspective) with Flemish technique and detail. The central image represents St. Peter, patron of the church or chapel that this multipaneled altar once adorned. Here the art of painting is closely associated with that of church furniture. Bright reds and gold unify the disparate parts of a complex construction, seemingly suspended above its predella of paired Apostles.

Mention of Flemish painting brings us to the outstanding example in New England, one of the masterworks of Roger van der Weyden of Tournai (1399/1400–64). The subject is *St. Luke Painting the Virgin*,[66] a fascinating combination of Gothic religious icon and modern artist-and-model picture. St. Luke (for whom many of the guilds and academies of painting were named) holds a silverpoint, and we may discern here the making of just such a drawing as the Dieric Bouts portrait at Smith College (MA 170). The setting flows easily from indoors out to a balcony overlooking a characteristic Flemish cityscape. An early work of the master from about 1436, it is more than usually influenced by the great Bruges painter Jan van Eyck, whose *Madonna of Chancellor Rolin* (in the Louvre) inspired its main conception. Nevertheless, van der Weyden's picture became famous in its own right: there are three other versions in major European museums, but the Boston example is acknowledged to be the original work. Bought at auction in New York by Henry Lee Higginson in 1889 and given to the museum by him in 1893, it was the earliest major Flemish painting to enter an American public collection. Its subject suggests that it was done for the Painters' Guild in Brussels, where Roger chiefly worked. Contemporary with the activity of the first generation of painters of the Florentine Renaissance, it seems to be indebted to them for its converging perspective, although this new device is not systematically employed here. While van Eyck's detail and something of his limpid atmosphere dominate Roger's art, the figures have much more sculptural volume, but without the anatomical coherence of those in the paintings of Masaccio or the sculptures

65

66

of Donatello (see MA 68). Details not to be missed are the simulated carved group of Adam and Eve and the Tree of Knowledge on an arm of the Virgin's throne, and behind St. Luke his symbol—an ox—in the lower compartment of a bookcase.

Acquired in 1964 as the gift of R. Thornton Wilson in memory of President Kennedy is a magnificent *Portrait Bust*,[67] about 2 feet high, made c. 1500 at Salzburg in Hafner ware—fired earthenware with colored glazes of tin and lead. A century later than the Rhenish tapestry just discussed, it still belongs to a disquieted late Gothic age—paradoxically contemporary with Michelangelo's great marble *David* of 1501–04. Compared with the peaceable art of Roger van der Weyden, the bust expresses emotional tension, in the face, in the tightly clasped arms, and in the jagged folds of the drapery. Roger's simple reds and blues could not be substituted for the dour browns of these glazes. Such inner expressiveness foretells the art of the modern Germans, and of another Austrian, Oskar Kokoschka (see MA 105), whose 1908 polychromed clay *Self-Portrait* (in the contemporary section of the museum) projects similar feelings. Clearly a donor image rather than a purely secular one, the Hafner-ware bust may also be a self-portrait—by a master of the Salzburg Hafner Guild.

After viewing these several expressions of the late Gothic spirit, to come upon Donatello's glistening white marble relief of the *Madonna of the Clouds*[68] is to enter a new world, that of the humanistic Florentine Renaissance. A 13-inch-square plaque in very low relief known as *stiacciato*, it dates from around 1430, well into the long career of Donatello (1386–1466). This is perhaps the only work in America by the hand of the greatest sculptor between Greek antiquity and Michelangelo—some would say the greatest sculptor of all time, and Michelangelo in his own time might have supported such a statement. Experts disagree about Donatello's authorship of a fifteenth-century unfinished *David* in the National Gallery, Washington, but generally agree that the conception of the Boston relief is Donatello's and likewise the carving of the Virgin, while the little background angels may be the

67

68

work of an assistant. The powerful form of the Virgin, at once gracious and sublime, clearly foreshadows the art of Michelangelo. We know that Donatello visited Rome and that he was enthralled by ancient Roman art, but his own work managed to recapture the spirit of a Greek art he could not possibly have seen, and to infuse it with a new emotional warmth and tenderness. We also know that this relief was treasured in Florence after the master's death. A certain Piero del Pugliese had it enshrined in a wooden tabernacle with movable wings painted by Fra Bartolomeo; and in Vasari's time (mid-sixteenth century) it was in the collection of Duke Cosimo de' Medici. The most perceptive account of the *Madonna of the Clouds* is by Sir John Pope-Hennessy in *Essays on Italian Sculpture* (London: Phaidon Press, 1968, pages 54–55).

Boston's representation of fourteenth- and fifteenth-century Italian painting cannot match that of the Gardner Museum or the Fogg Art Museum in Cambridge. Mention should be made, however, of the small gold-ground altarpiece of the *Crucifixion*, with wings representing the bishop saints Nicholas and Gregory, of which the center panel is either by Duccio di Buoninsegna (c. 1255–1319), the founder of Sienese painting, or possibly by a very faithful follower. In the section on the Mount Holyoke Museum of Art we discuss a small panel said to have come from Duccio's great *Maestà*, a multipaneled altarpiece for the high altar of Siena Cathedral (MA 204).

Outstanding among the museum's fifteenth-century Italian paintings is the *Presentation of the Virgin in the Temple*[69] by an anonymous artist known as the Master of the Barberini Panels, who flourished in the 1460s. A companion panel of similar size (height 58 inches), representing the *Visitation*, is in the Metropolitan Museum of Art. Both were acquired in the 1930s from the Barberini Gallery in Rome. Efforts to link them with the work of a known artist have met with little success. Whoever he was, he carried the Florentine passion for architectural perspectives to a kind of Surrealist extreme, and so populated his compositions with incident and extraneous characters (who nevertheless help us measure the planar recession) that it is not easy to find

69

the main subject. All the elements of this fantastic building relate to Renaissance architecture, but such a building clearly could not exist; it is best understood as painter's architecture. The two angels atop the main cornice suggest that the picture may have had a very elaborate frame.

The *Dead Christ with Angels*,[70] signed by the Florentine painter known as Il Rosso Fiorentino (1494–1540) brings us past the High Renaissance art of Raphael into the so-called Mannerist art of about 1525. A large oil on panel over 4 feet high and in superb condition, it is not only the most important work of this master in America but probably our finest Mannerist picture. Inspired by both Leonardo da Vinci and Michelangelo, Il Rosso broke with most of their artistic premises: axial balance is dislocated, space is telescoped into a narrow shelf of recession, light and shade run to violent contrasts, and color turns vivid. The naked body of Christ, neither dead nor alive, is set on an altar attended by angels. Perhaps it is resurrected. Its sensuality seems contradictory to its iconic function. We feel at once a weakening of dogma and a heightening of aestheticism. The message here seems to be a celebration of art itself, tinged with highly equivocal overtones of what it is that these androgynous angels are worshiping. In sum, a picture both shocking and marvelous.

The seventeenth century, like the nineteenth, was a century of great painters, and El Greco (1541–1614) lived long enough to initiate it. The seated portrait of the Trinitarian monk, *Fray Felix Paravicino*,[71] often cited as one of El Greco's masterpieces, dates from 1609. The light and color give the monk a kind of phosphorescent energy. The fluid brushwork helps convey the sense of a moment in time. On all these accounts we approach Baroque art, though the Baroque emphasis on physical bulk is conspicuously absent. This is because Domenico Theotocopoulos, called "The Greek" in Toledo to the end of his life, came from Byzantine Crete. The longer he painted, the more closely he returned to the mystical art of his origins.

That this picture was purchased on the specific recommendation of John Singer Sargent is as astonishing as the date of the purchase itself

70

71

—1904, four years before Manuel Cossio's pioneering biography of El Greco and six years before Julius Meier-Graefe's *Spanish Journey* established him as an artist for our time. Sargent's insistence, based on what the European avant-garde was beginning to say about El Greco, resulted in the first acquisition of his work by an American museum. The price—seventeen thousand dollars—was not inconsiderable for an "unknown" at the time. All of this made possible by the creator of the Gardner Museum's *El Jaleo* (MA 51)!

Diego Velázquez (1599–1660), the leading painter of the Spanish Golden Age, is represented in the museum by superb examples of both his earlier and his mature work. The *Portrait of Luis de Góngora*,[72] the poet, painted when Velázquez was twenty-five, is marked by the sharp line, the bony structure, and the thin proportions of Mannerist art of the previous century. (These are also found in El Greco.) Very Spanish are the detachment and pride in this intense personage. The *Don Baltazar Carlos and His Dwarf* was painted some ten years later, after Velázquez had toured Italy and returned to Madrid as chief court artist. Full of enthusiasm for the Italian Renaissance painters, especially Titian and the Venetians, he now used opulent colors, notably deep reds and violets. He developed a play of silvery texture over transparent darks, and generally relaxed the intensity seen in the early Góngora portrait.

In Holland the great figure before Rembrandt was Frans Hals (c. 1581–1666), and Boston's magnificent *Portrait of a Man*,[73] dating c. 1664–66, is one of his last surviving works. Thus it should be thought of in the revolutionary terms of the last water-lily canvases of Claude Monet (much later than any discussed in this book), for Monet too lived to the age of eighty-six—or considered with the late Pietàs of Michelangelo, who died at eighty-nine. The unknown sitter fancied himself. He acquired (or borrowed) a deep rust-red kimono of shot silk, of the sort first given by the Japanese Shogun to officers of the Dutch East India Company and later exported to a fast-growing European market. His extravagantly long brown hair (possibly a wig) awkwardly apes the style then fashionable at the court of Louis XIV. Accoutred in these status symbols, he observes us with a rather smug smile (I have

72

73

made it, he seems to say). What a contrast to the usual stark black-and-white images of Dutch burghers and their wives!

So much for the subject, but what of the artist? In the twenty years that elapsed since Hals painted *Mevrouw Bodolphe* (Yale University Art Gallery, CT 73), his brushwork has grown increasingly looser and more transparent, as if to express the disillusionment that has crept into his soul. Our status-hungry sitter thus became an occasion for mordant satire. Note, in contrast to the Yale portrait, the total concentration on the head (but do not miss the expressiveness of the hand), peering out from all this foolish finery. If the kimono is brushed with almost nonchalant speed, it is nevertheless a miracle of execution. Two centuries later, its quality was not lost on Edouard Manet. A fine account of the Boston portrait will be found in Seymour Slive, *Frans Hals* (3 volumes; London: Phaidon Press, 1970, 1974, catalogue number 220).

The museum owns an important pair of full-length portraits of Reverend and Mrs. Johannes Elison, painted in 1634 by Rembrandt van Rijn (1606–69)—a year later than the Gardner Museum's *Lady and Gentleman in Black* (MA 48). Other Dutch pictures of note include the Dirk Baburen *Procuress* that appears on the back wall of the Gardner Museum's *Concert* by Vermeer of Delft (MA 50), a marvelous little *Cavalier in the Saddle* by Gerard Ter Borch (1584–1662), and Jacob van Ruisdael's *A Rough Sea*,[74] which we now consider.

Among the younger contemporaries of Rembrandt who specialized in landscape painting, none was more distinguished than Ruisdael (1628/9–82), a native of Haarlem. Indeed, Rembrandt's own landscapes are so personal and psychological (compare the example in the Gardner Museum (MA 49) that it is doubtful they should be considered as landscape in the usual sense of the term.

Ruisdael excelled in all categories of landscape: sky, land, and water, and in all their combinations. His marines, embodying the Dutch love of the sea and of sailing, are perhaps unequaled in the history of art, though they inspired a rival in the young Turner (an example is at the Malden Library, MA 165) early in the nineteenth century. *A Rough Sea* is considered one of the finest marines of his whole career. Painted about 1670, it shows an estuary outside Amsterdam. The broad expanse of water zigzags back in alternating light and dark triangles, with counter-accents of darks and lights in the foreground pilings and the near

74

and distant sails. The brisk lapping of the waves sets up a nervous tension through its sharp linear rhythms, felt again in the shapes of the clouds. Earlier works by Ruisdael are discussed at Springfield (MA 211) and at Manchester (NH 24).

Because Peter Paul Rubens, Nicolas Poussin, Antoine Watteau, and J. B. S. Chardin—major figures of seventeenth- and eighteenth-century painting—are discussed in other museums, we regretfully pass over fine examples of their work in the Museum of Fine Arts. In connection with a superb Poussin (*Achilles on Skyros*), however, the visitor is fore-warned to look up the story of how Achilles' mother concealed him in woman's attire among the daughters of Lycomedes and how a sword destroyed his cover.

Short of his grandiose ceiling paintings in the palaces of Venice, Würzburg, and Madrid, it would be difficult to cite a more sumptuous example of the art of Giovanni Battista Tiepolo (1696–1770) than *Time Unveiling Truth*,[75] an oil nearly 8 feet high dating from c. 1745, in the full glory of the long career of this Venetian decorator. A pen-and-wash drawing, *Hagar and Ishmael*, in Williamstown (MA 266) sets up expectations of power and energy fulfilled here in the oil medium. Tiepolo provides the essential link between Baroque grandeur and Rococo sensuality. The darkish Baroque color—bronzed greens, deep ochers, and wine reds—sets off the lightly keyed flesh tones and sky blues found in French Rococo painting (as in the museum's *Return from the Market*, 1767, by François Boucher [1703–70]). Note how Time's scythe introduces, as at the beginning of a symphonic movement, two major visual themes: a bold curve and a rapidly receding strong diagonal. As we climb up this complex composition these motifs are intertwined in complicated variations. A fluted column at the rear provides a forceful note of stability.

In the city-dominated eighteenth century, views of natural landscape were in little demand. Views of cities, however, and other sights included on the Grand Tour were extremely popular. Often these pictures were rather small, and more often they were replicas turned out in quantity by some well-organized atelier. Antonio Canale, called Canaletto

75

(1697–1768), the leading Venetian painter of such views, like the slightly later (and, to sharp eyes, very different) Francesco Guardi, ran such an establishment. His large (49 by 60 inches) and superbly painted *Bacino di San Marco*[76] (c. 1740–45) shows us Canaletto at his best, and the picture is probably entirely by his hand. In mid-distance before the Doges' Palace, amid a vast array of shipping, is the impressive *bucintoro,* the golden, many-oared barge wherein, on great occasions, the Doge was enthroned as the symbol of the Most Serene Republic. The painting was purchased from the artist himself for Castle Howard, in England, whence the museum acquired it in 1939. The view is taken from near the Customs Building at the entrance to the Grand Canal, with the Piazzetta and the Doges' Palace on the left, and the island church of San Giorgio Maggiore on the right. Richard Parkes Bonington's view at the Malden Library (MA 166) looks in exactly the opposite direction.

Far to the north from Tiepolo's and Canaletto's Venice, but hardly sixty miles from the Residenz at Würzburg—with its great Tiepolo ceiling frescoes of c. 1750—the ceramic sculptor Johann Martin Mutschele (1733–1804) may be said to have absorbed and transposed Tiepolo's forms into a new medium. His imposing *Madonna of Victory,*[77] 4 feet high, in white glazed Schrezheim faience, once adorned the portal niche of the residence of the Teutonic Knights (now the Rathaus) at Wolframs-Eschenbach, in Franconia. A unique creation, it is the most important single work of German faience. The date, 1771, appears with the artist's monogram. The Tiepolo influence, referred to above, was not at the expense of German tradition, for eighteenth-century German piety—so pronounced that it amounted to a virtual medieval revival— is strongly in evidence here. The source of the theme is biblical (Revelation: 12): "And there appeared a great wonder in heaven, a woman clothed with the sun and the moon under her feet and upon her head a crown of twelve stars." The museum's *Bulletin* for 1965 carries a fine article on this piece by the then curator, Hanns Swarzenski. Filled with the Baroque sense of drama, the figure at the same time has the intimacy and refinement of Rococo art, further marked by the emphasis on C-shaped curves originally derived from the forms of the conch shell.

Perhaps the least significant fact about John Singleton Copley (1738–

77

76

1815) is that his celebrated *Portrait of Paul Revere,*[78] painted about
1768–70, was almost exactly contemporary with Mutschele's *Madonna
of Victory.* Such gratuitous information nevertheless helps us measure
the immense gulf that separated American Colonial culture from that of
Rococo Europe. As we have seen in the discussion of the great portraits
at Bowdoin College (ME 10–12), Copley was among the first to establish the art of the American colonies as other than a provincial offshoot
of British art. Perhaps the same can be said for Paul Revere, Boston's
patriot-silversmith. We may take special pride that these two artistic
forebears come together in Copley's memorable portrait. Like the painting, the silver teapot (very similar to one by Revere in the same room)
shows a high order of craftsmanship, painstaking detail, strongly simplified shapes, avoidance of anything showy or ornate. The Revere portrait was painted several years before Copley settled in London and
gradually yielded his American heritage to English tastes. Its informal
air is in sharp contrast to the many fashionable images in the museum's
collection of more than sixty works by Copley. Here his ever-sharp eye
and disciplined hand have caught the subject's physical girth, his intense
facial expression, and his blunt fingernails—doubtless worn down in
the practice of his craft. For other Boston portraits by Copley, see the
examples at Dartmouth and Smith colleges, and for an English one the
Mrs. Seymour Fort at Hartford (CT 25).

Landscape painting, in contrast to cityscapes so popular in the eighteenth century, became the dominant theme of Romantic art. In the same
way, nature dominated poetry in the age of Wordsworth. England took
a leading position in both arts. The poetry of nature in oils, as landscape
painting might be called, moved in two distinct directions: the serenity
of the homeland and the exotic appeal of natural wonders abroad. John
Constable (1776–1837) stands for the former and Joseph M. W. Turner
(1775–1851) for the latter, though this contrast admits of some exceptions. In any event, the museum's Constable, *Weymouth Bay,* with its
cloud-swept coast plunging us miles into untroubled distances, contrasts
violently with Turner's huge and crashing *Falls of the Rhine at Schaffhausen*[79] (c. 1806). In the one, a little figure walks the moors while
in the distance a farmer—his shirt a miraculous speck of light—con-

78

79

tentedly plows his fields. In the other, a knot of figures, horses, and wagons is dwarfed by nature's wild power. A rainbow arches the spume, and the great rock seems to push like an animate being against the roaring torrent. In both, nature, not man, is the protagonist: nature is space, and air, and moisture, and light, and, above all, weather. Indeed, Constable (see CT 57–58) used to make quick sketches out of doors, and mark them with the location, the date, and the direction of the wind. If he is England's closest parallel to Wordsworth in painting, Turner comes nearest to Byron's great apostrophes to the sea.

Despite its extremely unfinished state, nothing could better demonstrate the mysterious power of Honoré Daumier (1808–79) than the *Man on a Rope*.[80] What is the man doing? Is he a circus acrobat? Is he escaping from prison? Is he, as some have said, merely a house painter? We shall probably never know, and even if we did, it would make little difference. The first explanation seems the most likely. The second is possible. But because Daumier could transform the most insignificant incident into a theme of Michelangelesque grandeur, one is tempted to think the third explanation may lie closest to the truth. Balzac, one of Daumier's admirers and in many ways his equivalent in literature, once said of him: "There is something of Michelangelo in that fellow." The date is probably c. 1858–60, well after Daumier's somewhat Neoclassical forms in his lithograph of 1834, the *Rue Transnonain* (CT 41).

Edouard Manet (1832–83) and Edgar Degas (1834–1917) were both closely associated with the circle of the Impressionists in Paris, yet both remained strangely aloof. Essentially this was caused by their basic temperament. Manet and Degas were much more deeply committed to the traditional values of painting than their somewhat younger colleagues in Impressionism. This becomes especially clear in their early works, of which Boston owns examples of the very first order. *The Street Singer* by Manet dates from 1862, the year of Yale's *Young Woman Reclining* (CT 79) and the year before the famous *Olympia* and the *Déjeuner sur l'herbe* (in the Louvre), and the same model, Victorine Meurend, posed for both of them. Degas's portrait of his sister and her titled husband, *The Duke and Duchess of Morbilli*,[81] was painted in 1867. Both Boston

80

81

pictures are low in color intensity, with restrained grays, browns, and greenish ochers underlining the well-bred reticence of the persons portrayed. Both have an aristocratic air, despite Manet's choice of a rather tawdry subject. While Degas's hauteur was partly a matter of natural inheritance, the solid bourgeois background of Manet did not commit him to accepting its social point of view. At this time he found his inspiration in Velázquez, whether in the few attributed works then available in Paris or in black-and-white reproductions we do not know. Degas's sources were Ingres, Mannerist painters like Bronzino, and the purity of line of some of the fifteenth-century Italians. A drawing of the head of the duchess, also in the Boston Museum, is very close to such a Florentine master as Ghirlandajo.

The *Portrait of Madame Cézanne*[82] was painted by Paul Cézanne (1839–1906) about 1877, several years after he had worked with Camille Pissarro at Pontoise (see MA 255) and absorbed Impressionist technique with its high-intensity palette. Here he unites it with his powerful sense of volumes and replaces the Impressionist sense of a fleeting moment with his characteristic solemnity and timelessness. Long his mistress before becoming Cézanne's wife in 1886, Hortense Fiquet patiently posed for him for some twenty-seven portraits over a period of thirty years. He is said to have preferred her to still life because she did not rot. Much of Cézanne's effect is due to his elimination of the camera's illusion of spatial recession (faithfully adhered to by the Impressionists). Thus the figure resembles relief sculpture against a flat plane. Strokes of paint brushed on in small flat rectangles in a close value range lose their impact in the black-and-white photograph, for the hues differ. You soon learn to "read" a change of color as a shift in direction, so they participate in the rounding of a volume. Characteristically, the eyes are sightless, as in many Greek and Roman heads. There is no psychological focus. Indeed, this is a still-life portrait.

Pierre Auguste Renoir (1841–1919) is the leading figure painter among the true Impressionists, as Claude Monet was the leading landscapist. Both of them were notable painters of still life (for Renoir see MA 128 and MA 256). Boston's *Bal à Bougival*,[83] signed and dated by

82

83

Renoir in 1883 and measuring a generous 71 by 38 inches, is one of his masterpieces from the vintage years of the early 1880s, just before he began to move away from Impressionism toward a style marked by more incisive outline and more substantial modeling. Already in this work the process has begun; it approaches a Rubensesque hymn to joys of the flesh. But the color, soon to become both hotter and drier, retains Impressionism's rainbow palette of unmixed prismatic hues, their sparkle enhanced by deft turns of the brush. The foreground figures are more massive than in earlier Renoirs of this sort, but as we move back into the distance the language of Impressionism gains in purity. For this picture, sometimes called *La Danse à la Campagne*, Suzanne Valadon—painter, model, and the mother of Maurice Utrillo (see ME 40)—posed with Renoir's brother.

Two sides of American life in the later nineteenth century may be observed in *Long Branch, N.J.*, an early landscape by Winslow Homer (1836–1910), and *The Daughters of Edward D. Boit*,[84] painted in 1882 by John Singer Sargent (1856–1925). Homer came from Boston, and though Sargent was born in Florence, Boston was his spiritual home. In later life Homer's genius led him to the solitudes of the New England coasts; Sargent's led him to Europe and a fashionable career as a portraitist. Thus we have a clear opposition between native and expatriate art. Sargent belonged to the world of Henry James, whose castigations of Homer for his "vulgarities" (see CT 80) can only be understood in this context. *Long Branch* (1869) is exactly contemporary with the beginnings of Impressionism in Paris, from which Homer had recently returned after a period of study. His concern with light and his subject are the only connections: all else is as different as a Copley from a Gainsborough portrait in the preceding century. Sargent, too, makes poetry of American innocence; but he has left a telling document of a somewhat inbred society. The picture was painted in the Boits' Paris apartment. The big vases, which made many journeys back and forth from Boston, are important in establishing the size of the little girls, and in completing the blue-and-white scheme that helps unite this 87-inch-square canvas. The picture was called "four corners and a void" by a hostile critic when it was shown at the Paris Salon of 1883; but Henry James, in an essay on Sargent written ten years later, much preferred "The Hall with the Four Children," as he called it, to *El Jaleo* (Gardner Museum, MA 51). "If the picture of the Spanish Dancer illustrates, as

84

it seems to me to do, the latent dangers of the Impressionist practice, so this finer performance shows what victories it may achieve . . . [an] astonishing work on the part of a young man of twenty-six" (Henry James, *The Painter's Eye*, edited by John L. Sweeney; Cambridge: Harvard University Press, 1956, page 223).

In the company of Renoir's *Bal à Bougival*, Sargent seems very conservative, especially in his muted colors in this darkened interior. In his youthful years he was an Impressionist more in the vein of the early work of Degas and Edouard Manet—whom he followed in his enthusiasm for Velázquez's hushed illusionism. Similarly, the early work of Vincent van Gogh (1853–90)—born only three years before Sargent—is marked by the dark tones of Pre-Impressionism, as seen in Boston's *Weaver*,[85] painted in 1884. In January of that year Vincent wrote to his brother Theo: "Soon I hope to start another two of weavers, where the figure comes in quite differently, that is to say, the weaver does not sit behind it, but is arranging the threads of the cloth. I have seen them weaving in the evening by lamplight, which gives very Rembrandtesque effects." A pen drawing for the Boston version of this subject (one of several he painted in 1884) is in the Van Gogh Museum at Amsterdam; it includes a lighted lamp not seen in the painting. In some versions the weaver seems almost imprisoned in a kind of cage; but here the effect is less troubled. If the loom is seen in the pale gray light of a sunless day, the pinks and reds of the woven cloth and the blue of the weaver's coat give out a little warmth. For an actual loom like this one, see the Merrimack Valley Textile Museum, North Andover (page 263).

After these tentative but moving beginnings, van Gogh went on to master Impressionism in Paris and then to his great achievements in Arles (CT 81), Saint-Rémy (ME 27), and Auvers. Boston has the marvelous *Postman Roulin* from the Arles period (1888) and the tumultuous *Ravine*, painted a year later at Saint-Rémy. We discuss his 1888 *Self-Portrait*, dedicated to Paul Gauguin, in the section on the Fogg Art Museum of Harvard University (MA 130). As for Gauguin (1848–1903), Boston has impressive examples of his painted wood sculpture and an unsurpassed oil. Over 12 feet wide, it was painted at Tahiti in 1897 as his final testament.[86] At that time Gauguin had planned to

85

86

commit suicide. Signed and dated at the upper right, the canvas carries its provocative title in the balancing corner at the left: *D'où venons-nous? Que sommes-nous? Où allons-nous?* Gauguin's answer to these eschatological questions is organized in a cycle from right to left (counter to expected Western readings). A running dog somewhat obviously starts us off. We are born, we enjoy the fruits of life, we end grayed and shriveled, accompanied by a symbolic bird, described later by Gauguin in a letter as "a strange white bird, holding a lizard in its claw [*sic*] . . . [It] represents a futility of words." Some may find this—and much additional—symbolism excessive. If you are anthropologically inclined, you will discover that the exotic deities—the one at the left, Gauguin wrote, "seems to indicate the Beyond"—have little or nothing to do with Tahitian religion, but are an admixture of the artist's memories of non-Western arts in the Paris museums. In his obsession with such material, however, Gauguin was far ahead of modern enthusiasms; and his example, not lost on Picasso and the German Expressionists, had a profound influence. Still more important were his sense of flat mural design and his revolutionary color. In these respects Henri Matisse was his true twentieth-century follower. In these, too, Gauguin is most respected today. His high opinion of himself was on a different level: discussing the Boston picture, he wrote, "I have finished a philosophical work on this theme, comparable to the Gospels. I think it is good." The title, he insisted, is "not a title, but a signature."

The acquisition in 1958 of *Standing Figure*[87] by Pablo Picasso (1881–1973) brought the museum's collections abruptly into modern avant-garde art, an area in which it had been sadly deficient. This statement holds true even though the picture, 5 feet high, was painted as early as the spring of 1908, a few months after the completion of the celebrated *Demoiselles d'Avignon* (Museum of Modern Art, New York). In the Boston oil Picasso has narrowed the color range to the warm pinks, orange browns, and sky blues of the *Demoiselles'* more complex palette. *Standing Figure* carries nascent Cubism farther along than in that path-finding earlier work. During 1908 and 1909 Picasso further reduced his color range to warm cinnamon browns and subdued greens; and in the next two years it reached a state of virtual grisaille—pale tans, browns,

87

grays—until around 1912/13, when color made its reappearance (as in Dartmouth College's *Guitar on a Table*, NH 11). A study for the central figure in *Three Women* in the Hermitage, Leningrad, the Boston painting was once owned by Daniel-Henry Kahnweiler, a Paris dealer who wrote important treatises on Cubism and a major book on Juan Gris (see MA 184). Interest in the forms of primitive art, inspired by the example of Paul Gauguin, led Picasso in 1906/7 to find fresh sources of creative energy in ancient Iberian and in African and Oceanian sculpture. Into these forms he injected his own sense of violence through sharp edges and angular collisions. He achieved further aggressiveness in *Standing Figure* by making it occupy the full height of the picture surface (contrast Renoir's *Bal à Bougival*), even to the extent of chopping off the top and bottom extremities.

In 1964 the museum purchased Picasso's large *Rape of the Sabines*, painted the year before as a sort of challenge to Jacques Louis David's painting in the Louvre; and eventually a new department of contemporary art was established. "Contemporary" is a less polarizing word than "modern," but modern is what was intended. The first purchase, in 1971, by the department was Jackson Pollock's *Number 10, 1949*. The collection, now fast growing, includes no fewer than six major paintings by the important "color-field" painter, Morris Louis (1912–62). In modern sculpture, David Smith (1906–65) is strongly represented at the museum by two large works, *Cubi XVIII* (1964) and *Zig VIII*,[88] over 8 feet high and fashioned in 1965 in welded and polychromed steel. The title was suggested both by the zigzag directions of the design and by ancient Babylonian ziggurats—winding pyramidal towers ornamented with glazed brick. Against the perfection of a white-rimmed red circle, the girderlike black arms stretch in diagonal opposition.

A glass lamp of the fourteenth century from Mohammedan Syria[89] must stand as a single example of the museum's remarkable collection of Near Eastern decorative art. The ornament, in colored enamels and gold, has a dedicatory inscription around the body, and on the rim a verse from the Koran: "God is the light of the heavens and the earth; His light is as a niche in which is a lamp, and the lamp is in a glass,

89

88

the glass is as though it were a glittering star." Such intricate repetitions and variations in symbolism closely parallel the complexities of the interlaced design.

Our earliest selection from the museum's fabulous Asiatic collections is a *Yaksi Torso*,[90] sandstone, about 29 inches high, from one of the gateways of the Great Stupa at Sānchī, in central India. A masterwork of Buddhist sculpture of the first century B.C., it formed part of the outdoor complex that celebrated the myriad aspects of the phenomenal world. This figure of a tree-dwelling dryad illustrates perfectly the union of spiritual and sensual abundance that is a constant theme in Indian religious art. We must await the nudes of Correggio and Rubens to find anything comparable in Western expression. This transformation of stone into flesh is achieved by lush contours, swelling interior folds, powerful twists of the body, and by the abrupt contrast of the rigid thrust of the thighs. For a discussion of the Great Stupa, including a plan and an elevation, see Benjamin Rowland, *The Art and Architecture of India*, Pelican History of Art.

While Boston's collection of Indian art is outstanding, and its Indian painting reputed to be greater than any collection in India itself, its Chinese and Japanese art is the finest in the Western world. Among the great masterpieces of early Chinese sculpture may be cited the seated *Bodhisattva Maitreya*[91] of the late fifth century A.D. (northern Wei dynasty), and the dedicatory bronze group of the *Buddha Amitabha Trinity and Attendant Deities*,[92] dated A.D. 593 (Sui dynasty). The re-

90

92

91

semblance of such sculpture, especially in the case of the *Maitreya*, to Romanesque art has often been noted: compare the paintings of Boston's Catalonian chapel and the twelfth-century wooden *Virgin and Child* at Worcester (MA 293). The flat plane dominates. There is a minimum of undercutting and of spatial recession: thus their particular appeal to modern eyes. The connection is, of course, purely coincidental, but it has led, with other evidence of widely differing cultures, to a theory of cultural cycles running from the taut "Archaic" stage (seen here and in Romanesque art) to the serene "Classic," to the freewheeling "Baroque." We should be gravely in error to assume that cultures must evolve in this way, for Egyptian and Byzantine cultures did not. Yet it is interesting to speculate whether modern art has created a new archaic stage after the baroque of the nineteenth century.

Both the *Maitreya* and the Sui dynasty shrine are included by Laurence Sickman in the authoritative Pelican History of Art volume on *The Art and Architecture of China*. Of the former (page 49), Sickman notes its purely frontal character and as well its "serenity of spirit." "An anonymous stone-carver," he continues, "has with some naivety and complete sincerity captured a convincing vision of the great Bodhisattva destined to be the Buddha of the future." The shrine is praised (page 61) as an exceptionally complete example of Chinese Buddhist art "in its most vital creative period, the sixth and seventh centuries." He notes that the Buddha and the two Bodhisattvas have "the benign, tender expressions that mark the best Buddhist concepts from the later sixth century."

For discussion of the high "classic" art of the T'ang dynasty (618–906) the reader is referred to the examples discussed at the Fogg Art Museum (MA 134 and 137) and the great stone head at Worcester (MA 311). By the time of the Southern Sung dynasty (1127–1279) painting had so liberated itself from the limitations of drawing and the effects of modeled sculpture as to reach a stage not unlike that ushered in to Italian painting by the great Venetians. In this period Chinese sculpture became markedly pictorial. The seated *Kuan-yin*,[93] one of the Bodhisattvas, or lesser Buddhist deities, is among the greatest known examples of Chinese sculpture of the Sung dynasty. Carved in wood, it dates from the twelfth century. The typical "royal-ease" position suggests a baroque freedom of movement, though it would certainly be an

93

exaggeration to compare it to anything as extreme as a Rubens or a Bernini. The distance in forms that Chinese art has traveled since the late fifth century may be gauged by a comparison to the *Bodhisattva Maitreya.*

Chinese painting followed roughly the same development that we have traced in the selections of Chinese sculpture. If there is any truth in thinking of Sung art as relatively baroque, the great flowering of painting in this age may be cited in support of such a contention. In a Baroque age, architecture and sculpture generally yield their dominant position to painting, and in turn are marked by a desire to compete with painting on its own ground. However this may be, the *Nine Dragons Scroll*[94] by Ch'ên Jung (c. 1210–c. 1261), nearly 36 feet long and one of the most celebrated of all Chinese paintings, unwinds its mysteries in volutes of mist and water. We can learn to respond to the subtleties of the Chinese mind only by repeated exposure and long contemplation. With the least of means—a few scratches and washes in ink heightened by pale suggestions of color—the artist has achieved, almost five hundred years before Leonardo da Vinci, what Leonardo sought to achieve in his drawings of the waters.

Another scroll from the Sung period, *Ladies Preparing Newly Woven Silk*[95] by Emperor Hui Tsung (1082–1135), will strike the observer as much more restrained and much less atmospheric than the preceding example. An explanation may lie in the fact that a later inscription tells us that the imperial artist copied it from a picture by Chang Hsüan, a court painter of the earlier T'ang dynasty. This much smaller scroll, under 5 feet in length, emphasizes elegance and dainty coloring rather than the unearthly mystery of the *Nine Dragons Scroll.* Our illustrations of both are limited to the final section, that is, the left end of each scroll. In accordance with Far Eastern reading habits, such scrolls are regularly unrolled from right to left. It is, of course, as arbitrary to cut off any section as it would be to do the same to a musical score. In these and other ways Far Eastern art challenges our Western conception of the

94

95

framed picture, and even our assumption of the separate categories of the several arts.

Japanese culture, profoundly influenced by the Chinese, increasingly developed its own inflection and style. If the tenth-century (Fujiwara) *Buddhist Deity* at Yale (CT 65) is a harsher, more earthbound variant of T'ang dynasty sculpture, emphasis on warlike exploits in Japanese art left little opportunity for such cosmic expressions as the *Nine Dragons Scroll*. (The dragon was the ultimate symbol for the *Tao*, the elemental vital force of the universe.) A vast cultural divide separates that Sung dynasty masterpiece of the twelfth century from *The Burning of Sanjo Palace*,[96] a scroll of the thirteenth century (Kamakura period) almost 23 feet long that is said to rival anything even in the imperial collections in Tokyo. There can be no hesitation in calling it one of the great war pictures in the world. Our illustration, from near the central portion of this epic, shows approximately a fifth of the whole. Unrolled from the right, it rises gradually to a great crescendo; then, following the conflagration, the action subsides until at the extreme left a single horseman leads the triumphal procession. An analogy to Western symphonic movement is inescapable. Our segment also exemplifies the Japanese method of describing spatial recession—not by converging parallels, but by parallel diagonals. An advantage of this system over Western one-point perspective is that objects in the distance that we know are the same size as foreground ones appear that way here—and we can see them with equal clarity. Furthermore, no illusionistic "hole" is pierced through the paper ground; thus the medium itself is respected.

Monkeys,[97] a six-fold screen, ink on paper dated 1491, is the work of Sesshū (1420–1506), a leading painter of the Muromachi period. That he was a contemporary of such Western artists as Dieric Bouts (MA 100) merely reinforces the difficulty of adjusting our sights as we approach the art of another world. After we study Sesshū's subtle brush-work and peer through his vapors, it is not surprising to learn that he traveled in China and visited Zen monasteries, nor that at this time the Japanese venerated Sung dynasty painting.

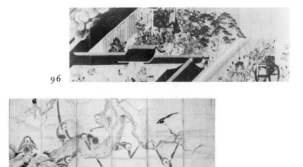

96

97

Brockton Art Museum

Location: Oak St., in D. W. Field Park; take exit 18B from Route 24, west of the city; follow Oak St. (Route 37) east. The museum is on your left

Hours: Open daily except Mon. 1-5; on Thurs. 1-10 P.M. except in July and August

Admission: Charged

Opened in 1969, the museum was made possible by the generosity of Myron Leslie Fuller. In that year the architect, J. Timothy Anderson, received the national blue-ribbon award for excellence from the Society of American Registered Architects. The building was cited as "one of America's finest small museums . . . in a brilliantly achieved environment, growing naturally and gracefully out of its surrounding woods and rocky grounds." I suspect you will have no quarrel with that estimate.

The museum maintains an active program of temporary exhibitions, lectures, and art classes, and its public is both numerous and enthusiastic. While the permanent collection is not large, it has range and it is growing. Two of the finest paintings are on indefinite loan from the Brockton Public Library: the *Portrait of Walter Copeland Bryant*, a late work of 1903 by Thomas Eakins, and that of *Abel Willard Kingman* by the stylish Italian master Giovanni Boldini. Both Bryant and Kingman were distinguished residents of Brockton. Emphasis within the collection as it develops is on contemporary American art of a conservative character.

Busch-Reisinger Museum,
Harvard University

Location: 29 Kirkland Street, at Divinity Avenue
Hours: Mon.-Sat. 9-4:45; in July and August Mon.-Fri. 9-4:45
Admission: Free. Ⓗ by arrangement

The museum was founded in 1902 as a center for the study of Germanic culture. A part of Harvard University, it is administered by the Fogg Art Museum. The building, erected in 1921 in a style that visitors to Munich will quickly recognize, contains a large Romanesque hall, with casts of German medieval sculpture, and generous space in smaller galleries. As a result of the rapid growth of the Fogg Art Museum, rich holdings in Netherlandish art have in recent years been moved to the Busch-Reisinger Museum; today it thus offers a superb survey of northern European art, that of France and England excluded. The collection is very strong in modern German art, including study material relating to the famous Bauhaus movement (1919-33) and to the architect Walter Gropius and the painter Lyonel Feininger (see MA 277). Organ concerts are given in the Romanesque hall on an instrument fashioned on authentic Baroque design.

Four colossal sandstone statues of *The Seasons*, of which we reproduce *Summer*,[98] occupy the corners of the great hall. Attributed to Johann Joachim Günther (1717-89), they came from the gardens of the palace at Bruchsal, summer residence of the Prince Bishop of Speyer, and were acquired by the Fogg Museum in 1952. The low bases have appropriate seasonal reliefs with frames of rocaille design marked by the irregular C-shaped element that is so characteristic of the Rococo style. The figures are loaded with allegory, but through their svelte undulation, carried through from top to bottom, and through fluid twists of head, torso, and limbs, they take artistic precedence over these accessories. The German Rococo lilt is heavier than its French counterpart, and the nudity is a bit more self-conscious, but these signs of provincial-

98

ism are surely more engaging than detrimental. The date is about 1760–65.

From the excellent casts, one can study masterpieces of German sculpture from the eleventh-century bronze doors of St. Michael's at Hildesheim to the great stone rood screen of the thirteenth century at Naumburg and the Golden Gate of Freiburg Cathedral. An original unpainted wood statue of *St. John Evangelist*, c. 1490–1500, is close to the art of Tilman Riemenschneider, Germany's most expressive late Gothic sculptor. From the neighboring Austrian Tyrol comes a 5-foot painted wood *Madonna and Child*,[99] c. 1430, standing on a crescent moon and crowned with one of the most elaborate examples you are ever likely to see. Note how the swinging lines of the drapery, beginning at Mary's feet, lead you up to it. The rustic innocence of this version of the theme contrasts greatly with the regal poise of the larger example at the Boston Museum of Fine Arts, dating from c. 1450–60 (MA 63). In the base is a small shelf for exhibiting a relic or an offering.

Outstanding among the many fine early Netherlandish paintings are a *St. Jerome in His Study* by Joos van Cleve, c. 1520, and a white-robed *Angel* against a blue-green landscape by an unidentified artist whose expressive power was considerable. But finest of all is a *Half-length Madonna and Child*,[100] oil on panel, by Dieric Bouts (c. 1420–75), the probable author of a precious silverpoint drawing at Smith College (MA 170). Bouts, born at Haarlem, worked in Louvain after the late 1440s. His early pictures combine the meticulousness of Jan van Eyck with the broader, more sculptural style of Roger van der Weyden; but by the mid-1460s, when he must have painted the *Half-length Madonna and Child*, Roger's influence was much the stronger. Comparison with Roger's *St. Luke Painting the Virgin* at Boston (MA 66) will make that clear, especially in the figure of the Child. Another Bouts *Virgin and Child*, in the London National Gallery, dated about 1465, is nearly a mirror image of the Busch-Reisinger example. There is great sensitivity in Bouts's hands (and feet), but the faces are characteristically impassive. The scale is large and imposing, despite an actual height of only 12 inches. An accentuation of the vertical, crossed by rather rigid diagonals, avoids tenderness in favor of the effect of a spiritual icon.

99

100

Infrared photography has revealed a great rarity beneath the *Madonna and Child*: a study of a full-length female nude. No painting by Bouts of this subject, unaccompanied, is known, and only a couple by other Netherlandish masters of the period. An Eve is immediately suggested, but there is no Adam. We are left with two mysteries: who she is, and why Bouts abandoned his original project.

Impassive is surely the word for the *Portrait of a Lady Holding a Flower*,[101] by Barthel Bruyn the Elder (1493–1555), painter of Cologne. This north German contemporary of Hans Holbein the Younger (see MA 43) was a much less incisive portraitist—though the face has a certain charm in its fugitive expression—but he produced superb ornaments in the guise of portraiture and he seems to have had an obsession about fingers in contorted frozen positions. The wiry activity of crisp line and small detail descend from German late Gothic art; and while there is some evidence of a Renaissance understanding of anatomy, the figure conveys no such sense of ease as do Holbein's.

For the eighteenth century, apart from many fine porcelains, there are two three-dimensional models for altars, a red chalk *Assumption of the Virgin* attributed to the architect-sculptor Egid Qurin Asam; and an upper Austrian *Crucifixion* group, c. 1700–25 in pearwood, with the customarily charming flying *putti* and a Rococo cartouche. Most impressive, however, is a *Return of the Holy Family from Egypt*, in painted and gilded wood some 3 feet high, the work of Meinrad Guggenbichler (1649–1723). This fine sculptor, whom we shall discuss in more detail at Wellesley College (MA 235), flourished in the lovely lake region north and east of Salzburg. The date of the Busch-Reisinger altar group is probably just before 1700.

Emil Nolde (1867–1956) was an early and commanding figure in the development of modern German painting. Born Hansen, he took his artistic name from his birthplace just south of the Danish frontier. Of humble peasant stock, he found little to interest him in the slick productions of the later nineteenth-century German academies. He managed to travel a great deal outside Germany, and he was a pioneer, after Gauguin, in responding enthusiastically to the art of primitive cultures. The *Mulatto*,[102] painted in 1915, has the inner expressiveness

101

102

and the formal simplification of African masks, here accentuated by color of an almost savage brilliance. The composition in concentric circles, like that sometimes used by Vincent van Gogh, has a hypnotic effect. The juxtaposed reds, pinks, oranges, and yellows are inherited from Gauguin, but the strong accents of black are Nolde's own; a head-band of green provides exciting contrast. At a size of 30½ by 28¾ inches, this vivid oil is not likely to be missed.

As we consider further Harvard's extraordinary riches in this field, a catalogue by Charles L. Kuhn with an introductory essay by Jakob Rosenberg, *German Expressionism and Abstract Art: the Harvard Collections* (Harvard University Press, 1957), should be mentioned for its fine background coverage as well as its complete listing. As you turn its pages—and study the original works—it is worth remembering that all these artists were declared "degenerate" by the Nazis. All of them proclaim the primacy of the artist's imagination; and in a totalitarian society that cannot be endured. Such artists as were still alive in the 1930s and had not left Germany were deprived of working materials, their market shut off, or were otherwise persecuted. Museums that owned their art were forced to sell it.

As early as 1905 a group of painters born in the 1880s joined together at Dresden, and later in Berlin, under the name of Die Brücke (The Bridge). The name signified their sense of connection with Germany's great medieval past, overarching the worldly extravagance of the Renaissance and Rococo eras and especially the hollow academicism of the nineteenth century. They invited the older Emil Nolde to exhibit with them. He did in 1905–07 but then preferred to pursue his own solitary career. The leading spirit in this movement was Ernst L. Kirchner and his most important associates were Erich Heckel, Karl Schmidt-Rottluff, Max Pechstein, and Otto Müller.

Erich Heckel (1883–1970) painted *To The Convalescent Woman*,[103] a triptych 7 feet long, in 1912/13. Like the sculptor Ernst Barlach, he was deeply influenced by Vincent van Gogh, a variant of whose sunflowers appears in a totally new and sickly color scheme at the right. The nude figure at the left suggests African sculpture, another source of inspiration for these intense and primitive-oriented artists. This is easily the most important German Expressionist painting in New England, and it is Heckel's acknowledged masterpiece. Formerly in the Folkwang Museum at Essen, it was forcibly sold during the Nazi regime as "degenerate" art. Both Heckel and Kirchner produced woodcut variants of the central panel. The museum owns an impression of Heckel's version.

103

Woodcut was as important a medium for the German Expressionists as oil painting, and many critics find in their prints (frequently based on their paintings but even more concentrated and powerful) an even higher degree of expressiveness. They made superb lithographs and etchings; but it was the woodcut process, so closely allied to wood sculpture—with its cracks and splinterings—that had a special affinity with these artists' sense of violence in a soon-to-be-war-torn world. The *Convalescent* surely attains a symbolic significance.

The early paintings of the Bridge Group were marked by the cur- vilinear forms of Nolde and of other older artists (Toulouse-Lautrec, Matisse); but after 1910 the angularities of Cubist art (and of African sculpture) replaced them. This can be seen not only in the Heckel just discussed but in *Self-Portrait with a Cat*,[104] by Ernst L. Kirchner (1880– 1938)—even though the pink-red-orange-green palette of Gauguin- inspired Nolde still remains. The date is 1918. The splintered forms aspire to Gothic verticality in this 4-foot-high image of psychological torment. As almost invariably in modern German art, the blacks thunder ominously.

The pen drawing of *Herwarth Walden*[105] by Oskar Kokoschka (1886–1980) may serve to remind us that great masters of line are not limited to the distant past. Kokoschka, an independent Austrian artist, was especially active in avant-garde circles in Berlin, where Herwarth Walden published *Der Sturm* (The Storm), an influential magazine sup- portive of modern art. Observe the variety of line here, its range of thickness, its shorthand conventions for indicating projections, hollows, shadow, and even the glint of light on glass. Not a stroke is wasted, and each one is set down with a skilled surgeon's decisiveness. The date is 1910; the world evoked is surely that of Sigmund Freud. When not on exhibition, the drawing is kept at the Fogg Museum.

We continue with two watercolors by painters, neither of them Ger- man by birth, who exerted a tremendous influence on modern German art. Wassily Kandinsky (1866–1944) came from Russia; Paul Klee (1879–1940), from German Switzerland. In Munich they formed a

104

105

friendship that was to last throughout their lives. In revolt against the worn-out teachings of academic artists, Kandinsky founded in Munich the so-called Blue Rider group (1911) in association with Klee, Franz Marc, and others. The group took its name from one of Kandinsky's early paintings. Soon after the opening of the Bauhaus at Weimar in 1919, the director, Walter Gropius, called both Kandinsky and Klee to its staff; they taught at the Bauhaus until Nazi pressure forced its dissolution in 1933. (Gropius, who later taught architecture at Harvard, was the chief designer of the Harvard Graduate Center.)

Landscape[106] (1918), by Kandinsky, is a work of his rare "Russian period." He was in Moscow during the war, but few of the works of that time are known outside Russia itself. Perhaps under the influence of currents then prevailing in Russian art, Kandinsky sharpened his lines and reduced the atmospheric effects of his better-known "Blue Rider" works, but their animated movement still prevails. Klee's gentle little fantasy *Magnetic Apparatus for Plant Cultivation*[107] (1921) is almost like a Swiss toy. In its expressive atmosphere and its textures and brooding color, it is thoroughly Germanic. Klee's world of magic is seen as if under a magnifying glass, but the forces he evokes tell us, obliquely or not, of life and death.

Self-Portrait in a Tuxedo[108] (1927) by Max Beckmann (1884–1950) is characteristically German in its inner force, in its acid hues dominated by blacks, whites, and grays, and in its starkly angular shapes. The informality of the pose, including the cigarette, strikes a contemporary

106

107

108

note. Like many German painters from Dürer onward, Beckmann was an important printmaker. A refugee from Nazi tyranny, he became a very influential teacher in America, first in St. Louis and later in Brooklyn. A natural sympathy seems to bring modern German and younger American artists together.

At first glance, one assumes that Beckmann's self-portrait is life-size; but the actual height is 56 inches, and since the figure is cut off well above the knees, that would make him very tall indeed. Actually, Beckmann was under six feet, and of broad, muscular build. Again, German-Gothic verticality carries the day: the rigid axis, the line of the window at the side, the direction of a thumb and of the all-important cigarette, and finally the acute spear-shaped angle between the legs. Furthermore, observe how the starched shirt is divided vertically by gray shadow (its tone repeated in the claustrophobic non-view out the window), the vertical steps of black shadow up the face, modeling it, and two strokes of reddish brown (borrowed from the color of the window frame) in the center of the lower forehead—adding yet another touch of grimness to this severe face. The powerful angular pose of the black arms is echoed in the position of the left hand. And what blacks in this image!

Well represented in this museum are the leading figures in modern German sculpture, for the most part by several works each. Born in the 1870s are Ernst Barlach and Georg Kolbe; in the 1880s, Hans Arp, Rudolf Belling, Wilhelm Lehmbruck, Gerhard Marcks, and Renée Sintenis. Associated with the Bauhaus movement (whether in Germany or in its later manifestation at Chicago) are Josef Albers, Herbert Bayer, and László Moholy-Nagy. Arp is best seen, however, in the Harkness Commons of the Harvard Graduate Center, for which he designed a large plywood screen; and Bayer, in the same location in a mural painting, *Verdure*, and in an unglazed tile mural adjacent to a brick relief by Josef Albers. (The center also boasts an oil mural by Joan Miró and an outdoor metal sculpture by the American sculptor Richard Lippold.) Since the building itself is by Walter Gropius, the Graduate Center may be thought of as an extension of the Busch-Reisinger Museum's coverage of the Bauhaus and its activities.

Gerhard Marcks (born 1889) is the author of *Prometheus*,[109] a bronze of 1948, some 30 inches high. He was strongly influenced by Wilhelm Lehmbruck (see MA 240), whose late masterpiece, the *Seated*

109

Youth (1918) at Duisburg, the *Prometheus* somewhat resembles. Marcks's forms are more angular than Lehmbruck's and thus closer to those of Barlach. Their inner tension is strongly felt. Note how the tied hands of the figure are balanced against the bent head across the void of the torso framed by the arms. As you move around the *Prometheus* the empty spaces take their place as positive elements in the composition.

The 7-foot figure of a *Crippled Beggar*[110] by Ernst Barlach (1870–1938) should be compared in its emaciated forms to the reproduction of the Romanesque bronze Crucifix of the abbey of Werden, in the stairwell off the Romanesque hall. Nothing could better illustrate the dependence of modern German art on its own early medieval traditions. This most important work by Barlach in the United States is a second casting in dark vitreous clay (it may be called clinker) of one of three figures that Barlach completed by 1930 for niches in the facade of the fourteenth-century brick Gothic church of St. Catherine at Lübeck. The extra cast was made to be sold to help defray the expenses of the project. Using a medieval language of expression, Barlach evokes a modern world of sorrow and suffering. Comparison with New London's cast of *Singing Boy* (CT 93), of 1928, will show similar Gothic angularities in a theme of gentler import.

We have left to the end a brief description of Moholy-Nagy's highly complex *Light-Space Modulator*, of 1923–30, exhibited in a special gallery. A photograph would tell you what it looks like, but it could give no idea of what it is meant to be. Its aluminum and chrome-plated surfaces are designed to be activated by an electric motor equipped with chain belts. Lighted by spotlights in the darkened room, and casting moving shadows on walls and ceiling, it echoes the modern cityscape as seen at night.

In closing, mention should be made of Harvard's rich collection of modern German prints, housed with other graphic treasures at the Fogg Art Museum. Some decades ago, Jakob Rosenberg, then the curator of prints, and Charles L. Kuhn, then the curator of the Busch-Reisinger Museum, took advantage of current low prices (which have subsequently skyrocketed) to develop one of the outstanding collections in the modern German and Austrian field. With this superb supplement to its holdings in German painting, drawing, and sculpture, Harvard dominates

110

the German field in this country in much the same way that Yale dominates the British field with its new British Center.

Excellent catalogues of the collection are available, including a selection of one hundred works, each with a full-page illustration, published in 1980. In the summer of that year a selection of the same magnitude was exhibited at the National Gallery in Washington.

Fogg Art Museum, Harvard University

Location: Quincy Street at Broadway
Hours: Mon.-Wed. and Fri. 9-5, Thurs. 9-9, Sat. 10-5, Sun. 2-5
Admission: Free. Ⓗ

The Fogg Art Museum houses the most extensive collection of art owned by any university in the world, England excepted. Founded in 1891 and first housed in the former Hunt Hall (1895), it moved to the present building in 1927. From the earliest days of art-historical studies at Harvard the importance of having original examples at hand was clearly understood. Boston was, of course, not so easily accessible from Cambridge; even today there is no substitute for direct and immediate contact with the original work of art.

The college (or university) museum is little known in Europe outside England. This is partly a matter of geography, for the European universities are situated in great cities with their huge artistic resources, while American colleges and universities are usually to be found in the country or in the smaller towns. Whatever the reason, the early collections at Bowdoin, Yale, and Harvard have led to the founding of so many college museums that they have become a unique feature of American cultural life.

The visitor should realize, therefore, that a museum such as the Fogg has a different function from the city museum. It must play an active part in liberal education at both the undergraduate and the graduate level. Its exhibits must change frequently to satisfy the demands of many departments in the university. The visitor should not expect, therefore, to find all of my selections on view at any one time.

Among the special features of the Fogg Museum is a research laboratory for the preservation and restoration of works of art, a collection of drawings rivaled in America only by those of the Metropolitan Museum and the Morgan Library in New York, a superb collection of European art of the late eighteenth and early nineteenth centuries, and holdings of extraordinary quality in Far Eastern art. The latter were established by the late Langdon Warner, who conducted archaeological expeditions to enrich them, and in 1943 they were vastly enlarged by the Grenville Winthrop bequest, also rich in early nineteenth-century art. Today, with the combined resources of Boston and Harvard University, the area is unsurpassed in the world as a center for Far Eastern studies.

A cooperative lending policy links the important print collection of the Fogg Museum with the superb collections of rare illustrated books and illuminated manuscripts owned by the Widener and Houghton libraries at Harvard. Photography is also included in the Fogg's print department.

Construction of the Carpenter Center, designed by Le Corbusier, on the adjoining Quincy Street property brought the practice of art to a level commensurate with the study of art history. Growth of the Fogg's collections has proceeded at such a rate that, as of this writing, plans are well advanced toward the construction of an extensive addition. When this is completed, Quincy Street will become a kind of Avenue des Arts with its sequence of the Carpenter, the Fogg Art Museum, its new extension, the School of Design, and at the far end the Busch-Reisinger Museum, then beyond it, on Divinity Avenue, the Peabody Museum.

Following its opening in 1927, the Fogg exerted influential leadership in conservation of works of art and in the training of museum personnel. These were the respective fields of the two co-directors, Edward Forbes and Paul Sachs. During the 1930s and until other institutions began to catch up with Harvard, an overwhelming proportion of younger directors of American art museums were Harvard-trained. Mr. Sachs, who was not a tall man, objected to the then current habit of hanging pictures well above his line of vision. His influence in lowering them dominated American museum practice for several decades; but today's growth of collections has often necessitated superimposing them.

The representation of ancient art at the Fogg Museum is not extensive, but there are superb examples. The finest work of Graeco-Roman sculpture is a life-size marble figure of the hunter *Meleager*.[111] In style it is close to what is known of the work of Scopas, a leading artist at the time of Alexander the Great. Like most surviving antique statues, this is a later copy, probably Roman in date, but the copyist was unusually competent and spirited. Best known for the twisted action and inner expressiveness of his figures, Scopas is sometimes referred to as the initiator of the Baroque point of view in Western art. Note how the body contours of the *Meleager* make the eye wind around and behind the figure, and break up the sense of the frontal plane. Note also the expressive use of shadow produced by undercutting at the eyes and mouth.

Warburg Hall, on the ground floor, contains some of the Fogg's important collection of French and Spanish capitals of the Romanesque period. Thirteen of these come from Moûtier-Saint-Jean, in Burgundy (about 1130). The material (limestone) is the same as that from which the church and its monastic cloister were constructed. While this identity

111

of materials also occurred in Greek sculpture and architecture (marble), it was not characteristic of the Romans, who thought of sculpture as a part of a veneer of precious materials to be applied to the entire surface of a core of brick and rubble. Observe how the Romanesque designer adapted the form of the Corinthian capital, inherited from ancient Rome, to the special demands of telling the story of *Cain and Abel*,[112] symbolizing the conflict of good and evil. Necessarily, he departs from Greek canons of proportion, warping the figure to make it fit the architectural shape. Below Cain and Abel, who present offerings under the Hand of God, the base is strengthened by an altar in the form of a symmetrical double-headed eagle—a frequent device inherited from the early Christian Near East and, in turn, all the way back to ancient Mesopotamian art. It makes an interesting comparison with the Toulouse capital at Amherst College (MA 3), where the device shifts to two birds with a single head.

A 4-foot marble statue, *The Angel of the Annunciation*,[113] attributed to Arnolfo di Cambio (1260–1302), is said to have come from the facade of the old Cathedral of Florence. Its rough, plebeian character parallels that of Florence's chief contemporary painter, Giotto. It diverges markedly from the elegance of late thirteenth- and early fourteenth-century French art, favored in Siena. Though the large painting attributed to Giotto's chief pupil and godson, Taddeo Gaddi (active 1334–66), *St. Francis Receiving the Stigmata*,[114] is in very damaged

112

113

114

condition and is at best an echo of a similar picture in the Louvre, a comparison of it with the squat proportions of Arnolfo's angel and the blunt turns of heavy drapery hiding the figure's articulation will be instructive. This very large tempera panel, $7\frac{1}{2}$ feet high, and the small one we have discussed at the Gardner Museum (MA 33), give the best idea of Giotto's art that can be found in American museums. For the study of Giotto himself, so celebrated that Dante praised him, there is no substitute for a journey to Padua and to Florence.

Siena, Florence's great rival in the fourteenth century and only fifty miles away, seems ages apart in basic attitude. Though Sienese painters also worked in fresco, egg tempera on gold-ground panel was their preferred medium. Here the exquisite refinement of color and of the goldworker's craft found freer expression. A small *Crucifixion*[115] by Simone Martini (1285–1344), chief painter of Siena after Duccio and chief rival of Giotto in Italy, is a prime example of Sienese art, despite the much larger size of the stiffly Byzantine polyptych in the Gardner Museum (MA 34). One is reminded of manuscript illumination, in which Simone engaged at the papal court of Avignon, where he may have executed this little panel late in his career, and of the svelte figurines of Parisian ivory carving of the same time, such as the superb example at Worcester (MA 294).

Fra Angelico's *Crucifixion*,[116] one of the major possessions of the Fogg Museum and indeed of any American museum in the field of Early Renaissance painting, displays a Florentine resilience in the figures not to be found in Sienese art. Everything about Fra Angelico (1378–1455) would seem to have turned him away from the secular interests of the Florentine Renaissance. He was a Dominican friar, an extremely pious man, and a pupil of entirely medieval masters. We should note, however, that the *Crucifixion* is a very late work, probably from the time of his frescoes in the chapel of Nicholas V in the Vatican.

116

115

We turn now to one of the master drawings in the Fogg's great collection, the *Portrait of Susanna of Bavaria*[117] by Albrecht Dürer (1471–1528). A late work (1521), it was drawn in indelible silverpoint, or zinc point, on prepared green-tinted paper. On the sleeve there are traces of heightening in white to increase the sculptural modeling. Like most great German artists, including Goethe and Thomas Mann, Dürer felt the pull of the South, and so he became a European artist without forsaking his deep Northern roots. Compared with a High Renaissance work of the time, such as the slightly earlier Raphael at the Gardner Museum (M A 41), this portrait is more individualized, but without any sacrifice in formal clarity and construction.

Orazio Gentilleschi (1563–1639), whose *Madonna and the Sleeping Christ Child*[118] we now consider, is usually grouped with the followers of Caravaggio. This is true to the extent that, after arriving in Rome as a teenager from his native Pisa, he was eventually attracted to the early work of that master, as exemplified by Hartford's *Ecstasy of St. Francis* (CT 12); but he did not follow Caravaggio's dramatic and tenebrous later style. What attracted him was the master's new informality and intimacy, and his love of light playing on smooth fabrics. Gentilleschi developed a special palette favoring lemon yellows and pale blues, seen in the Fogg's fine example, dating from c. 1610. In 1621 he moved to Genoa, then on to Turin and Paris, and finally to London, where he remained from 1626 to his death. He had apparently met Van Dyck in Genoa, and through him became a court painter for King Charles I. In his excellent survey, *Italian Baroque Painting* (London: Phaidon Press, 1960), Ellis K. Waterhouse aptly summarizes Gentilleschi's art as having an "odd combination of naturalism, intimacy, and elegance." His daughter Artemisia became the most important woman artist of her time —and one of the first.

Cutting across time and space, let us compare two magnificent examples of the Baroque style in painting. Small as they are, Rubens's 1635 oil sketch for a composition (now in Dresden, *Quos Ego, Neptune*

117

118

Commanding the Waters[119] (from Virgil's *Aeneid*), and Delacroix's *Giaour and Pasha*[120] of 1856 (from the poem by Byron) surpass many larger works by these masters where the execution was entrusted to assistants or where for other reasons the inspiration faltered. For Delacroix (1798–1863) the Romanticism of the new century implied a return to the vehement art of Peter Paul Rubens (1577–1640). As often happens in the history of Western art, a revolution finds its source by skipping over the previous hundred years. It is worth pointing out that both these masters of Baroque energy were highly disciplined and intellectual men. In both, the heart was subject to the mind. Both moved in complex social circles. Both were inveterate correspondents, and Delacroix kept a journal that rivals Dürer's and Leonardo's in profundity and extensiveness of observation. Both paintings come from the final ten years of the artists' careers. Fundamentally, Delacroix and Rubens are so similar that it is hard to realize the passage of over two hundred years and the shift of taste from classical literature to the exotic Near East.

The Rubens sketch, oil on panel about 20 inches high, dates from 1635. It celebrates allegorically what is described in the full title: *The Happy Voyage of Cardinal Infante Ferdinand of Spain from Barcelona to Genoa*—that is, with Neptune's help, on his way to a triumphal entry into Antwerp as the new governor of the Netherlands. In this sketch, as in another at Yale's British Center (CT 52), we see Rubens at his most spontaneous, his forms at their most fluid.

Similar spontaneity, expressed in the medium of terra-cotta, can be seen in Rubens's alter ego in sculpture, Giovanni Lorenzo Bernini (1598–1680). The life-size *Head of St. Jerome*[121] is one of the most

119

121

120

spectacular in a series of twenty-seven studies (*bozzetti*) owned by the Fogg and designed by Bernini for some of his most important marble sculptures. The marble *St. Jerome* fills a niche in the Chigi Chapel of the Cathedral of Siena. The chapel, designed by Bernini himself, also includes a figure of *St. Mary Magdalen*. The date is 1661–63. The Fogg's head closely resembles the final version, but spontaneity was inevitably lost in the transfer to marble. In the terra-cotta we can almost participate in the action of modeling and scraping. Tool marks are evident, and we half expect to find the master's fingerprints, as we do in Carpeaux's terra-cotta head at Wellesley (MA 237). At the time of the Rubens and Delacroix paintings just discussed the artists were both fifty-eight; Bernini was in his mid-sixties when he molded the *Head of St. Jerome*. All three were at the height of their careers.

Another *St. Jerome*,[122] this time a three-quarters figure in oil 50 inches high, is by Jusepe de Ribera (1588–1656). Signed and dated 1640, it is a first-class example of the work of this Sevillian who moved to Spanish-owned Naples about 1616 and worked there until his death. Deeply influenced by the later art of Caravaggio, he infused it with his Spanish reserve and austerity, and with his intense observation of detail. The subject was a favorite of his, and it afforded him an opportunity to enrich his somber black and brown palette with the deep red of the saint's traditional robe. Perhaps the skull, held in his left hand, is the finest element in this moving picture of quiet meditation.

In the century of the Grand Manner, dominated by Baroque explosions of Rubens and Bernini, we forget too easily the counterforce of Classicism—important for understanding Rubens as well, for he developed an impressive collection of ancient marbles in his great house in Antwerp and many of his painted figures were derived either from them or from celebrated examples he saw in Rome. Nicolas Poussin (1594–1665) is the outstanding Classicist in the Baroque Age. If Rubens was inspired by the late proto-Baroque style of Titian (see MA 45), Poussin reverted to that of Raphael (see MA 41). Arriving from France in his youth, he matured in Rome under the influence of conservative painters like Domenichino. Occasionally, as in the Hartford *Crucifixion* (CT 16), he worked in the dramatic spirit of the era, but more frequently, as in the Fogg's *Holy Family*,[123] c. 1650, his art was as intellectually ordered as the reasoning of Descartes. Note the pyramidal construction capped

122

123

by rectangular solids, and the suggestion of early Corot and Cézanne in the landscape on the right. Yet Poussin's pen-and-wash drawings are strongly Baroque in style. This fact helps us understand that his painting was a process of shaping his initial image to fit a dominant ideal. In a Baroque century, he felt, like Milton, a need for clarity, and achieved it through emulation of classical forms. Visitors should not miss another superb Poussin, *The Birth of Bacchus*, an elegiac, hushed work of 1657. Here he speaks of death as well as of generation. As the infant Bacchus is entrusted to the care of the Nymphs, Echo sorrows for the death of Narcissus—whose passing brings to life a beautiful white flower.

To the superb works of Rembrandt van Rijn (1606–69), painted in the 1630s, which we discussed at the Gardner Museum—and the imposing Elison portraits of 1634 at the Museum of Fine Arts—we now add a modest but magical *Head of Christ*,[124] painted about 1648–52. On an oak panel only 10 inches high, it dominates any gallery in which it is hung. We can quickly orient the reader as to Rembrandt's development by a reminder that *Dr. Tulp's Anatomy Lesson* was painted in 1632, the *Night Watch* in 1642, and *The Syndics* in 1661. The date of the *Head of Christ* can be bounded, so to speak, by the *Supper at Emmaus* (Louvre) of 1648—the two Christ heads have similarities— and *Aristotle Contemplating the Bust of Homer* (Metropolitan Museum of Art, New York) of 1653. From there he moved on to such master- pieces of the final decade as the *Self-Portrait* in the Frick Museum, New York, the *Portrait of Jan Six* (Six House, Amsterdam), and the tran- scendent *Self-Portrait* of about 1663 at Kenwood, outside London. Of the last-named work, Kenneth Clark, in *Looking at Pictures* (Boston: Beacon Press, paperback, 1968), wrote that "the humility of Rem- brandt's colossal genius warns the art historian to shut up." That is what I propose to do about the Fogg's *Head of Christ*.

The museum also owns two early paintings by Rembrandt, one a self- portrait, and a wonderful selection of drawings by the master and his followers; in the print department there is much more. The paintings and drawings are studied in an authoritative article by the director, Seymour Slive, in *Apollo* magazine, June 1978, pages 453–63.

If we skip over the Fogg's riches in eighteenth-century art—drawings

124

by Watteau and the Tiepolos, top-grade portraits by Gainsborough and Copley, and much more—that is only because we discuss these masters elsewhere.

Jacques Louis David (1748–1825) is seen here in one of his finest portraits, of *Emmanuel Sièyes, Aged Sixty-nine*,[125] signed and dated in 1817. It came to Harvard in 1943 in the bequest of Grenville Winthrop. One easily understands that Raphael was David's chief source of inspiration, as he was for Poussin. Never was the French sense of disciplined energy more in evidence than in this portrait of a colleague in the days of the Revolutionary Convention, or in the celebrated *Death of Marat*. David's place in history as the leader of the Neoclassic movement is secure when based on such compositions of Greek and Roman history as *The Death of Socrates* and the *Oath of the Horatii* (painted in Rome in 1784); but his portraits demonstrate that he was more than that. It would not be an exaggeration to call him the Classicist among the Neoclassicists. With the exception of Ingres, his disciples—their name is legion—seem to have been caught up in a fashion rather than to have been great pioneering spirits.

It is now well understood that Neoclassicism was a preliminary form of the Romantic movement; and David must be credited with that development too. One of the most dominating figures of any age, he inspired reaction as well as idolatry. He was Géricault's point of departure, and after Géricault Romanticism reached its highest pitch in Delacroix, whose *Giaour and Pasha*, already discussed, marks its flaming and passionate end.

Jacques Ange Dominique Ingres (1780–1867), the most important pupil of David and his assistant in the execution of the celebrated *Portrait of Madame Récamier* (Louvre, 1800), injected a potent element of sensuality into the forms of David as he developed his own style. While his male portraits have much in common with David's, his female ones, and especially his nudes set in an exotic Oriental harem environment, mark the new and clearly Romantic direction that this irascible pundit of classical theory actually followed in his painting. *Odalisque with Slave*,[126] painted in 1839, could hardly differ more from David's athletic nude Greeks and Romans—males all, with only a few

125

126

exceptions. Never has sinuous line been more sexually evocative; and color, with touches of Leonardesque shadow, runs to oblique, secondary tones (David liked red, white, and blue). Ingres's anatomy is distorted for similar sensual effect. André Lhote, a minor Cubist painter but a major teacher in the Paris of the 1930s, made his models attempt the impossible—to assume Ingres's exact poses—in order to convince his classes that distortion can be artistically indispensable. The stomach of the Slave is a masterpiece of soft sculpture. Like an apple seen from the top, it is observed as a larger breast with an indentation in lieu of a nipple. Followers of Ingres, more faithful than he to Academic rules—like Bouguereau and Gérôme—missed these subtleties.

The formidable drawing of a *Negro Soldier*,[127] in sepia and gray wash over pencil, is a consummate example of the art of Théodore Géricault (1791–1824). In the history of nineteenth-century French painting Géricault stands midway between David and Delacroix. As in David's *Sièyes*, the figure is placed squarely across the picture surface in a formal and geometric arrangement; yet the play of light and dark is as rich as in Goya or Rembrandt, and the subject (Moorish) also opened up new possibilities for Delacroix, who found in Géricault his most immediate inspiration. Note how the grays take on a bluish tinge in the context of the sepia washes, so that the whole range of warm and cool tones is suggested, but with the utmost economy of means. This is one of many master drawings given to the Fogg Art Museum by Paul and Meta Sachs.

That Pierre-Auguste Renoir (1841–1919) was already an accomplished composer and colorist by the age of twenty-five can be seen in *Spring Bouquet*,[128] an oil 3½ feet high, signed and dated 1866. Eight years before the first exhibition of a rebellious, Salon-scorned group called Impressionists (by a caustic critic who applied to them that word in the title of an atmospheric sunrise picture by Claude Monet), Renoir was already well launched in the new direction. The subject, of course,

127

128

was traditional, but Renoir found joy in flower painting to the end of his life—or rather until arthritis in his old age made it impossible for him to hold a brush. In this floral cascade lavender grays and fugitive pinks and yellows linger from the work of earlier masters; but during the 1870s they would be outdazzled by the Impressionist "rainbow" palette, as in the celebrated *Moulin de la Galette* (Louvre). The same sequence has been discussed in connection with Claude Monet's *Boats Leaving the Harbor*, painted very likely in 1865, when Monet too was twenty-five (CT 5). However much we rightly admire the will to develop that kept these masters from settling down into routine production, their Pre-Impressionist works are not necessarily inferior to what followed.

With the bequest of the collection of Maurice Wertheim, the Fogg became rich in both Impressionist and Post-Impressionist painting. The latter term is useful for purposes of chronology but it is otherwise meaningless, and even its chronology is misleading. Cézanne, surely a leading Post-Impressionist, was born a year before Monet and two years before Renoir; and as for Monet—the leading Impressionist of them all —his late work (MA 254 and thereafter) makes him an outstanding Post-Impressionist. Such younger painters, born between 1848 and 1864, as Gauguin, van Gogh, Seurat, and Toulouse-Lautrec have little in common except that they mastered Impressionist techniques and then departed from them.

Paul Cézanne (1839–1906), represented in the Wertheim bequest by a fine *Still Life*[129] of c. 1885, had spent many months with Camille Pissarro painting Impressionist pictures at Auvers-sur-Oise. That was in the mid-1870s, but thereafter he steadily moved away from an attempt to catch fugitive effects of light on objects and toward a world out of time. He wanted, as he said, to make of Impressionism something durable, like the art of the great museums. In this *Still Life*, geometry comes to his aid: solid spheres and flat circles, ovals flattened at their ends toward a circular shape, cylinders, flat rectangular planes. The tablecloth, if observed for itself and out of context, is startlingly similar to the geometric rock formations of his favorite motif, the Mont-Ste.-Victoire. Impressionist space, like that of the camera which influenced it, is seen from a single point of view, and everything happens *behind* the picture surface—or seems to do so. Cézanne has changed all this. He looks down at the tabletop, but straight ahead at the large jar, and again somewhat down at the jar's lip. The tablecloth winds back, but

129

not very far, because its farther white peak, strongly contrasted against the dark red-brown commode, leaps forward toward the picture surface. In other words, Cézanne is sacrificing illusion in order to assert the claims of painting as color applied to a flat canvas. The whole composition is full of adjustments: solid bodies and their relationship to flat shapes, spatial continuum as against rhythmic two-dimensional design. It is through these relationships—often spoken of as inevitable—that a sense of permanence is achieved, and one of solemnity and silence. These modest objects are nowhere and no-when. They endure.

In his *Self-Portrait*[130] of September 1888, Vincent van Gogh (1853–90) is represented at the Fogg by one of his finest pictures. It has the additional interest of an inscription across the top to his friend Paul Gauguin, who was soon to join him at Arles. Van Gogh had just received a self-portrait from Gauguin and so he reciprocated. In a letter to his ever-faithful brother Theo, Vincent describes his own picture, which he considered superior to Gauguin's: "It is all ashen gray against pale malachite (no yellow). The clothes are this brown coat with a blue border, but I have exaggerated the brown into purple, and the width of the blue borders. The head is modeled in light color painted in thick '*pâte*' against the light background with hardly any shadows. Only I have made the eyes 'slightly' slanting like the Japanese." In Paris Japanese prints had helped turn van Gogh from Impressionist illusion toward the flat arabesque. As later in Nolde's *Mulatto* (MA 102), concentric strokes radiating from the head give it an almost hypnotic effect.

Yet another masterpiece is *Maternity*,[131] painted in 1901 by Pablo Picasso (1881–1973). A prime example from his "Blue Period," it was painted when he was still nineteen. By age sixteen he had passed the examinations at the Barcelona Academy and had taken prizes in competition with mature artists. A trip to Paris in the fall months of 1900 had exposed him to the later developments of Art Nouveau and to the work of the Intimists, especially Bonnard and Vuillard. But his Spanish heritage was strong, and a return to Barcelona in December, to stay until

130

131

May of 1901, fortified it. A second trip to Paris lasted until the end of
the year. Whether *Maternity* was painted in Barcelona or Paris need not
concern us, for his Paris pictures of 1901 were as profoundly Spanish
as his Barcelona ones. The elongated, emaciated figures echo those of
El Greco (but without his flamelike strokes) and behind them Spanish
Romanesque frescoes (MA 61) and sculpture. Picasso's choice of a
dominant deep blue color may have been suggested by the late works of
Cézanne, but he chilled it with suggestions of green. The figure of the
mother is a wonderfully interlocked chain of flattened Art Nouveau
shapes; but her tight embrace is counteracted by the two impassive faces
and by her limp, virtually Byzantine hand. The commonest of themes,
perhaps suggested by the images of Jean François Millet, here becomes
ennobled. It speaks to us through the language of painting, not through
external sentiment. Various stages of Picasso's later career are covered in
examples from other museums.

Upper Deck,[132] painted in 1929 by Charles Sheeler (1883–1965),
has the look of a photograph—a medium in which the artist excelled,
especially in industrial subjects—until you come upon the original oil.
Here an extraordinarily subtle range of off-whites delights the eye, and
this is strengthened by sharp edges, darkest dark ovals in the ventilator
outlets, and by all-important diagonals of guy wires and railings. Such
art by Sheeler, Charles Demuth (MA 276), Niles Spencer, and Preston
Dickinson earned them the term of "The Immaculates."

Our selections of Far Eastern art can do no more than draw attention
to the wealth and high quality of these collections. An unexpected
parallel in forms is presented by two of the Fogg's most precious items,
a *Ceremonial Bronze Vessel*[133] probably of the Shang dynasty (1700–
1050 B.C.) and a glazed terra-cotta *Horse*[134] of the T'ang dynasty
(A.D. 618–906). Because the vessel approaches the shape of an animal,
the resemblance is perhaps less surprising. Yet, over a gap of two
thousand years or more, in different materials, and in objects serving
widely varying functions, there are striking similarities: in the rhythmic
surge of reverse curves, in sculptural compactness and economy of statement, and in a kind of inner alertness. Note the proud arch of the
horse's neck, the circular perfection of the rump, and in sudden contrast
to these the vibrant diagonal thrust of the legs. In the Shang vessel, of

132

133

the type known as *kuang*, the advanced skill of bronze casting at several levels of relief—occurring over thirty centuries ago—is something to ponder.

How large are these two objects? Do they not suggest the grandeur of monumental art? The fact is that they are not large; but what is important, aesthetically, is not their *size* but their *scale*. Still, they are not mere decorative trinkets. We should not overlook the high ceremonial purpose of the *kuang*, or the destiny of the horse to be buried with a personage of exalted station. Actual maximum height for the vessel is 9¾ inches; for the horse, 14½ inches.

An elongated limestone *Head of a Bodhisattva*,[135] as strong as it is elegant, comes from the Northern Wei period (A.D. 383–565) and probably dates from the fifth to sixth century. Its superficial resemblance to certain Archaic Greek heads of the sixth century B.C. is purely coincidental, but not entirely without significance. Chinese culture evolved through an Archaic-Classic-Baroque cycle in much the same pattern that we can trace in Greek culture, and in the sequence from Romanesque through late Gothic art, and in Renaissance art from its beginnings in Giotto through the Baroque seventeenth century. Such sweeping overviews of cultures are intellectually stimulating, but they run the danger of dogmatic prediction (Egyptian and Byzantine art went through no such evolution) and of denying to the individual artist the freedom to do the unexpected. In the *Head of a Bodhisattva* the Archaic flavor of rough-hewn strength is apparent in the nameless sculptor's respect for the shape of his original block of stone; yet nothing could be more sophisticated than the elegance of the features, the elongation of the ears, or the Modigliani-like slenderness of the neck. The head is about 1½ feet high.

It is generally accepted that the T'ang dynasty (A.D. 618–906) achieved the classic phase of Chinese culture—roughly comparable, that is, to Greek art of the fifth century B.C., to Gothic cathedral sculpture of the thirteenth century, and to the High Renaissance art of Raphael and Michelangelo. The superb fragment of a wall painting, represent-

134

135

ing a *Bodhisattva*,[136] from the caves of Tun-huang (Kansu Province), supremely exemplifies these qualities. It was brought back in 1923 from a Harvard expedition to these caves. Compared with Raphael's *Portrait of Inghirami* in the Gardner Museum (MA 41), the Bodhisattva similarly emphasizes capacious circular and spherical forms, circular curves used for modeling neck contours, and an overall psychological detachment. If our earlier Northern Wei *Bodhisattva* suggests Greek heads of the Archaic sixth century, this one has something of the timeless impersonality of the fifth-century sculptures of Olympia and the Parthenon. A close equivalent in T'ang stone sculpture will be found in the majestic head at Worcester (MA 311).

The Fogg also offers a fine example of a complete stone figure of the T'ang period, a *Seated Sakyamuni Buddha*[137] 4 feet high, from the caves of T'ien Lung Shan. Here the head is very broad, in greatest contrast to the elegant attenuation of the Northern Wei head. But as in the two other T'ang works just cited—the wall painting and the Worcester head—the circular curve again dominates, here in the drapery and in the articulation of breast and neck. The sophisticated ovoid projections of the knees, however, are in seeming contrast, but they provide a forceful base. As a whole, the figure radiates a sense of command and at the same time one of impenetrable detachment. The circular perfection of the eyebrow lines very likely contributes to this effect. Note, in the earlier Northern Wei head, how the oval lift of the brows and a slight suggestion of a smile about the mouth produce an effect of secret self-awareness.

Comparison of the T'ang statue of the Buddha with the Gandharan example at Yale (CT 64), of the first to third centuries A.D., will show surprising continuities in sculptural tradition across great leaps in time and in space—indeed across much of the Asian continent, Gandhara being in modern Afghanistan. While Buddhism united India and the Far East, there was another common denominator in sculptural traditions: the conquests of Alexander the Great. Gandhara formed part of the Bactrian kingdom at the outer reaches of Alexander's empire. It was

136

137

on a basis of Hellenistic Greek art, therefore, that much of the great sculpture of Central and Eastern Asian art developed. To sense the presence, even in echo, of Greek art in the Fogg's T'ang *Seated Sakyamuni Buddha* quickens the imagination.

Harvard is also rich in the art of the Persian and Moghul miniaturists. In this abbreviated account, a fifteenth-century manuscript illumination, *Giraffe with Its Keeper*, at the Worcester Art Museum (MA 313), must suffice for the former. For the Moghul illuminators of Islamic northern India, inheritors of the great Persian traditions, we have chosen an example from the Fogg: an *Elephant Hunt*.[138] Painted at the beginning of the seventeenth century, it is about 15 inches high. On the reverse is a depiction of a palace courtyard with figures and animals. With little sacrifice of the high quality of Persian design and color, such Moghul painting aimed at, and caught, a more homely realism.

Not surprisingly, Harvard scholars have published a wide range of handbooks, catalogues, and special studies of works in the Fogg collections—works estimated as of this writing to number some thirty thousand. In 1978 the London magazine *Apollo* devoted two of its issues to the Harvard collections; they serve as an excellent introduction with many more works discussed and illustrated than could be included in this book.

138

Peabody Museum of Archaeology and Ethnology, Harvard University

Location: 11 Divinity Avenue
Hours: Mon.-Sat. 9-4:15, Sun. 1-4:15; closed July 4, Thanksgiving, Christmas, and New Year's Day
Admission: Charged. ⓗ (via the adjacent Tozzer Library)

The Peabody Museum contains one of the great archaeological and ethnological collections of the world. If we add its contents to those of the Fogg Art Museum, the Busch-Reisinger Museum, and the rare books and illuminated manuscripts owned by the Widener and Houghton libraries, the total wealth of Harvard's artistic resources puts it in a class by itself among universities the world over. The collections of the Peabody Museum have been amassed from all quarters of the globe, primarily through expeditions sponsored by the university. Coverage here can be only symbolic. The selections were very kindly made by the museum's director and staff, my own knowledge of these areas of art history being anything but authoritative.

Until recent years the museum was more of a storehouse of magnificent treasure than a display showcase. In 1978, however, under the direction of Professor C. C. Lamberg-Karlovsky, "Masterpieces of the Peabody Museum" were superbly shown in a ground-floor gallery, newly appointed for the occasion. The catalogue, well illustrated and with authoritative comment by twenty-one specialists, covers some sixty examples. It is warmly recommended, and my debt to it is great. In his introduction, the director pointed out that "today it has become universally recognized that the art of the tribal people of Africa, Asia, Oceania, and the New World, far from being 'primitive,' attained levels of aesthetic production at times fully meriting the term 'masterpiece.' . . . It should be remembered, however, that the collections . . . are primarily of scientific value."

The museum was founded in 1866 by the same George Peabody (1795–1869) to whom the Peabody museums of Salem and of Yale University—as well as the original concept of philanthropy that later gave rise to the Carnegie, Rockefeller, Ford and other foundations—owe their existence. It has now embarked on an ambitious program of installing in modern galleries selected examples from its vast collections while still keeping the main body of its possessions available to an interested public.

The stone head of a *Maize God*[139] from the ruins of Copan in Honduras is one of the most famous examples of Maya sculpture in the world. A half-length figure in the British Museum is perhaps its only real competitor in artistic grandeur from this culture. Carved from andesite tufa and about 11 inches high, it is one of several such heads from Temple 22 brought back from the Peabody Museum expedition to Copan in the 1890s. (One of these was acquired from Harvard in 1954 by the Cleveland Museum of Art.) Unlike the rendering of other Maya gods, the Maize God was always shown as a handsome young man. The sprouting vegetation above his head is his special attribute. The date is A.D. C. 700–800, when Europe was still in the pre-Carolingian age, while China was producing the wonders of T'ang dynasty civilization. In the century before its abandonment, which apparently took place about A.D. 800, Copan reached its height. A scientific center, it has been called the Alexandria of the Maya world.

The masterly carving of the Peabody head, with its massive ear spools and rugged strings of hair contrasting with the finely chiseled features, was probably enhanced by the suitability of the local tufa for sculpture. At most other Maya sites, the limestone is much more intractable. The Copan head was originally coated with fine plaster and painted red, with the eyes outlined in black.

The fearsome hammered *Gold Disc*,[140] about 7 inches high and dating from A.D. C. 500–700, comes from Sitio Conte, Cocle, Panama. Probably worn as a breastplate, it may represent a trophy head, since the eyes are closed in death. The gold content is over 97 percent. The technique seen here of working in sheet gold was first developed in the New World in Peru in the first millennium B.C. How different are the gold death masks from Mycenae (c. 1500 B.C.), in the release of eternal slumber, as one sees them in the National Museum of Athens!

Crowned by the brilliant red-and-blue tail feathers of the macaw and circled with a spectrum of other feathers and down—whites, blacks, yellows, greens, and more reds and blues—the *Wayana Headdress*[141] is

139

141

140

surely the Matisse of the Peabody Museum. Nearly 4 feet high, it was collected in 1871 by Louis Agassiz, Harvard's renowned professor of zoology and geology, on one of his trips to the northern coasts of South America. Now reduced to under one thousand souls, the Wayana live in small villages in Surinam and southward into neighboring Brazil. Despite its magnificence, such a headdress is not necessarily reserved for a shaman or chief, for it can be worn by a ritual male dancer. It is made on a plaited basketwork base. While the feathers are collected from specified parts of particular birds, they are sometimes tinted to acquire the exact shade desired. Present knowledge of the Wayana does not allow a satisfactory interpretation of the significance of these head-dresses, but everything about them suggests that it goes deep.

The beautiful *Wooden Bowl*[142] with the head of a loon (?) is the work of a Blackfeet Indian artist. Such bowls were sometimes used to hold medicine water in the Sacred Feast and Mystery Dance of the Dakota Sioux. From bird's head to tail the bowl measures 15 inches; the wood is probably maple. It was acquired by exchange with the Worcester Historical Society in 1928. What a magical achievement, to make a wooden bowl come alive!

One of the most startling facts about this 20-by-15-inch *African Plaque from Benin*[143] is its date, late sixteenth to early seventeenth century. Another is that it is in brass (generally miscalled bronze) cast by the lost-wax process. African wood sculpture is said not to survive much beyond 150 years of the local climate, and bronze (or brass) casting is foreign to African art except in the West African kingdom of Benin, Nigeria, discovered by the Portuguese in 1485, which rapidly grew rich through the resulting trade. European bronze-casting technique was presumably introduced in this way, and the wonder is how thoroughly it was mastered.

Weighing no less than 37 pounds, the plaque represents a spear-bearing chief flanked by two warriors, perhaps on their way to honor the Oba, Benin's absolute monarch. In the upper corners, small in size and in much lower relief, are Portuguese soldiers, recognizable by their

143

142

helmets, curved mustaches, and muskets. They are as ancillary to the main purport of the relief as the little angels in Donatello's marble relief of the *Madonna of the Clouds* in the Boston Museum of Fine Arts (MA 68). Such plaques, of which some nine hundred are known, adorned pillars in passageways in the Oba's palace leading to his chamber.

The head of the Benin chief should be compared with the large memorial bronze heads of royalty of the same period. Examples are owned by the Peabody Museum but we illustrate one at the University of Vermont (VT 2). These outstrip our chief in neck adornment as well as in the sense of regal status. Note in the relief the *horror vacui* apparent in the black plane, completely filled with a repeated floral motif and ubiquitous dottings.

The *Great Scoop*,[144] or ladle of carved wood, about 28 inches long, comes from the agricultural Dan ethnic group of Liberia and the Ivory Coast. Collected in 1927 by Dr. George Schwab, a Presbyterian missionary, it can be attributed to a sculptor known locally as Sra, meaning "god," a name given him because of his beautiful work. As in the case of the Blackfeet Wooden Bowl, an ordinarily simple utilitarian object is brought to life through art that responds to its special ritual function. In Dan society there are competitions for the most honored *wunkirle*, or hospitable woman; and each village entrant is already established as a *wunkirle* through her generosity to all, especially to itinerant troupes of singers and dancers. In the ritual dance, while singing her ritual song, each *wunkirle* swings her spoon—large to symbolize her generosity— and then portions out rice into bowls for the invited families.

The head at the handle symbolizes the Dan canon of female beauty, in which narrow eyes rimmed with paint are an important feature. The elaborate hairstyle ends in plaited fiber edges. The sloping shape of the ladle itself, however, speaks in universal, not local, terms.

The two-faced *Helmet Mask*[145] for the female Bundu Society comes from the Gola tribe of Liberia, and it is closely related to masks of the Mende tribe of Sierra Leone. The Janus type, with faces in opposite directions, is very unusual. Worn by women at their initiation to the

144

145

society, it shows the typical high forehead, high headdress, and crown. Hair and neck folds are stylized in chevronlike sequences with powerful effect.

This mask was collected by George W. Harley, a medical missionary. A word should be added about Harley and George Schwab, the Presbyterian missionary who collected the *Great Scoop*. Both men were made Associates in Anthropology at Harvard in recognition of their services as donor-collectors and researchers for the Peabody Museum. Schwab worked in Cameroon and Liberia from 1897 to 1947, Harley in Liberia from 1926 to 1948. Harley's paper, *Masks as Agents of Social Control in Northeast Liberia*, published by the museum in 1950, points out the difficulty for outsiders to learn the most important things in the lives of these people. It is hard to get beyond such statements as that they are known "only by the old men." Should such a devotee be successful in actually joining one of the secret societies, he would have to swear never to reveal what he had learned. Harley and Schwab, however, managed to learn a great deal as the many masks they collected were brought to them. (One hundred fifty, for example, in eight years.) Harley notes that "a mask is the same word used to designate the human spirit and the spirit of the ancestors"; and his general conclusion is that "the masks are visible manifestations of a type of ancestor worship, debased, perhaps, by the necessity of using the masks as practical implements to guarantee the smooth working of a system of government founded on strict adherence to custom." He became especially interested in the Poro Society in Liberia, donated a large collection of their masks to the Peabody Museum, and in 1941 published brief notes on them in the museum's *Papers*.

Massachusetts Institute of Technology

Hours: Open daily (works are on the grounds and in lobbies of buildings)
Admission: Free. Ⓗ

The institute is assembling a collection of modern art that already
makes it the most important center in that field in the immediate
Boston area. In modern painting, however, its leadership is challenged
by the collection of Brandeis University at Waltham. The well-appointed
Hayden Gallery, on Memorial Drive, is used primarily for temporary
exhibitions (often of considerable importance); there is the smaller
Compton Gallery for exhibitions of lesser magnitude. Visitors are
strongly advised to call at the office of the Committee on the Visual Arts,
Room 145 in Building 7 (turn left from the main entrance on Massachusetts Avenue, ground floor), and ask for a map and a list of the
collection, with location of the whereabouts of the many works that are
on public view. The institute has a vast complex of buildings and you
will need guidance.

In addition to the works discussed below, you should visit Eliel
Saarinen's Chapel (across Massachusetts Avenue from the main entrance), both as a fine modern building and for its steel altarpiece and
45-foot aluminum bell tower by Harry Bertoia (1955). The music
library in Hayden Memorial Library (Building 14) has a cast of Emile
Antoine Bourdelle's powerful bronze *Tragic Mask of Beethoven*
(1901); and in the Hayden Library itself there is Rodin's *Large Head
of Iris* (1890/1). Other indoor sculptures worth seeking out are by
Varda Chryssa, Nicholas Schöffer, Ernest Trova, and Isaac Witkin.

The Iceberg and Its Shadow,[146] designed in 1975 by Larry Bell (born
1939 in Chicago), is his most ambitious sculpture to that date. It is
composed of 56 glass panels, square, triangular, or trapezoidal, each
having a common base width of 60 inches but of varying heights. The
panes, either clear or gray glass, are vacuum-coated with metallic
inconel and quartz. It can be installed in an almost unlimited number
of configurations. As of this writing, two of them can be seen in the
ground-floor lobbies of the Sloan and the Bush buildings (numbers
E52 and 13 on the map). Bell's imaginative title is most appropriate:
it describes the jagged profiles of the work as well as suggesting the

146

substance of the iceberg (clear glass) and its shadows (gray glass). One wonders what Frederic Church, that painter of icebergs (see CT 102), might have thought of it. Bell is concerned with twentieth-century phenomena: the dissolution of solid form in light, color, and space; and the shifting ambiguity of disappearing images of the environment (and of yourself as viewer), mirrored in the glass panes—something initiated by Marcel Duchamp in his celebrated *Large Glass* (Philadelphia Museum of Art). As in Duchamp's work, sculpture here departs from its traditional concerns with mass and weight in discrete, fixed objects. Instead, it invites us to enter a world of evanescence and illusion.

Outdoor sculpture includes *The Big Sail*, 40 feet high, by Alexander Calder (1966)—the model for it is in Building 9 Plaza; a bronze by Dmitri Hadzi; a steel *Cenotaphe* by Jean Ipousteguy (1957); the corten steel *Dunes I* by Beverly Pepper; and steel sculptures by Tony Smith and Isaac Witkin (VT 13). In front of the Hermann Building (E53) is a cast concrete enlargement by Carl Nesjar developed from a wood maquette of 1958 by Pablo Picasso; the interior engraving was done by sandblasting.

Transparent Horizon,[147] by Louise Nevelson (born 1899 in Kiev, emigrated with her family in 1905 to Rockland, Maine), is a painted corten steel piece dating from 1975 and some 20 feet high. It will be found in the plaza between the Landau Building (number 66 on the map) and Buildings 62 and 64. Nevelson's career, New York oriented, was enriched by travel and study abroad and by her own collecting of African, American Indian, and Pre-Columbian art. At first she produced human and animal figures, usually in wood, plaster, or terra-cotta. During the 1940s she turned to assemblages of found wood objects, and these grew in the next decade to walls of stacked boxes filled with such wood forms, painted black, gold, or white. In the 1960s she turned to other materials, especially welded steel, and gradually perforated what had been compact massings. Her large outdoor sculptures date from 1969 and after. *Transparent Horizon*, commissioned by MIT in 1974, is a composition in two related parts, both derived from works of 1972 and 1973. The shorter portion was inspired by the projections of a tropical tree; the taller one, by floral elements including spiked leaf forms and a capping of petal shapes. In the ensemble there are suggestions of a gate, and of an enveloping landscape. Nevelson describes herself as "an architect of shadows."

147

Visible from Memorial Drive is *Three-Piece Reclining Figure, Draped,*[148] a bronze of 1976 reaching a length of over 15 feet and a height and depth of nearly 9 feet. Comparison with Yale University's *Draped Seated Woman* of 1959 (CT 69) will show Henry Moore's extraordinary development from more traditional norms to a split-up abstraction that invites you to reassemble it into a single reclining form. A germ of this idea is already visible in Amherst College's *Stringed Figure* of 1938 (MA 13). Actually, the effort of connecting these split elements is powerfully guided by the artist through the orientation of his massive shapes, by their rhythms, and by the sympathetic correspondence of solid and void. Moore's wide exposure to the art of primitive cultures has been discussed in the examples referred to above. Those who have admired the enormous split figure in Lincoln Center, New York, will respond here to the suggestions of prehistoric majesty that so often mark his work. From the back view, in ·particular, the great hooded head, the massive shoulders and hips, and the tremendous force of the jutting knees are clearly apparent.

In a book so dominated by painting as this one is, I have taken advantage of the opportunity at MIT to redress the balance somewhat. That is not to say, however, that the painting collection should be overlooked. While some of the examples I shall list are in private offices, most of them can be seen (with the help of MIT's list and map) in public locations. My own selection of artists represented will give some idea of the riches available: Albers, Anuszkiewicz, Bush (a Canadian artist who has also found an enthusiastic reception at the Museum of Fine Arts), Gene Davis, Hans Hofmann, Léger and Lurçat (tapestries woven from their designs), Olitski, Rosenquist, Stamos, Trova, Vasarely, and Youngerman. There is also a small group of paintings by the Hudson River School (Bierstadt, Cole, and Doughty), by Homer and Inness, and a portrait by Charles Willson Peale.

Plans are under way, as of this writing, for a new building to house arts and media facilities, and for a much-needed handbook in the form of a walking tour.

148

In an institution devoted primarily to the sciences, it is a pleasure to record a deep concern for the humanities. This should come as no surprise when we recall that Einstein was a violinist on the side and that one of his greatest friends was the art historian Erwin Panofsky; and that Robert Oppenheimer owned paintings by sublime modern masters, including one of the finest van Goghs. Great scientists, like great artists, venture creatively into uncharted lands.

Historic Deerfield, Inc.

Location: Off Route 5, midway between Greenfield (Route 2) and South
Deerfield (Route 116). From I-91, take exit 24 traveling north, or exit 26
traveling south
Hours: Mon.-Sat. 9:30-4:30, Sun. 1-4:30 throughout the year, except
Thanksgiving, Christmas Eve, Christmas, and New Year's Day. For hours
of specific buildings, inquire at the Information Center. For group tours write
ahead (Box 321, Deerfield, MA 01342) since ordinarily house tours are limited
to six persons
Admission: Charged (per house visited). Phone for further information

Because the interest here is primarily architectural and historical, as is
also true at Old Sturbridge Village, the reader is referred to the companion volume in this series by Margaret Supplee Smith, *Historic Houses
of New England.* American decorative arts are here in great abundance,
however, and several paintings of importance. These we shall consider
briefly.

Historic Deerfield, Inc., was founded in 1952 by Mr. and Mrs.
Henry N. Flynt to carry on the tradition of historic preservation
initiated by the Pocumtuck Valley Memorial Association (founded in
1870) and Deerfield Academy. It offers ten house museums, including
Hall Tavern (c. 1760), where the Information Center is located, a
Silver Shop in a restored farmhouse of 1814, and the Helen Geier Flynt
Fabric Hall in a refitted barn of 1872. Paintings we shall discuss are
located in the Dwight-Barnard House (c. 1725, moved from Springfield) and the Allen House (c. 1720).

According to the diary of the Reverend William Bentley of Salem,
who visited Deerfield in 1782, "The Street is one measured mile,
running North and South. . . . There is a gate at each end of the Street,
& about 60 houses in better style, than in any of the Towns I saw."
Such was the rebirth of Deerfield during the eighteenth century, following the burning of half the town by the Indians in 1704 and the
tomahawking of over half its inhabitants. In later times many of the
houses were moved to other sites in Deerfield, and not a few fell into
ruin. The restoration has brought a significant number back to their
original sites and four more have been saved by removal from the
neighboring area to Deerfield's Street. Today more than fifty houses
front it to compose one of the greatest concentrations of fine old houses
in any New England town.

Mrs. Flynt's collection of textiles, needlework, and costume is taste-
fully displayed in Fabric Hall. While the emphasis here is on American
work of the eighteenth and early nineteenth centuries, English and
European examples are also included, some of them from the seventeenth century. In the superb group of coverlets, a finely quilted
Bedspread[149] has a bold floral design in green and red worthy of Henri
Matisse. This American masterpiece dates from the nineteenth century.

The white background has minute quilting hardly a quarter-inch apart, with seven to ten stitches per linear inch. An inner lining gives the coverlet a triple thickness. It is conjectured that this example may have been for a bride, who for reasons of superstition worked only on the floral design. Friends would have done the quilting of the background; indeed, close inspection shows considerable variation in the workmanship.

Among several paintings in the Dwight-Barnard House is the fine *Portrait of John Barnard*—no relation to the Dr. Ebenezer Barnard who practiced medicine there from 1772 to 1790, but a deacon of Cotton Mather's church in Boston. The artist is Peter Pelham (1697–1751), who arrived in Boston from London in 1726 and thereupon painted Mather's portrait and from it made a mezzotint engraving in 1727—the first known American example. The Barnard portrait is also dated 1727, when the subject was seventy-four. He surveys us with Puritanical mien, but the vigor of the modeling is thoroughly English, in the Baroque manner of Kneller. It contrasts with the puffy forms of Smibert's *Bishop Berkeley and His Entourage* (CT 74), painted in 1729 just after *his* arrival in America. Peter Pelham had some influence on the very young John Singleton Copley, for he married Copley's mother in 1748, when the boy was ten years old. Although Pelham died three years later, his studio equipment—and boyhood memories of him—were benefits that accrued to his stepson. In the Allen House, Copley's *Portrait of Reverend Arthur Browne*, painted in 1757 when Copley was only nineteen, shows him already superior to the best of Smibert.

Also in the Dwight-Barnard House is a pair of portraits by the Connecticut Valley painter William Jennys (see CT 87), known from these very portraits to have been in Deerfield in 1801. The sitters are Dr. William Stoddard Williams and his wife. Jennys received twenty-four dollars for the pair. Another, equally fine pair, of Captain Elijah Arms of Deerfield and his wife, hangs in Memorial Hall.

Memorial Hall is an independent historical museum relating to Deerfield. The exhibits include sturdy pieces of furniture, a rare overmantel painting from Bernardston (near Greenfield) attributed to Jared Jessup about 1810, a fireboard representing the very fireplace it shielded, and

149

the Jennys portraits. The brick building was designed in 1798 by Asher Benjamin as Deerfield Academy's first home. It was acquired in 1878 by the Pocumtuck Valley Memorial Association largely through the efforts of the town historian, George Sheldon, who recorded that in the collection "not a single article here is preserved on account of its artistic qualities. . . . The collection is founded on purely historical lines, and is the direct memorial of the inhabitants of this valley, both Indian and Puritan." Period rooms here shown are believed to be the oldest such displays in the United States. (Closed November to April.)

Adjacent to Memorial Hall is the Henry N. Flynt Library, erected in 1970 and named in memory of Mr. Flynt in 1972. Supplementing the archival resources of Memorial Hall itself, the library is an active research center, and the education offices of Historic Deerfield, Inc., are located here.

Deerfield Academy is the fortunate recipient of the Charles P. Russell collection of European and American Paintings, the gift of his daughters, Mrs. Lucius Potter and Miss Lucia Russell, of Greenfield.

As the paintings are undergoing conservation treatment and scholarly research, they are not currently on view, but they are eventually to be displayed in a special gallery. In date they range from the 17th century to shortly after 1900.

Among the European examples are portraits of high quality by Jacobus Leveck (1634–75), a German pupil of Rembrandt, by Nicholas Maes, and by Sir Joshua Reynolds of *Miss Franks* (1766). An early nude (1846) by J. F. Millet is a precious example of the work of his pre-Barbizon years. Landscapes by Théodore Rousseau, Courbet, and by Pissarro in early career (1859) are memorable.

Not surprisingly, most of the American examples are portraits. Those by John Wollaston, Jeremiah Theus, James Peale, and William Jennys are outstanding both in quality and in condition. There is a fine Eastman Johnson genre scene, *Whittling in the Barn* (1866), and as well a diminutive J. F. Peto *Still Life* painted on a palette. Two rainy urban scenes of 1866 and 1891 by Childe Hassam, providing strong contrast with such late works as the *Isle of Shoals* landscape at Smith College (MA 182), are among the finest pictures in the collection.

A preliminary catalogue was published in 1969.

Duxbury Art Complex

Location: 189 Alden St., off Route 3A (from Boston or Plymouth take exit 33 from Route 3 onto Route 14)
Hours: Fri., Sat., Sun. 2-5
Admission: Free

Opened in 1971 in a rural setting not far from the sea, the Art Complex appears as a delightful surprise. It is a graceful, free-flowing building of wood and glass with an undulating roof and skylights that allow natural north light into two galleries. The architect, Richard Owen Abbott, developed the design from original sketches by the late Ture Bengtz, artist and first director of the museum. Its unusual openness and freedom allow the outdoors to blend naturally with the indoors.

The Art Complex was made possible and is supported by the Carl A. Weyerhaeuser family. It includes the large Weyerhaeuser collection of American painting. From this we select a joyous marine landscape by George Bellows (1882–1925), *Farm of John Tom*,[150] painted in September 1916 on the island of Matinicus in Maine. It measures 21½ by 27½ inches. In contrast with the ominous tone of the Farnsworth Museum's *Boating out to Sea* (ME 32), painted in 1913 on Monhegan Island, it proclaims a sunny optimism in intense blues and greens with the foamy effervescence of the breaking surf. Other painters well represented here include Bengtz, Burchfield, Doughty, Hassam, Inness, Homer Martin, Sargent, and Andrew Wyeth.

Another branch of the collection consists of Shaker furniture and artifacts.

The extensive collections of traditional and modern Japanese art had the advantage of the advice of Kojiro Tomita (1890–1976), curator of the Asiatic department of the Boston Museum of Fine Arts for over thirty years and a longtime friend of the Weyerhaeuser family. He was also instrumental in commissioning the construction of a Japanese Tea House, in which demonstrations of the tea ceremony occasionally take place in the summer season.

150

Fine examples of modern Japanese ceramic art are to be seen here, and among the printmakers color woodcuts signed by Kaoru Kawano (born 1916) are especially sensitive. His *Moonlight Night* (with an Owl) and *Twilight* (with Fish) hold their own in the company of celebrated examples in the same medium by Hiroshige (1797–1858).

Since both galleries are used for temporary exhibitions, much of the permanent collection may not be on view at any given time. Free lectures, concerts, and demonstrations of the tea ceremony are added attractions for the visitor. The large art library is particularly strong in books on Japanese art.

Fall River Historical Society

Location: 451 Rock Street
Hours: March-December, Tues.-Fri. 9-4:30, Sat. 2-4
Admission: Free. Ⓗ partially

Fall River Public Library

Location: 104 North Main Street
Hours: Mon.-Thurs. 9-9, Fri., Sat. 9-5, but closed Sat. in summer
Admission: Free

The two institutions, particularly the Historical Society, offer an opportunity to study the work of a gifted local still-life painter, Robert Spear Dunning (1829-1905). Born in Brunswick, Maine, Dunning came to Fall River at the age of five, studied in New York, and returned to Fall River for the rest of his life. A portraitist and landscape painter at first, he turned to still life in 1865. Many of his works are in local private collections. The Public Library staged a Dunning exhibition in 1911 with forty-six; and in 1970 the Greater Fall River Art Association included twenty examples in an exhibition of the Fall River School, 1853-1932. As a longtime teacher he contributed greatly to the local development. There is a good section on Dunning in Gerdts and Burke, *American Still Life Painting* (New York: Praeger, 1971).

Our selection, in the Historical Society, showing a spill of *Potatoes, Onions, Carrots, and a Turnip*,[151] is signed and dated 1879. It makes an interesting comparison with Renoir's *Onions* (1881) in the Clark Art Institute (MA 256). In their elegant company Dunning's American produce seems modest indeed, as if these homely objects had just come out of the ground. They tumble from the brass pail in no such preordained order as Renoir gave to his onions, and they lack the svelte

151

rhythms and color echoes in the tablecloth that make Renoir's picture so much a work of high art. Yet, like Eakins's portraits and Peto's pile of books (both at Smith College), they have an uncompromising honesty. On occasion, as in the Historical Society's large *Still Life of Fruit*, 1883, Dunning included more luxurious accessories (the Victorian silver pitcher) and—following Dutch practice of the seventeenth century —a self-portrait (here on a support of the carved mahogany table). Dunning enthusiasts tend to pick out our plain fare as their favorite, and on a standard of originality we find no reason to disagree with them.

Thomas Badger's *Still Life with Melons and Fruit* at Colby College (ME 36) belongs to an earlier generation, and it retains much of the polish of Colonial and Federal art. Dunning, at least in the example we have chosen, seems to have had the earthy sensibility of a Jean François Millet, as in the Malden Library's *Woman Churning* (MA 167).

Among other local painters of still life, Bryant Chapin (1859–1927) is well represented at the Historical Society, particularly in his specialty, baskets of strawberries.

The society's granite building, stern and finely proportioned, was formerly the home of the Brayton family. Built in the 1840s, it was moved, block by block by oxen, in 1870 to its present site and reconstructed. The style agrees with that of the scores of magnificent factories that are Fall River's chief claim to architectural splendor, although the many fine houses on Highland Avenue are not far behind in interest. Within, the society's possessions are handsomely displayed.

Elsewhere in the city are the Marine Museum (70 Water Street, admission charged), with ship models, marine paintings, lithographs, and posters relating to the growth of maritime steam power; the U.S.S. *Massachusetts* of Second World War fame (open daily, admission charged); and for the criminologist the Lizzie Borden House (230 Second Street). The great granite and brick factories once made Fall River the largest cloth-manufacturing city in the world.

Fitchburg Art Museum

Location: Merriam Pkwy.; from Main St. (Route 2A) turn east at Upper Common onto Merriam Pkwy. Parking available
Hours: Tues., Wed., Fri., Sat. 10-5, Thurs. 10-9, Sun. 2-5; closed July and August, and Thanksgiving, Christmas, and New Year's Day
Admission: Free

The museum was established in 1925 through the generosity of Eleanor Norcross, daughter of the first mayor of Fitchburg. The original building, opened in 1928, was destroyed by fire in 1933. The present fireproof building was constructed in the following year. It houses the permanent collection and provides space for adult and children's art classes. The museum's annual regional exhibition attracts entries by artists from more than forty neighboring towns.

An active program of temporary exhibitions, on an average of one per month, is supplemented by lectures by visiting artists, scholars, and critics; by crafts demonstrations; and by bus tours to Boston, Worcester, Manchester (N.H.), and other leading centers. A large and enthusiastic membership is evidence that Fitchburg enjoys one of the better small art centers in New England.

The collection, not large but steadily growing, is richest in works on paper. An impressive print collection, maintained in well-designed storage racks, is strongest in Japanese woodblock prints and in work by twentieth-century Americans, but a large example by Joan Miró (see CT 32) should not be missed. There are fine watercolors, too, including a pair by Charles Burchfield, and Edward Hopper's *Two Lights, Maine*. Prints by Mary Cassatt and the German Expressionist Kaethe Kollwitz are of fine quality here.

Among the oil paintings in the permanent collection are a small study for Sargent's *Hosea* in the Boston Public Library (MA 29); *Theophila Palmer Reading "Clarissa,"* by Sir Joshua Reynolds (1771); and *The Wedding* (1903) by Edward Lamson Henry (1841–1919)—that infinitely patient observer of American life.

Set in its magnificent original Chippendale frame, the *Portrait of Mrs. Sarah Clayton of Liverpool*,[152] measuring 50 by 40 inches and painted in 1770 by Joseph Wright of Derby (1734–97), is the outstanding Old Master work in the collection. Mrs. Clayton sits in dignity at a mahogany table holding an architect's plan of the St. Nicholas Church at Liverpool. The subtle color scheme runs from the mauve and lavender of her taffeta dress and bows to the green curtain blown across the inevitable status-column—of the sort that belatedly (and unnecessarily) exalts Thomas Jefferson in the Gilbert Stuart portrait of 1805 at Bowdoin College (ME 13). Apart from a trip to Europe in 1773, Wright spent most of his life in Derby, far removed from the fashionable London of his slightly older contemporaries, Reynolds and Gainsborough. Trained under Thomas Hudson (1701–79), Wright did not venture, as a portraitist, much beyond the models set by his teacher, who was also the master of Reynolds. Of Hudson, Ellis K. Waterhouse, in the Pelican History volume on *Painting in Britain*, has said that for all that he was Reynolds's teacher, his work is "straightforward and solid, with no graces and no nonsense and no poetry about it." (The visitor to the Fleming Museum at the University of Vermont, after seeing Hudson's *Portrait of Miss Ann Isted* (VT 4), may take issue with this judgment.) Despite Wright's clear advance in subtlety and in psychological penetration beyond Hudson's attainment, he seems closer to his Boston contemporary, John Singleton Copley, than to the leading portraitists of London. By London standards, Wright—again as a portraitist—was a provincial, as was Copley; but, as in the case of Copley, these standards are not relevant.

Wright is known today less for his portraits than for his pictures of candlelight scenes of scientific experiments, for moonlight landscapes and scenes of grottoes and caverns, and for views of Mount Vesuvius in eruption. In such works he was among the forerunners of the Romantic movement. There is no hint of any of this in his portrait of Mrs. Clayton, but the lavender-mahogany-green color scheme is similar to that in many of his landscapes.

If the Wright portrait offers us high competence without aesthetic surprises, that cannot be said of our second selection, *Still Life with a Bottle of Olives*,[153] by William M. Harnett (1848–92), signed and dated 1877. This Irish-born Philadelphian supported himself until that year as an engraver of silver in Philadelphia and New York. His first oils date from 1875, and when in the following year a depression in his regular trade cut off his livelihood, he took up painting as his new profession. The surprise offered by Fitchburg's small picture, therefore, is double: that he so quickly achieved competence, and that he initiated a form of still life that would be difficult to parallel in the long-sustained American interest in this theme during the nineteenth century. We can find minutely spotted apples and sharply detailed descriptions of cut melons, but where such a sentinellike bottle of stuffed olives, its contents huddled behind a streak of light on glass? All this before

152

153

Harnett set off in 1880 for a six-year stint of study in Europe, chiefly in Munich. After his return, he went on to such expansive tours de force as Springfield's *Emblems of Peace* (MA 220). In the section on the Smith College Museum of Art (see MA 187), we shall have more to say about this Jan van Eyck of American painting, including some curious developments that took place after his death.

Archaeologically minded visitors to Fitchburg will be interested in a dig on the edge of town, sponsored by the museum and the local Historical Society and conducted by the museum's director. With meticulous care, vestiges of the Spofford Garrison, one of the area's earliest sites, are slowly reemerging into the light of day.

Danforth Museum

Location: 123 Union Ave.; take exit 13 from Mass. Tpke. to enter the city on Route 126; from Route 135 turn north to the business district. Parking available
Hours: Wed.-Sun. 1-4:30; closed major holidays
Admission: Free. Ⓗ

Development of a flourishing art center in Framingham has overcome two great disadvantages: its proximity to the artistic riches of Boston and the fact that the museum opened as recently as 1975. With commendable imagination and initiative, public-spirited citizens took over a vacated school building, renovated it, established an ambitious program of classes in arts and crafts and of lectures, films, and exhibitions, and quietly began assembling a permanent collection. The emphasis here is on prints, including good examples by the great masters and very fine ones by the German Expressionists.

The small collection of oil paintings includes a pair of Gilbert Stuarts and a somewhat simpering, but characteristic, Bouguereau (see MA 257); and excellent examples of the landscape art of Jasper Cropsey (1832–1900), Samuel Gerry (1813–1906), and Frank Shapleigh (1842–1906).

Outstanding is a modest but lovely early work by Albert Bierstadt (1830–1902), *Near North Conway, N.H.,*[154] measuring 18 by 24 inches and painted about 1860. Beyond a screen of dark evergreens a wide prospect opens out under a pale gray sky, climaxed by the silvery sheen of a distant lake. A very different response to Conway scenery is offered by a large Inness at Mount Holyoke College (MA 206). As for Bierstadt, he later expanded onto enormous canvases like *Domes of the Yosemite* (1867) at St. Johnsbury (VT 14), and let himself go in Wagnerian Romantic fervor as in *Seal Rock* (1872) at New Britain (CT 44).

154

Cape Ann Historical Association

Location: 27 Pleasant St. Ask for map and directions at information booth on the waterfront, reached at end of Route 133 from Route 128
Hours: Tues.-Sat. 11-4
Admission: Charged

There is no more attractive small museum in New England than the Cape Ann Scientific, Literary & Historical Association. Housed in sea captain Elias Davis's 1804 home and a tasteful gallery added alongside in 1936, the association dates from 1875. In addition, it owns and maintains two eighteenth-century houses in the town. Apart from a library of historical documents relating to Gloucester's seafaring life, its displays —arranged with impeccable taste—include fine antique furniture, silver (some by Paul Revere), pewter, china, and glass; ship models and ship portraits; and fishing gear. Much care and expert knowledge have been expended on the explanatory labels.

The major attraction is the collection of thirty-two oils and over one hundred drawings by Fitz Hugh Lane (1804–65), born and died at Gloucester, and one of the most precious masters of mid-nineteenth-century America. While examples of his work may be seen in many other museums (notably in the Karolik collection of the Boston Museum of Fine Arts), none comes near to matching what can be seen here. A superbly designed and illustrated catalogue, with text by John Wilmerding, was published for the Historical Association in 1974 by the Stinehour Press. Three oils by Lane were included in the Museum of Modern Art's memorable 1976 exhibition, "The Natural Paradise: Painting in America, 1800–1950." Lane and Martin J. Heade (1819–1904) form a close pair in what is now called American Luminism; the fact that thirteen oils by Heade were shown in the Museum of Modern Art's exhibition should signify no lesser rank for Fitz Hugh Lane, but only that his career as a painter, delayed by a period of earning his living in Boston as a lithographer of town views, hardly spanned a quarter century, whereas Heade's long life made possible a career of over twice that length. While the two have much in common and it would be easy to believe that the older Lane inspired Heade's early development, there is no solid evidence that they ever met, or even that Heade knew Lane's work. For a discussion of both artists, see Barbara Novak, *American Painting of the Nineteenth Century* (2nd edition, New York: Harper and Row, 1979), chapters 5 through 7. For Lane, see the brilliant monograph by John Wilmerding (New York: Praeger, 1971) on which his catalogue for the Cape Ann Association's collection is based.

Partially paralyzed in his legs, Fitz Hugh Lane worked mostly at Gloucester and inland on Cape Ann, but there are memorable paintings of the Maine coast, which he often visited in the company of a younger Gloucester friend, Joseph L. Stevens, Jr. The Stevens family had a house at Castine, on Penobscot Bay. Arriving there by train and boat, Lane and his friend cruised the coast, with Rockland a favorite subject for sketching. Wilmerding suggests that Lane traveled light, making only pencil sketches and color notes, and that the resulting oils were painted in Gloucester "with a sense of reverie, now seen to be an enviable characteristic of the nineteenth century."

Gloucester Harbor from Rocky Neck,[155] signed and dated 1844, is the earliest oil in this collection and one of Lane's largest pictures (29½ by 41½ inches). It has the crispness and meticulous detail of his early lithographs—indeed, he made a lithograph version of it—and of his pencil sketches. It also achieves a sense of tranquillity extending into great distances. But it is through a pervasive, limpid light and discreet spottings of color that he turns description and topography into poetry. Patience is sometimes the enemy of feeling, but not here.

Riverdale,[156] signed and dated 1863, more concentrated as a composition and ever so slightly looser in technique and richer in color, shows us how faithful Lane remained to the standard he had set two decades before. Hardly twenty miles to the north by crow's flight from Gloucester, and at exactly the same time, Heade was painting similar haying scenes on the salt marshes near Newburyport. We illustrate an example of c. 1865–70, at Bowdoin College (ME 14). Heade's vision of an Emersonian harmony between man and nature is gently disturbed by a passing shower (frequently he introduced ominous storms, as in CT 100, an oil of 1863). But for Lane, Cape Ann's salt marshes were serene and untroubled. Wilmerding, who holds out for the likelihood—notwithstanding the lack of evidence—of a connection between the two artists, suggests that in such late works as *Riverdale* Lane was influenced by Heade's haying scenes.

However that may be, in Lane's magical idyll, a mushroom-shaped load of hay has passed by some bread-loaf rocks, and in good time will reach the gate in a stone wall built by patient hands. The trees do not stir. In the pale distance a village rests in summer slumber.

155

156

The Hammond Museum

Location: 80 Hesperus Ave., west of the town. Exit from Route 128 onto Route 133 and follow it to the waterfront; at the town's information booth ask for a map and directions
Hours: Open daily 10-4, except in winter; December-March, Tues.-Fri. 10-3, Sat.-Sun. 10-4; closed during January and on Thanksgiving, Christmas, and New Year's Day
Admission: Charged

The home of Mr. and Mrs. John Hays Hammond, Jr., was established as a museum in 1931, soon after its completion. Designed by Allen and Collens, later the architects of the Cloisters in New York, it provides a medieval setting for an extensive collection of architectural fragments, sculpture, painting, furniture, and decorative arts dating from the Roman period to the Renaissance. It is situated picturesquely on the rocky coast somewhat west of Gloucester, not far from the reef of Norman's Woe, celebrated in Longfellow's "Wreck of the Hesperus." Chief element in the design is the Great Hall, which is based on the proportions of the Gothic transept of the church of St. Nazaire at Carcassonne. This contains the largest pipe organ in private possession. Organ recitals, early music concerts, and other musical events are open to the public throughout the year.

Because the guided tour, lasting about an hour, is very competently conducted, only the outstanding exhibits will be mentioned here. The finest architectural elements, incorporated in the conservatory-court, are two timber house fronts of the fifteenth century, one from Amiens and the other from the neighborhood of Tours, and a large flamboyant Gothic portal in limestone from the Loire region. Opposite the fireplace in the Great Hall are three examples of architectural stone carving of Italo-Byzantine provenance: an altar frontal, a round-arched portal, and a bishop's throne. The last-named piece comes from Lecce, near Bari in southern Italy. Late as these examples may be, their style is of the sort that filled the time gap between the fall of Rome and the Romanesque age of the eleventh and twelfth centuries. The emphasis in these carvings is on flat ornament, strongly Eastern in character. They differ from early Byzantine art chiefly in their rugged crudeness.

Over these carvings is a gilt organ screen from the Marienkirche in Lübeck, in northern Germany. Johann Sebastian Bach used to hear Buxtehude play the organ there, and later he became the organist. The screen itself is of late Gothic date. The reverse curves ending in floral finials mark the flamboyant style, of which the French limestone portal in the conservatory-court is an example on a larger scale.

As of this writing, the collections are undergoing scholarly study and attribution. Since they are primarily of architectural or decorative character, they fall outside the scope of this book.

In one wing there is a series of Colonial American rooms with excellent examples of furniture, glass, pewter, a marine painting, and a small bronze statue of Thomas Jefferson.

The museum has an active program of temporary exhibitions, a lecture series, and sponsored trips to other museums. As a whole, it offers a free-ranging early twentieth-century Romantic interpretation of a medieval castle-residence. Unlike some historical reconstructions, it has the good sense not to dress up the guides in historical costume.

An attractive illustrated handbook is available.

Hancock Shaker Village

Location: On Route 20, 5 miles west of Pittsfield and near the New York State line; do not approach via Hancock Center, which is on Route 43. Parking provided
Hours: Open June 1-October 31 only, daily 9:30-5; use of library at other seasons by appointment only
Admission: Charged. Ⓗ within limits

In preparation for a visit, which should be unhurried, to this model preservation of a not quite extinct phenomenon of American culture, you are enthusiastically advised to seek out, in the nearest available library, the December 1966 issue of *Harper's* magazine. There you will find a most engaging account of this enterprise by Russell Lynes. Failing that, all is not lost, since you will receive a well-organized orientation in the attractive Visitors' Center.

On a pasture, woodland, and meadow site are some twenty buildings, several of them dating from as early as the 1790s. From 1779 to 1790 residents of Hancock, Richmond, and Pittsfield heard Shaker testimony and joined together in Hancock. In 1783, the year before her death, the founder, Mother Ann Lee, visited Hancock and Richmond; and by 1786 the Believers had raised a meetinghouse—dismantled in 1938 but replaced in 1962 by a similar building moved from Shirley, Mass. In 1790 Hancock—the "City of Peace"—was formed as the third covenant Shaker community under the leadership of Father Calvin Harlow and Mother Sarah Harrison. The true name for the Shakers is the United Society of Believers in Christ's Second Appearing.

Important construction in the early nineteenth century included the Trustees' House (c. 1800, modernized at the end of the century); the Schoolhouse (c. 1820, reconstructed in 1976 on the original site); the celebrated Round Stone Barn (1826); and the Brick Dwelling House (1830). By the time of the last-named building, the community had reached its numerical peak of 247 members; the Dwelling housed 100 brethren and sisters.

In 1960 Shaker Community, Inc., was formed, under a dedicated board of trustees, to save the buildings and to perpetuate the Shaker traditions. In that year the community had officially closed, and the buildings were threatened with destruction by a neighboring racetrack (which subsequently also closed).

An extensive program of reconstruction and repair was inaugurated immediately after the formation of the corporation, and this was accompanied by major collecting activities geared to illustrating all phases of Shaker life and manufacture. The capacious Brick Dwelling is only the most sizable of the many fascinating exhibition areas to be seen here. A varied sampling of Shaker work greets you in the Visitors' Center, but a vast assemblage of furniture, tools, wooden models for making bonnets (strangely similar to the simplified nature abstractions of Brancusi), and all manner of crafts will be found in the various buildings.

An experimental program of inviting craftsmen to demonstrate the Shaker techniques—on special summer occasions—proved so successful that a second barn, near the Round Barn, has recently been equipped for year-round activity by resident artisans. Their products, made strictly in accordance with Shaker practice, will be sold at the sales shop of the adapted structure.

An extensive library of Shaker materials has been assembled, and a complete Shaker bibliography, by Mary Richmond, published. The library is now actively used by scholars and other specialists in Shaker life. Another branch of Shaker activity, cooking, has also received devoted attention. You can purchase publications of Shaker recipes, and on special occasions you can savor a Shaker repast.

Most precious of Shaker creations are the Inspirational Drawings—divinely inspired visions of the spirit world. A group of forty-two examples formed the centerpiece of a Shaker exhibition, "The Gift of Inspiration," held in 1979 at Hirschl & Adler Galleries, New York; of these, half were lent by Hancock Shaker Village, many of them done at Hancock itself. Well attended and enthusiastically reviewed, the exhibition was a Hancock benefit.

In many instances the author of the drawing is duly inscribed. At Hancock, Hannah Cohoon (1788–1864) appears to have had exceptional talent, or, to speak more reverently, to have been vouchsafed more inspirational revelations. Four of the finest drawings are by her hand. *The Tree of Light or Blazing Tree* is inscribed [*sic*]: "Seen and received by Hannah Cohoon in the City of Peace Sabbath Oct 9th 10th hour A.M. 1845. drawn and painted by the same hand." The three other drawings date from the 1850s—comforting evidence that inspiration was not short-lived. *Tree of Life*,[157] 18 by 23 inches, is inscribed: "City of Peace Monday July, 3rd 1854. Seen and painted by, Hannah Cohoon." And on the back: "Aged 66." We also learn that on October 1 at 4:00 P.M. the design was identified to Hannah Cohoon by Mother Ann, "writing" its title through the hand of a medium. The inscription further reveals that ". . . the spirit shew'd me plainly the branches, leaves and fruit, painted or drawn upon paper. The leaves were check'd or crossed

157

and the same colors you see here." The leaves are green-green; the fruit dark green and vermilion-vermilion. To other Believers the revealed colors were gentler and subtler; many of the drawings feature yellows, pinks, and sky blues.

The activities of the village are strengthened by programs in research and in education. In addition to the work of local and visiting scholars, there are frequent visits by student groups from schools, colleges, and centers of graduate study—some from as far away as Michigan.

Nearby, in New York State off Route 295, is Old Chatham, with a Shaker museum containing another huge collection of Shaker materials. While the range of objects rivals Hancock's, there are no Shaker buildings, for no community was established there.

Fruitlands Museums

Location: Prospect Hill (P.O. address R.R. 2, Box 87); from Route 2, exit south on Route 110, turn right on Old Shirley Rd. and follow the signs
Hours: Open May 30 to September 30, Tues.-Sun. 1-5; closed Mon. except when a holiday
Admission: Charged

Founded in 1914 by Clara Endicott Sears, the Fruitlands Museums include an early eighteenth-century farmhouse where in 1843 Bronson Alcott and other Transcendentalist leaders founded a new social order known as the Con-Sociate Family; a Shaker house; an American Indian museum; and a picture gallery. A library is open throughout the year to qualified research workers. These buildings are situated on a beautiful two-hundred-acre estate that commands a superb view of Mt. Wachusett and Mt. Monadnock.

The gallery contains Miss Sears's collection of portraits by itinerant American painters of the nineteenth century and landscapes by members of the Hudson River School. In both fields Miss Sears was among the first collectors.

Mt. Ascutney, Vermont[158] was painted in 1862 by Albert Bierstadt (1830–1902). Often this master impressed through sheer size or through the choice of a melodramatic landscape subject (VT 14). While this is a fairly large picture, about 6 feet in length, the effect could hardly be more unassuming. Like George Inness in his earlier pictures (see M E 23), Bierstadt simply communicated his own peace of mind as he contemplated the serenity of a broad New England prospect. He was born in Düsseldorf, but his family emigrated to New Bedford when he was only two years old. In 1853 he returned to Germany to study painting and remained for six years, including travels to Italy, Switzerland, and the Rhine. Characteristically, he went to the Rocky Mountains in search of extraordinary scenery. In later life he made three more trips to Europe. Bierstadt painted this lovely pastoral near Claremont, N.H., looking across the Connecticut River to Vermont. Note how gently, but firmly, he leads us down the center of the broad panorama to the elms in the middle distance, where the river takes us to the farthest mountains. There is much to be seen at the sides, but our attention is never dis-

158

tracted. While this picture is more ambitious than the lovely small example of 1860 discussed at Framingham (MA 154), it is in a similar spirit.

The *Portrait of a Lady*,[159] from the Walter Perkins House in Brookline, is attributed to Alvan Clark (1804–87). Of the many tightly compressed images that stare out from these walls, this is perhaps the most memorable. Furtive and reclusive, the face is framed in a blue headdress that looks exactly like ribbon candy. The lady has black hair, she is dressed in black velvet, and there is a black ground. A dark red curtain provides a little relief in color, but adds to the feeling of ominous tension. The scale of the figure is enhanced by meticulous dottings on the headdress, at the throat, on the gilt buckle at the waist, and on the wrist and the cuff. The lady may be described as a Puritan Bloody Mary played by Lillian Gish. There are finer portraits here, but none so alarming. What would Dr. Freud have made of it?

Subsequent donations have greatly enriched Miss Sears's collection of nineteenth-century American painting, but within the same scope. Not previously represented is Thomas Chambers, a landscapist who was born in London in 1808, came to America in 1832, and frequented New York, Boston, and Albany during the 1850s and 1860s. His subjects included the Delaware Water Gap, the falls of the Genesee at Rochester, and Niagara, but his favorite was the Hudson River at West Point. One of the last-named, fairly similar to the version at the Albany Institute of History and Art, can be seen here. More characteristic, however, is *View from Mount Holyoke*, showing the Oxbow of the Connecticut River. The setting is nearly identical to one by the French-born Regis Gignoux, who came to America in 1844 and painted in what may be called the normal Hudson River School style, especially that of Frederic Church. Chambers, on the contrary, seems to have based his compositions on popular prints. He gave them a strongly personal stamp, marked by a play of rich oranges, greens, and whites, and by crisp contour lines. Born more than thirty years before the self-taught Henri Rousseau (*le douanier*), he prefigured to a surprising degree Rousseau's fresh and modern point of view.

William Matthew Prior (1806–73), son of a Maine shipmaster and now firmly established as a portraitist of ability, was already represented in Miss Sears's collection by six examples, but many more have now come to Fruitlands, including a large picture of *The Sons of Edwin A. and Sarah R. Hill*.[160] The date of 1853 on the red binding of the half-opened book agrees with the known ages of Edwin Lawton, Augustine Prentice, and John Pierce Hill: one, six, and four respectively—provided that we keep in mind that portrayals of Early American children invariably make them look older than they actually were. The arrangement is not unskillful, and the varying reds, blues, greens, and browns unite its parts successfully. If the bright red cherry and the bright green leaves on the floor, presumably dropped by Edwin, do not match the fruit he holds, they seem appropriate color accents for the bare lower-left corner.

Prior appears to have started out dutifully enough in the prevalent early Romantic manner of portraiture, as in the 1831 example of *H. B.*

Webb of Bath, Maine, and gradually to have turned to the manner seen in the Hill children. Yet as early as 1831 he advertised in the *Maine Enquirer* to the effect that "persons wishing for a flat picture can have a likeness without shade or shadow at one quarter price." An itinerant limner, he traveled as far south as Baltimore, but worked chiefly around Boston. He made a specialty of painting on glass, including copies of Gilbert Stuart's *George Washington*, one of which is in the Fruitlands collection.

Other paintings of note include portraits of a man and a woman of Sturbridge, by an anonymous master of considerable skill, and one of the earliest works of George Inness, *March of the Crusaders* (1824).

In the Tea Room behind the director's office is a photographic exhibit devoted to the founder, Miss Sears, clearly a person of great charm, style, and intelligence. Her vision for Fruitlands has been carried out in a manner that would surely win her approval.

159

160

The Holyoke Museum, Holyoke Public Library

Location: 335 Maple St. Take exit 4 from Mass. Tpke., or exit 16 from I-91
Hours: Mon-Sat. 1-5
Admission: Free

The museum provides an interesting reflection of collecting activities in the nineteenth and early twentieth centuries in this manufacturing city, when its mills were generating much wealth. In many ways it is as impressive as the Greek Ionic portico of the 1902 library building. Both the library and the museum were established in 1870, three years before the incorporation of Holyoke itself as a city.

Made possible by gifts, bequests, and the Joseph Skinner Art Fund, the collections cover American and European painting, decorative arts from the seventeenth through the nineteenth century, ceramics, glass, scrimshaw work, and American Indian basketry. While American paintings dominate, European landscapes, portraits, and genre subjects include examples of quality. American artists of note seen here are Asher Durand, Alfred Bricher, Eastman Johnson, William Merritt Chase, Frank Duveneck, and John Alden Weir.

Particularly sensitive is *Fog on the Cliffs*,[161] an oil measuring 17 by 36 inches, by Alfred Bricher (1837–1908), signed at the lower left. A comparable work, *Beach Scene at Sunset*—with no cliffs but instead a distant sailing vessel—is owned by the New Britain Museum of American Art; and the Wadsworth Atheneum at Hartford has *Fog Clearing: Maillon's Cove, Grand Manan*. Subtly atmospheric pictures like these, painted in the 1870s and conceived in the quiet vein of Fitz Hugh Lane and Martin Heade, add to our understanding of Luminism as a major development in American painting. Two other Bricher landscapes, also in his customary narrow horizontal format, were included in an important exhibition shown in 1976 at the Museum of Modern Art: "The Natural Paradise: Painting in America, 1800–1950."

Eastman Johnson's *The Kite*, with two figures on a hilltop, closely resembles early paintings by Winslow Homer (see CT 80), but at bolder scale and with more brilliant areas of white in strong light. *Young Girl* by William Merritt Chase, an oil in vigorous wide strokes in a deep brown key, reflects his early work in Munich; it contrasts strikingly with the much later oil at Dartmouth College (NH 10). His contemporary

161

—and companion in the Munich years—Frank Duveneck (1848–1919) is well represented by *Portrait of a Woman*.

Decidedly worth the visit in itself is a 50-by-40-inch *Seated Portrait of Sir John Skynner* (1703–1805) by Thomas Gainsborough (1727–88)—one of three ordered in 1785, of which at least two were completed by the following year. The others are at Christ Church College, Oxford, and Lincoln's Inn, London. The Holyoke example, included in the definitive monograph on the painter by Ellis K. Waterhouse, was given by bequest in 1975 from the estate of William Skinner II. Heavily bewigged and clad in a scarlet gown, the subject wears a long chain of elaborate goldwork, with a Tudor rose suspended from it. This insigne connotes no special order, but was awarded for service to the king (Henry VII had added the Tudor rose to such traditional chains). An identical chain is worn by Sir Thomas More in Holbein's celebrated portrait in the Frick Collection, New York. There is some probability of work in this picture by assistants, but on the whole—and in particular in the rich landscape detail at the left—it is a most impressive Gainsborough. See also CT 54 and MA 306.

The painting collection is well displayed on the second floor of the library in the Donald R. Taber Gallery.

De Cordova Museum

Location: Sandy Pond Rd., ½ mile from the village center; parking available
Hours: Tues., Thurs., Fri. 10-5, Wed. 10-9:30, Sat. 12-5, Sun. 1:30-5
Admission: Charged, except Wed. evenings 5-9:30

Opened in 1951 as the De Cordova and Dana Museum and Park, this is among the most firmly established and flourishing art centers in New England. Set in extensive grounds on a hilltop not far from Walden Pond, it is housed in a Rhenish-looking brick *schloss* converted in 1910 from the former residence of Thomas Dana by his son-in-law and law partner, Julian De Cordova (1851–1945). After a lifetime of amassing a miscellaneous collection of art objects, De Cordova gave the estate to the town of Lincoln in 1930; eight years later the house was opened to the public as a museum and that summer drew fourteen hundred visitors.

As of 1951, the focus here was placed on the creation of a community art center for direct participation in the arts. It has maintained ever since an active program of temporary exhibitions (such as the memorable and highly important one on the China Trade in 1979), lectures, and concerts; and now offers over three hundred classes in painting, drawing, printmaking, design, pottery, and jewelry. An amphitheater and workshop building have been added to the facilities, and large sculptures dot the nearby grounds.

Given the proximity of Lincoln to the great museums of the Boston area, and given the artistic value of what Mr. De Cordova collected, it was a wise decision on the part of the trustees to preserve his Thoreau-inspired dreams of the estate as a whole, but to transform entirely the character and the use of the house itself.

As for the permanent collection, the original intention was modest. The plan was to encourage local talent by occasional acquisitions from exhibitions held at the museum. Gradually the scope was extended to include contemporary New England artists, and ultimately contemporary American artists and a few European ones. Since the available exhibition space is completely taken up when major exhibitions are staged, the visitor will normally find it difficult to get much idea of the very large collection that now exists. A catalogue listing, which can be consulted at the entrance desk, is the best way to find out what is here; and you may be lucky enough to find a large selection on display. On my visit I listed a score of impressive works, and selected two for reproduction and illustration. The earliest examples on my list are *Thistles*, an oil of 1945 by the English artist Graham Sutherland, and *Cape Split*, a watercolor of 1949 by John Marin. It also includes works by Aaronson, Baskin, Frasconi, Georg Grosz, Hans Hofmann, Kepes, Levine, Liberman (*Cardinal Points*, a large steel sculpture of 1965 in the gardens), Maurer, Henry Moore (a large linen wall-panel representing two figures), Ohashi, Sheeler (*Hex Signs*, a small tempera of 1958), and an untitled gouache of 1954 by the German painter Fritz Winter (honored internationally but too little in this country, although Harvard owns a fine large oil).

Figure,[162] an oil of 1956 about 6 feet high by the New York Abstract Expressionist Franz Kline (1910–62), is perhaps the outstanding large painting in the collection. Characteristically rough-brushed in dense black strokes on a disturbed white ground, it exemplifies John W. McCoubrey's penetrating comment in his fine book, *American Tradition in Painting* (New York: Braziller, 1963, page 10). Contrasting another large Kline with a superficially similar work by the French painter Pierre Soulages, he writes: ". . . the American painting appears raw and violent, without any pretention to small imperfections. . . . The brush strokes reach to the very edge of the canvas and seem hardly contained by the frame. . . . It cannot be read, as can Soulages' painting, as a material object—or figure—against a ground." In short, we are faced with a brash New World, with all its energies and dislocations.

Among the outdoor sculptures, *Three Lines*,[163] by George Rickey (born 1907), offers the spectacle of three slim spears of stainless steel, 18 feet high, moving rhythmically with every passing breeze. Rickey's kinetic art is based on considerable engineering knowledge. It differs from Calder's mobiles (see NH 2), limited to movement in horizontal planes, in the introduction of action along vertical axes. This is achieved by carefully calculated counterweights clustered at the base. The approach of sculpture to the delights of ballet is thus closer than in the work of any previous sculptor; but Rickey's steel ballets are inspired by nature, by the movement of trees and grasses in the wind.

162

163

Malden Public Library

Location: 36 Salem Street (Route 60)
Hours: Mon.-Thurs. 9-9, Fri.-Sat. 9-6; closed Sun. and holidays; closed Saturdays June through Labor Day. But see last paragraph, below
Admission: Free

The library building, opened in 1885, is one of the masterpieces of the Boston architect Henry Hobson Richardson (1838–86). Designed in Romanesque style with a brown sandstone exterior and an oak interior featuring an impressive barrel vault over the main hall, it has the powerful massing, the spaciousness, and the richness of materials and ornament that characterize his work.

Since 1892 the library has been acquiring a small but fine collection of European and American paintings purchased from the Elisha S. and Mary D. Converse art funds. An illustrated brochure, *Thirty Paintings in the Malden Collection*, was published in 1976. In addition to the five examples discussed below, attention is called to excellent works by Albert André, George Loring Brown, John Singleton Copley (*General Picton*), Charles H. Davis (1856–1933, a Boston Constable follower whose skies are memorable), Jean Léon Gérôme, Francesco Guardi, Winslow Homer (*The Whittling Boy*, 1873), George Inness (*In the Berkshires*, c. 1878), Martin Lewis (*The Flatiron Building—Madison Square*), Anthonie Palamedesz (*Boy with Dogs*, 1656), Hubert Robert, and Constant Troyon.

The so-called *Armorer*,[164] by Nicolaes Maes (1634–93), a pupil of Rembrandt in Amsterdam, is no armorer, but a military or paramilitary person dressed up in a late seventeenth-century Dutchman's idea of classical garb—a reflection of the revival of interest in classicism that began in Holland in the 1660s. Maes's early work (such as *An Old Woman at Prayer* in the Worcester Museum) developed from Rembrandt's later style toward an unaffected, compassionate sentiment rich

164

in effects of color and shadow. In the 1660s, however, he went to Antwerp, where he fell under the sway of the fashionable Baroque school of Rubens. The *"Armorer"* clearly shows this influence. It should be compared with the great Rubens portrait of the Earl of Arundel in the Gardner Museum (MA 47). Though it will not hold up in such company, we may nevertheless admire the vigor of its modeling, and its honest middle-class look.

Seascape with Squall Coming Up[165] is considered one of the finest early Turners in America. The arrangement is generally similar to Turner's most famous work of this time, the *Calais Pier* in the National Gallery of London (1803). All these works were strongly influenced by such seventeenth-century Dutch marine painters as Jacob van Ruisdael (see MA 74). Turner, however, stepped up the value range, enriched the color intensities, and increased the sense of struggle between man and the waters. Note the dramatic opposition of light on dark at the left against dark on light at the right. Already Turner has sounded the basic theme of Romanticism: nature wild and untamed. He then went on to such feats as *The Falls of the Rhine at Schaffhausen* (MA 79) and later (1840) to *Rockets and Blue Lights* (MA 253), but his theme remained constant.

Doges' Palace,[166] by Richard Parkes Bonington (1801–28), measuring 64 by 45 inches, is one of his largest paintings and among his most important in America. The Fogg Art Museum owns a small variant or sketch for it. Guided by the perspective lines, our eye travels rapidly along the Riva degli Schiavoni, past the great pink Gothic marvel and Sansovino's Renaissance Library, and on to the far distance. The rich colors run to high intensities in the shadows. The effect is at once powerful and sensuous; it is an Englishman's Romantic reaction to a fabulous

165

166

world. We share the young bargeman's fascination in a passing religious procession. Just as Turner deepened the space of Dutch marines of the seventeenth century and stepped up their value contrasts, so did Bonington in comparison with eighteenth-century Venetian artists' views of their city. Malden has a shimmering little example: *View of San Giorgio Maggiore,* by Francesco Guardi—with which Bonington's should be compared. Note too how Bonington has enriched the colors as against the blond palette of Guardi's Rococo statement. One may admire Bonington's intimate little English scene at Yale (CT 59) even more than his more ambitious record of Venice, but the latter brings him closer to his Romantic French contemporaries, Baron Gros and Delacroix, who saw his work at the Paris Salons and were influenced by them. *Doges' Palace* dates from c. 1826, just before Bonington's death at the age of twenty-seven.

Woman Churning,[167] by Jean François Millet (1814–75), was exhibited at the Salon of 1870, where it was well received. Of Norman peasant origin, Millet studied in Paris and was enthralled by the work of Michelangelo and of Poussin (see MA 123). Like Daumier, his near contemporary, he adapted the grandiose forms of great past masters to a deeply felt interpretation of the life he knew so well. The churn is a powerful truncated cone, its axis reinforced by the instrument the woman handles so confidently. Her figure has the stability and the density of a limestone Gothic portal statue. The cat huddles against her. A deep space, defined by the paving stones and the rough oak beams, provides an ample continuum for this transformation of a moment in daily life into something majestic and monumental. The many objects in the back plane are appropriately subdued, but they run to stable geometric forms: squares, globes, cylinders. Color is likewise subdued in this serious, hushed world.

What a contrast in Frank Benson's *Hilltop,*[168] a big (71 by 51 inches) variant of French Impressionist art! Born in 1862, some twenty years

167

168

later than Claude Monet (who often painted the same theme in the 1880s but without the prettiness or the sentimental appeal of the small boy), Benson brushed this picture of sunny innocence in 1903. He outlived Monet by a quarter century, but never ventured into the complex and daring directions of Monet's later years (see MA 254). Despite the intrusion of "story" interest (what are the children seeing in the distance?), Benson's picture can be enjoyed as exhilarating painting, notably in the freshness of his whites and bright blues, and in the flutter of drapery and scarf. While the girl's figure has no sense of Millet's substance, the foamy billows of her dress can excite you.

Visitors should take into account that the library hours given above do not apply literally to the special gallery where the paintings are exhibited. Libraries are notoriously understaffed and underendowed. Plan your visit accordingly.

Museum of the American China Trade

Location: 215 Adams St. Follow Route 28 (Randolph Ave.) northerly from
Route 128, turn right on Adams St.; from Boston, follow S.E. Expressway
(Route 3) to exit 22, turn right
Hours: Tues.-Sat. 1-4; closed holidays
Admission: Charged

The museum is housed in the Captain Robert Bennet Forbes mansion, a
sturdy edifice of 1833 overlooking Quincy Bay. The style might be called
modified Greek Revival with an Oriental flavor.

The collection is a gem of its kind. If this were a book on the decorative arts, our account would be a long one and it would be generously
illustrated. The focus here is on one of the most exciting and important
developments of the post-Colonial age of sailing. Far Eastern wealth
was vital to American maritime and industrial growth. When the United
States entered the China Trade soon after the Revolution, it was not
with government backing, as with the Dutch and English companies,
but through the enterprise of individuals at their own risk. Smaller and
swifter than those of their competitors, American ships were able to de-
liver cargoes at a lower price. Trade was limited to Canton, where for-
eigners were restricted to a section of hongs (factories) on the waterfront.

Fine China export is often to be seen in other museums, but the displays here are dazzling. Cases of rare porcelain—green, blue, apricot,
and occasionally yellow—make the visitor wish he could finger their
subtle glazes. Ship portraits and views of the teeming Canton waterfront
bring this faraway world vividly to life. Fantastically ornate Chinese
Chippendale furniture, sometimes more interesting than inviting, attracted a new American taste emerging from its Puritan bonds. Not to
be overlooked is a vitrine on the upper floor filled with diminutive
samples of wares offered by the hongs to prospective buyers. Fine textiles and rugs will also whet your appetite.

Virtually all American households on the eastern seaboard that could
afford them coveted these luxury items. Backing up the displays are some
seventy-five thousand documents of the China Trade. Throughout the
year lectures and programs for all ages and interests related to this great
American venture are available.

Whaling Museum

Location: 18 Johnny Cake Hill (just south of Route 6 near the harbor)
Hours: Mon-Sat. 9-5, Sun. 1-5; closed Thanksgiving, Christmas, New Year's Day
Admission: Charged

Among the attractions offered in New Bedford are the Sandwich Glass Museum, the Seaman's Bethel, and the Whaling Museum. The first-named is unfortunately beyond the scope of this book. The second, administered by the New Bedford Port Society and located opposite the Whaling Museum, was dedicated in 1832 to the moral and spiritual improvement of seamen. The shoreside early portion of Melville's *Moby Dick* surely memorializes it, along with the oratorical sermon preached from its nautical pulpit.

The Whaling Museum was established in 1907 by the Old Dartmouth Historical Society, named for the Colonial township that included what is now greater New Bedford. Substantial additions have been made to the original building, given by the family of Jonathan Bourne, along with a sixty-foot model of his whaling ship, the *Bark Lagoda*. This is said to be the largest ship model in the world. Boardable, it is a complete and accurate reduced version of the typical sort of whaleship that set forth from New Bedford around the middle of the nineteenth century.

A full and enthralling account of the whaling industry can be obtained here, including paintings of the sea giants and their intrepid hunters. Figureheads and stern boards, of the kind visible at Mystic Seaport (CT 42) and the Peabody Museum at Salem, Mass., are much in evidence, as well as the expected array of scrimshaw work. A "jagging wheel," or pie crimper, is an especially elegant example, with its handle in the form of a unicorn. There is a large collection of marines and ship portraits.

The museum is also concerned with local history and the work of New Bedford artists. Albert Bierstadt and Albert Pinkham Ryder both grew up in New Bedford, and of lesser note are William Bradford, R. Swain Gifford, William Allen Wall, and Clifford W. Ashley. The museum owns a single Bierstadt and no Ryder, but of the others listed it has the largest existing collections. There are also portraits by Gilbert Stuart, Rembrandt Peale, and Chester Harding.

Bierstadt's *Gosnold at Cuttyhunk* (one of the Elizabeth Islands due south of New Bedford) is a precious record of his early years. Dating from 1859, it immediately precedes the lovely example discussed at Framingham (MA 154). R. Swain Gifford (1840–1905), too easily confused with his distant cousin Sanford Robinson Gifford (1823–80; see VT 16), will also enchant you. While the Giffords owed much to the older painters of the Hudson River School, their feeling for light and their delicacy of touch relate them to such Luminists as Fitz Hugh Lane and Martin Johnson Heade.

The New Bedford Free Public Library owns three more paintings by Bierstadt and several by Bradford. While not all of its paintings are on view, a visit is recommended.

Smith College Museum of Art

Location: Elm Street
Hours: Tues.-Sat. 11-4:30, Sun. 2-4:30; closed academic holidays; in June open by appointment only; in July and August, Tues.-Sat. 1-4
Admission: Free. Ⓗ

Smith College is fortunate in possessing one of the two most important college art museums in the United States. It shares this distinction with Oberlin College, and the two collections are surpassed only by those of such major universities as Harvard and Yale. Founded in 1881 as the Hillyer Gallery, in 1926 it received attractive new quarters by bequest from Dwight W. Tryon, an Impressionist painter of reputation who directed the gallery from 1886 to 1920. Steady growth of the collections and of the art enterprise at Smith forced a decision to build a whole new complex, involving the destruction of both the Hillyer and the Tryon facilities. During the period of new construction, fifty-eight of the Museum's finest nineteenth- and twentieth-century paintings were circulated by the American Federation of Arts to ten American museums, from Washington, D.C., to Seattle, from Texas to Ohio, and from Richmond to Utica, N.Y. Designed by John Andrews of Toronto, the new complex houses the collections, studios, lecture and seminar rooms, and the art library. It opened in 1973, the new museum building being named Tryon Hall.

Thanks to a generous endowment, the museum has assembled excellent works of sculpture and an impressive selection of prints, drawings, and photographs. It is chiefly known, however, for its paintings, particularly by nineteenth- and twentieth-century French masters. Many of these were acquired through the perspicacity and daring of its directors in the years 1920 to 1946, Alfred Vance Churchill and Jere Abbott; the collection continues to expand in this field. It also includes Dutch and English landscapes; French and Italian paintings of the eighteenth century; American painting in its entire development; and modern European painting.

To the discussion of Greek vases at Bowdoin College (ME 1–3) we happily add an *Archaic Red-figure Kylix*,[169] or drinking cup, dating from c. 520 B.C., about 5 inches high and with a diameter of 13 inches. Of exceptionally fine quality, it is attributed to the Nikosthenes Painter. The date places it at the earliest appearance of the red-figure technique

169

—discussed in the Bowdoin entry—and some thirty years before Bowdoin's *Black-figure Lekythos.* In other words, the transition from the earlier and more difficult black-figure technique to the more manageable red-figure method took place only gradually. (It took a comparable time for automobiles to cease looking like carriages.) The drawing style is remarkably free for its, or indeed for any, time. Satyrs and symposiasts ornament the outer rim; in the center a discus thrower bends in harmony with the surrounding circular frame, and the discus provides an echoing circle. Our illustration, however, is focused on the profile of this elegant vessel. The wide shape of its gently upcurved bowl is similar to the form of the bearing member (*echinus*) of Archaic Doric capitals of the same period. An authoritative study of this lovely possession, by Phyllis Lehmann, appeared in the 1957 issue of the museum's *Bulletin.*

Greek and Roman marble sculpture is well represented here, especially by a *Head of an Athlete,* from the fourth century B.C., powerful despite its damages and abrasions. There is a fine small mosaic, and from Easternized Roman antiquity comes a *Mummy Portrait* from Fayum, Egypt, of the first or second century A.D.—a starkly impressive foretaste of Byzantine art.

A small gold-ground wooden *Processional Cross,* painted in tempera on both sides, gives a fine impression of Italian painting of the thirteenth century as it infused Gothic feeling into Byzantine traditional forms.

In the large city museum, the public generally overlooks drawings, and it tends to forget that a painting is (or used to be) the end of a long creative process. The smaller, informal gallery, which can escape departmentalization, has a great educational advantage, and this has not been overlooked here. Perhaps the museum's most precious possession is an early Netherlandish drawing, *Portrait of a Young Man,*[170] attributed to Dieric Bouts (c. 1420–75). Such studies for small oil paintings on wooden panel are exceedingly rare. Here the delicacy of touch matches the fugitive beauty of the medium, silverpoint. The metal point leaves an indelible trace on the prepared paper, and thus the most disciplined skill is called for. This drawing is widely considered one of the masterpieces of its kind and few have hesitated to accept it as the work of the Haarlem-born master of Louvain, who painted the *Half-length Madonna and Child* in the Busch-Reisinger Museum (MA 100). But Erwin Panofsky, in his monumental and authoritative *Early Netherlandish Painting,* argued that while the tall cap was in vogue in the 1470s, everything about the drawing suggests that it is a self-portrait, and

170

thus much too young to be Bouts himself, who was at least fifty by 1470. Anyone who disputes Dr. Panofsky on Early Netherlandish matters does so at his peril.

Another drawing of prime quality and significance is a black chalk *Study of Drapery*[171] by Mathis Gothardt-Niethart, called Grünewald (1465–1528). This is presumably a study for the lost *Transfiguration of Christ*, once in the Dominican Church of Frankfurt-am-Main, dating from about 1512. The corner inscription, "A. Dürer"—a brave guess of long ago—can be discounted. Born about the same time as Dürer (1471–1528) and dying in the same year, Grünewald worked primarily in the Rhenish area of Mainz, but his masterpiece is the great multi-paneled altarpiece, completed in 1515, for the monastery of Isenheim, near Colmar, where it is preserved in that city's museum. The Smith College drawing is so close to the drapery of the Madonna in the Incarnation panel that it might have been a study for that figure. The Isenheim Altar, or rather, certain sections of it, inspired Paul Hindemith's Expressionist opera, *Mathis der Maler*. Expressionism is a modern term, but its extension backward to include such masters as El Greco and Grünewald is now accepted. The hypernervous wiggles of outline in the drawing, the sudden breaks, the cavernous recessions, the strangely fleshy appearance of the right knee despite the fact that it is covered with drapery—all these indicate the tumultuous spirit that produced the wild *Temptation of St. Anthony* and the agonized, even gangrenous *Crucified Christ* of the Isenheim Altar.

Among several fine Dutch seventeenth-century paintings, the *View of Rijnland*,[172] signed and dated in 1647 by Jan van Goyen (1596–1656), is outstanding. An oil on hardwood panel, only 16 inches high, it presents a vast panorama of the Dutch flatlands reduced to a 4-inch horizontal strip under a densely clouded, lowering sky. Gray and olive-brown tones set the mood of this restless image of infinity. A group of cows and a few figures establish the foreground—all very diminutive, but nonetheless telling—and a horseman starts us off on our long journey. Such views resemble less Rembrandt's *Landscape with an Obelisk* (1638, in the Gardner Museum, MA 49) than Vincent van Gogh's Dutch drawings of the years before he moved to Paris and then on to Provence.

171

172

We turn now to a series of portraits spanning time from the Age of Louis XIV to the beginning of our century. An oil sketch, 20½ inches high, of the great naval commander *Victor Marie, Marquis de Coeuvres, Duc d'Estrées,*[173] by Hyacinthe Rigaud (1659–1743) served for a full-dress, "paraphernalia" portrait in the grand manner of Rigaud's celebrated image of the Sun King himself (Louvre, 1701). Interestingly enough, in that portrayal the head of the monarch is painted on a separate canvas affixed to the main one. Louis, of course, sat for the head alone, and a retainer stood for the figure—as also occurred when Goya painted the Spanish royal family in 1800 (Prado).

Like Edouard Manet, in Smith College's fine *Portrait of Marguérite de Conflans* (1873), Rigaud worked rapidly and with confidence. Both artists observed their subjects and then set about ordering the features in a pictorial style. Both were excited by the medium itself, Rigaud in the shape of the shadow cast by the chin, the sensual bow of the upper lip, the liquid surface of the eyes—each with its spot of highlight—and the furry texture of the brows. Manet's subtle play of greens and black is matched by Rigaud's pink-orange flesh tones, the black wig, the natty little dabs of mustache, and the deep shadow of the chin.

Such continuities in the French approach to painting stand in contrast to the American one, as seen in portraits by McIlworth, Copley, and Eakins. Thomas McIlworth (active 1758–69), in his *Portrait of Dr. William Samuel Johnson,*[174] painted in 1761, strikes for the elegance of an ivorylike finish, long and lean features, and shoulders sloping to form an oval related to the inner oval framing the figure. There being no evidence of the flurry of brush strokes, we sense a personage taken out of time, rigidly posed, and set for long painting sessions. Rigaud captures the moment; his subject almost seems to be breathing, as in portraits by the Impressionists. While Dr. Johnson is forcefully characterized, our remarks about his physique apply to a whole range of McIlworth's portraits, and thus it may or may not have corresponded to the truth.

About the same time that McIlworth was painting in New York City

173

174

and the Albany region, John Singleton Copley (1738–1815) was at the top of his form in Boston, before he left for London (and forever) in 1774. His magnificent *Seated Portrait of John Erving,*[175] c. 1772, over 4 feet high, is much more deeply observed than McIlworth's *Dr. Johnson*; it is less rigid, and it has the peculiarity of a somewhat stunted physique. Nevertheless, it too has a high sheen; nothing moves; and the figure is approached in exactly the same painstaking and objective spirit as the inkstand and letter, the side chair, and Erving's cuffs, buttons, and wig. In short, it is a still-life portrait. In quality it matches Bowdoin College's *Thomas Flucker* of c. 1770 (ME 12).

Thomas Eakins (1844–1916) painted *Mrs. Edith Mahon*[176] in 1904. Allowance made for the passage of more than 125 years, we might almost be in the presence of another Copley image, for the subject has been observed with the same hard, uncompromising honesty. Eakins's picture came late in his career, almost thirty years after *Elizabeth at the Piano*, that dark masterwork at Andover (MA 17). The light is stronger, and details of the face thereby limned more clearly; but the expressive gaze is as fixed in reverie as John Erving's is riveted upon the spectator. Eakins has no interest in Edouard Manet's worldly sophistication, nor in the subtle evocations of Degas's portraits, but rather in the physical presence of a personality. Mrs. Mahon was an English pianist —yet another case of Eakins's obsession with music and musicians.

Of several paintings by J. B. C. Corot (1796–1875) in the collection, a small *View of the Romanesque Abbey of Jumièges*[177] is perhaps the finest. Painted about 1830, it shows the remains of now-vanished wall paintings in the central tower. This early work has a directness, to which the simple geometric forms no doubt contribute. Such works were far ahead of their time, though there is precedent for them in earlier French painters like Poussin. (Compare the landscape background of the *Holy Family* at the Fogg Museum, MA 123). Until Corot altered his style to

176

175

177

a softer, more ingratiating manner, which is shown in the museum's *Dubuisson's Grove* (1868), he was virtually unrecognized. After 1900 his early work was admired by the Cubists, but by that time it had become clear that Paul Cézanne had already brought fresh vision to Corot's discovery of durable forms beneath the shifting appearances and magical lights of nature. Smith was fortunate in acquiring the *Jumièges* in 1924, long before prices for early Corots ballooned. It has been widely exhibited and universally admired.

Alfred Vance Churchill, the director who enriched the Smith collections in these early years with so many French nineteenth-century masterpieces, produced his own in 1929 with the acquisition of a major work, measuring over 6 by 8 feet, by Gustave Courbet (1819–77).[178] Known as *La Toilette de la Mariée* until recently, it has now become *La Toilette de la Morte.* No Village Bride here, but the preparation of a dead girl's body for burial. X-ray, ultraviolet, and infra-red examination produced surprising revelations: the "bride" was originally nude, her head sagged toward her left shoulder, the left arm of the attendant (not of the bride) held the mirror, and the bride's arm lay limply across her lap. It was clear from the fumbling character of the alterations that Courbet did not make them; furthermore, the position of the mirror so close to the bride makes no sense unless it is held by the attendant for her own use. Off to the right, young friends recite prayers for the departed; any other interpretation is senseless. Ensuing research revealed that Courbet did indeed paint a *Toilette de la Morte* (not surprising in view of his 1849/50 *Funeral at Ornans*, in the Louvre), but there is no record of a *Toilette de la Mariée.* The alterations were made long after Courbet's death (for it never left his studio) in order to make it more salable, since morbid pictures do not ordinarily attract buyers. All this was duly recounted in the catalogue of the great 1978 Paris retrospective of Courbet's work.

No action has been taken by the museum to bring the picture back to its original appearance, partly because the picture itself is not finished (the upper left and right corners are by no means resolved) and partly out of respect for its actual history. As to its date, some time between 1850 and 1855 is generally agreed upon.

Despite these problems, the picture has enormous power. As a dark poem of village life it rivals the works of Emile Zola, Courbet's alter ego in literature. The rough brushwork gives many of the figures,

178

notably the central one leaning forward, the impact of French Gothic limestone sculpture. A dominant grayness underscores the stonelike character, as does the composition, with its strong rectangles and its many globular shapes. From this work we can understand why Courbet was criticized for painting "as if with a trowel."

Jephtha's Daughter,[179] 1858–60, is the largest and one of the finest of the early figure compositions of Edgar Degas (1834–1917). It measures 6½ by 10 feet. In a superbly fashioned circular design bracketed at the sides by standing men, the conquering Jephtha enters— to make the agonizing discovery that it is his daughter and only child who comes forth to greet him, across an expressively void space. (See Judges 11:30–40.) While the figure style emphasizes outline drawing, as instilled in Degas by his admiration for Ingres (see MA 126) and his own study of the Early Renaissance masters in Florence, the color has a range and a subtlety unknown to these precursors. The brushwork, though subdued, is as sensitive as Titian's. Observe, for example, the orange bandeau around Jephtha's head. From the point of view of compositional progression, circular and oval elements announce the advancing procession and prepare you for the oval plateau on which the daughter stands with her distraught companions. Right of center, the impressive figure of a foot soldier serves two artistic functions: he turns the action toward the daughter, but his curved sword (which helps to fill a nearby vacant upper corner) disguises by its counteraction what would otherwise be a too obvious hubless wheel in the composition as a whole. In Handel's late oratorio *Jephtha*, one finds similarly restrained passion, similar use of convention to reinforce clarity, and musical subtleties to be discovered only in repeated hearings. Unhurried study of Degas's great composition is likewise recommended.

If we were discussing a museum of lesser consequence, we should now consider paintings by Ingres (and a wonderful double portrait in pencil), two more masterworks by Degas, the Manet portrait already mentioned, two Monets, a portrait of an invalid woman by Renoir, and other Impressionist works. There is even an early Gauguin of a Paris suburb, signed and dated 1879, when he studied with the Impressionists —well before his characteristic Breton and Tahitian pictures.

179

We cannot fail, however, to consider *La Route Tournante à La Roche-Guyon*,[180] by Paul Cézanne (1839–1906). The date is 1885, when Cézanne spent some summer weeks with Renoir in this village not far from Giverny, where, the year before, Claude Monet had begun his visits and would later buy a house and develop his famous garden and lily-pad pool. La Roche-Guyon has a magnificent medieval donjon, but Cézanne paid no attention to it; his interests were not archaeological. *La Route Tournante* was acquired by Mr. Churchill in 1932—his last purchase. A certificate signed by Cézanne's son states that it was painted by his father and given to Renoir. For its mid-1880s date it is more loosely and thinly brushed than usual (compare the Fogg Art Museum's *Still Life*, MA 129). We may hazard a guess that Cézanne's momentary partial return to his Impressionist technique of the previous decade was, if not influenced by Renoir's art, intended as an oblique compliment to him. In every other respect, however, the picture is a denial of Impressionist premises. The camera's single point of view has given way to a multiple one (a photograph of the motif shows the hillside masonry at the left canted inward); the road curves upward rather than back (thus reinforcing the plane of the canvas itself); the high horizon brings the hill forward and effectively reduces what Cézanne called negative space—something to be avoided in the interests of making all parts of the picture function actively in an organic whole. As a result, Impressionism's single-instant image seen from a fixed position has been lifted out of the passage of time; Cézanne's view is not how "it looked," but how it will always be. We may argue that the work is unfinished; but to see a Cézanne in process, developing evenly in all its parts, is a precious experience.

In a memorable book, *Characteristics of French Art*, Roger Fry discussed the special French combination of a sense of actuality with a feeling for broad, monumental forms. Nowhere is this better seen than in the work of Georges Seurat (1859–91), whose masterpiece, *Sunday Afternoon on La Grande Jatte*, is a major possession of the Art Institute of Chicago. Smith College owns three studies for this work: a small oil of a woman with a monkey and two Conté crayon drawings. *Three Women*,[181] c. 1885/6, shares Cézanne's sense of permanence. The

180

181

wonderfully observed shapes are entities in themselves, their spatial position established merely by size and by the degree of pressure on the black crayon. The rough grain of the paper is not disguised; indeed, it may have suggested to Seurat the minutely dotted touches with which he laboriously executed his 8-by-10-foot canvas. Notice that in the drawing, as in the final painting, the overall texture supports the reality of a picture as a flat surface to which medium is applied. Note also that in the small oil sketch, painted quickly on the spot in Impressionist technique, both shapes and texture receive less attention. That will come later, in the studio, under no summer Sunday illumination, but, as Seurat preferred, by gaslight.

We have discussed Childe Hassam (1859–1935), the leading American Impressionist, in a stylish Parisian picture of 1888 at New Britain (CT 46). Eleven years later he painted *White Island Light, Isles of Shoals, at Sundown.*[182] This strong and brilliantly colored marine (for water is the main subject once you clear the great cliffs) has the high horizon of Claude Monet's *Rocks at Belle-Ile* and his *Haystack* series of the late 1880s and early 1890s, but the brush strokes are more regularized. While it would be a mistake to call them Pointillist, in the manner of Seurat, their ordered parallels do manage to achieve something of the same mosaic effect. A fascinating exhibition organized in 1978 by the Art Galleries of the University of New Hampshire, with text by Susan Faxon and others, included sixteen Childe Hassams painted on the Isles of Shoals between 1886 and 1912. Smith College's example was one of them. For its title, "A Stern and Lovely Scene: A Visual History of the Isles of Shoals," the exhibition borrowed a phrase from Nathaniel Hawthorne's description in *American Notebooks,* 1852. These rugged islands, some ten miles off Portsmouth, N.H., attracted many summer residents, and the list of painters included Olaf Brauner, William Morris Hunt, and William Trost Richards as well as Childe Hassam.

The briefest glance at *The Suitor*[183] (also called *The Workshop*), an oil of 1893 only a foot high by Edouard Vuillard (1868–1940), will indicate that Seurat's Pointillist technique had a following in France. In Vuillard, however, it served a different purpose. Although he painted

182

183

some large canvases, his work at the turn of the century favored the intimacy of a small format, and he crowded it with pattern upon pattern with an almost claustrophobic effect. The introduction of "story" interest here, in the peeping suitor, is unusual. Vuillard's interiors, into which natural light penetrates with difficulty, are frequently uninhabited; when people are present they sit in silence, or bend in total concentration on their household duties. The household, indeed, is Vuillard's chief subject. Its décor is out of fashion in today's antiseptic arrangements, but readers old enough to recall elderly hotels in France will understand what Vuillard was responding to. He lived quietly in Paris with his mother and did his work in their small apartment. Familiar with the painting theories of Maurice Denis, he emphasized the picture's flat surface. The Symbolist theories of the poet Mallarmé also attracted him. Like Mallarmé, who opposed "naming" an object in favor of an appeal to the reader's imagination through evoking and suggesting it, Vuillard knits his objects into a complex tapestry. Writing of the Smith picture in the catalogue for the Museum of Modern Art's retrospective in 1954, Andrew Ritchie observed: "By a process of telescoping planes in a picture . . . the foreground, middleground and background overlap and fuse into a pulsating space that bears a kind of relation to the fusion of imagery in a poem by Mallarmé." Echoes of Vuillard's strong influence on the young Matisse in the 1890s linger in the latter's painting of 1904 in the Gardner Museum (MA 52).

The developing theory of painting as first of all a flat surface, promulgated as the nineteenth century came to a close, and the influence of Cézanne's painting by flat planes that marked his mature and late work, led to the rise of Cubism in Paris. The seminal figures here were the Spaniard Picasso and the Frenchman Georges Braque, in their work of c. 1908–12. In general, Picasso was the daring pathfinder, Braque the more cautious creator of fine paintings. A younger Spanish friend of Picasso who took the name of Juan Gris (1887–1927, real name González) quickly followed their lead into collage, that is, the use of pasted papers as an additional element in what was to be applied to the canvas. Nothing could be flatter than these snippets of newsprint or wallpaper. If they happened to carry a printed message or to represent something, such meanings were rarely relevant to what the artist intended to convey; they were to be regarded as patterns, elements of scale in an organized design. With photographic illusion now left entirely to the photographers, the artist was free to make his statement without recourse to it. *Glasses and Newspaper*,[184] a Gris collage of 1913/14 some 2 feet high, remains true to Picasso's and Braque's "Spanish" grisaille scheme of tans, grays, blacks, and whites—current in their Cubist paintings and collages of c. 1910–12. If Gris's newsprint has browned with time, we may welcome this alteration on the same basis that weathering enriches medieval stained glass. The Cubists' subject was essentially the Montmartre bistro: a table with or without a cloth; glasses, bottles, carafes, siphons; playing cards, the game of chess; the day's newspaper, the guitar of a strolling musician. Gris's collage contains some of these elements of the new iconography. In line with Mallarmé's appeal to suggest rather than to name an object, none is completely represented.

All are fragmented (including the masthead of *Le Journal*). Such fragmentation implies multiple observation of the object from shifting points of view. Semitransparent and interpenetrating planes assist in the formation of a shallow space. You are looking *down* at the table instead of looking at objects *on* a table from the traditional viewpoint (as in ME 36). Cézanne's desire to make all parts function actively in the design is fully achieved here. Note, for example, the large glass at the upper left, in what would traditionally be an empty corner.

Jere Abbot's purchase of *La Table*,[185] an oil of 1919/20 by Pablo Picasso (1881–1973), did not make all Smithies happy even though the date of acquisition was 1932. Today, few would deny that it is a masterpiece of later Cubism; and none that the eye that chose it—and chose Degas's *Jephtha*, and Degas's portrait of his young brother René, and the superb *Blonde Gasconne* by Corot, and Seurat's oil sketch for *La Grande Jatte*, and Monet's *Seine à Bougival*; and the previously discussed van Goyen landscape, the silverpoint drawing by Bouts (*pace* Dr. Panofsky), and *The Suitor* by Vuillard—that this eye was anything less than sensitive.

By 1913 (as in the still life at Dartmouth College, NH 11) color returned to brighten Picasso's grisaille Cubist palette of the years just preceding, and his collages from that time on followed suit. From the beginning, collages had involved a witty give-and-take between reality and illusion: the illusionary representations on the *papiers collés* and the illusionary newsprint messages played second fiddle to the reality of the artist's abstract statement. Such oils as Smith's *Table* may be thought of as illusions of collages, since they contain no collage whatever. However that may be, it is fair to say that at his best Picasso expresses himself through sharp and angular patterns full of knife-blade shapes evocative of the nervous tensions of our age. All of this has its roots in the art of Picasso's Spain; and the trend was apparently set by the effects of seven centuries of Moorish impact on Spanish culture. Central to Picasso's art is the piling up of a construction rickety as a house of cards. Here as always his invention surpasses the apparent possibilities of the

184

185

subject: in this instance a table, a tablecloth, and a guitar. For the visitor who desires to arrive at an understanding of Cubism, prolonged study of this masterpiece cannot be recommended too highly.

Goat,[186] a drawing in pen and colored inks of 1925 by Paul Klee (1879–1940), was the gift of Jere Abbot in 1976; it had long been a treasured item on indefinite loan. We have discussed other small Klees of the same period at Colby College (ME 41) and the Busch-Reisinger Museum (MA 107); but this one attains a larger scale and greater mysteriousness, no doubt from the impact of the horns and the eyes. Note that only the right eye is a full circle; the other, bisected, suggests a turn back into space. Like the Chinese and the Japanese, Klee manipulates a few well-defined abstract notations through what we may call musical variations to describe only what is essential. One of these variations is in the color of the ink chosen.

Discarded Treasures,[187] oil on canvas about 19 by 29 inches, was purchased in 1929 as a work of William M. Harnett (1848–92), whom we discuss in a very early example at Fitchburg (MA 153) and a characteristic late one at Springfield (MA 220). Signed "W. M. Harnett" at the lower right, the Smith painting seemed authentic, though the signature did not have the customary dating, and the style was somewhat softer than usual. During the 1940s the San Francisco critic Alfred Frankenstein noted that a large group of supposed Harnetts had the same peculiarities, and this launched him on a voyage of fruitful research. Proof positive that something was awry came when he found that minutely painted postmarks on a letter and a postcard in one of these "soft" Harnetts (*Old Scraps*, purchased by Nelson A. Rockefeller and later given to the Museum of Modern Art) bore the date 1894— two years after Harnett's death. Further exploration, with all the twists and turns of a detective story, led to the discovery that some twenty of these pictures were the work of John Frederick Peto (1854–1907)—

186

187

and a trip to Island Heights, New Jersey, where the artist's daughter still lived, surrounded by his pictures and the very objects shown in many of the paintings under discussion. Peto was, at the time, little known except as one of many modest competitors of Harnett in fool-the-eye painting and influenced by him. Harnett, highly successful in his day with a clientele that paid high prices for his expensive-looking assemblages, was enthusiastically "resurrected" and sought after by museums and collectors in the late 1920s and 1930s, having earlier been edged into oblivion by the rise of modern art. Whether Peto's pictures were turned into Harnetts soon after Harnett's death or more recently is uncertain, but in either case it is clear that Peto was entirely innocent of the falsification. All of this is recounted in Frankenstein's *After the Hunt* (Berkeley: University of California Press, revised edition, 1969).

In 1950, forty-three years after Peto's death, the first one-man exhibition of his work—including Smith's picture—opened at the Smith College Museum of Art, and then traveled to the Brooklyn Museum and to San Francisco. On this occasion I bought *Pipe and Church Sconce* for Williams College, and learned that on Frankenstein's suggestion the staff at Smith had taken their "Harnett" out of its frame, discovered about an inch of additional painted canvas turned under at the base, and that on this strip the word E A C H completed the simulated sticker, "10 cents"—and that at the far right there was a clear indication of an erased signature under the Harnett one.

Subsequently, Peto—sometimes called the poor man's Harnett because of the relative plainness of the objects he portrayed—has been reinstated as indeed a worthy competitor. Some who have compared Harnett with Jan van Eyck because of his extreme precision have been reminded of Vermeer of Delft by Peto's painterly touch and less petrified vision. When the Smith College picture changed authors the event was a bit of a shock, but all's well that ends well.

Our next selection, a small watercolor of *Freight Cars*[188] by Charles Burchfield (1893–1967), differs so greatly from the jumbo-sized example discussed at New Britain (CT 49) that at first glance it appears to be the work of another artist. But the Smith watercolor dates from 1919, whereas *Lavender and Old Lace* was not begun until 1939 and not completed until 1947. A closer look at the weathered surface of the freight cars and the painting of their undercarriages will indicate similarities of touch—for example, compare the trees above the old house in the New Britain example. Burchfield's mastery of his medium, achieved by his mid-twenties, is everywhere apparent here. The subtlety

188

of his range of reds, heightened by a daring use of black, is exemplary. It would be easy, but unfortunate, to pass by this small gem, which came to Smith in 1970 from most knowledgeable donors—Mr. and Mrs. Alfred Barr, Jr.—to honor Jere Abbot.

Our lengthy discussion of Smith's paintings and its drawings (fine ones by Tintoretto and Daumier not even mentioned) should not distract attention from the collection of sculpture. Leaving to the sections on other museums discussion of ancient, medieval, African, and Pre-Columbian examples, we turn to works by two major French sculptors. Claude Michel Clodion (1738–1814), the sculptural counterpart of such Rococo painters as François Boucher and Jean Honoré Fragonard (see MA 252), is the highly talented author of a pair of terra-cotta groups, each a foot high above the handsome red marble base. A luscious *Nymph*, prefiguring Renoir but with more style and spirit, looks across at a Nijinsky-like *Satyr*.[189] Both are accompanied by playful or sleeping infants. They are among the finest acquisitions of the museum in the 1970s; and it is doubtful that they are surpassed by anything comparable, even in the Louvre. Their fluid modeling and varied textures rival any painter's brushwork; yet they retain, a century later, much of the strength of Bernini's marbles. As sometimes happens, but not very often, these terra-cottas expand beyond their small size through the bold scale of their design and the authority of their idea. We can easily imagine them executed at monumental size in stone, as in the contemporary German statues of the *Seasons* in the Busch-Reisinger Museum that once decorated the palace gardens at Bruchsal (MA 98). Discussions of Clodion's work too frequently miss his power. A definitive after-the-fact argument for it exists in the considerable influence Clodion had on the greatest French sculptors of the next century: Jean-Baptiste Carpeaux (see MA 237) and Auguste Rodin.

Both Carpeaux and Rodin broke with Academic insistence on smooth finish and general prettiness; and they were abused for it. The detailed textures of Clodion were a natural point of departure for them as they turned toward greater realism and deeper emotional expression. In Rodin's case the Clodion connection was limited to his youthful work, as in several enchanting plaster busts of young women modeled around 1865–70. Another point of contact was Rodin's training with the

189

sculptor Carrier-Belleuse, known as "the Clodion of the Second Empire," and work with him during this period at the Sèvres porcelain factory.

But Rodin's *Walking Man*,[190] a headless bronze 7½ feet high, is another matter. A late work of 1906, it immediately justifies its large size, even though it evolved as the enlargement of a much smaller study, executed almost thirty years earlier for the *St. John Baptist Preaching*, completed by 1880. First cast in 1907, the enlargement seen here is the ninth cast of an edition of 1965 from the celebrated Rudier foundry in Paris. *Man Walking* differs profoundly from the *St. John Baptist*. Minus head and arms, it avoids the overt moral message of a subject; its pocked and scarified surfaces are totally at variance with the relatively smooth torso and limbs of the *St. John*. If at first the Smith figure seems a mechanical expansion of a 3-foot-high study (which was also headless, armless and scarified), closer inspection reveals many changes, of which the most significant is the position of the right shoulder, which is shoved farther forward to increase the figure's driving force. *Walking Man* attains much of the grandeur of Michelangelo and Bernini, both of whom Rodin adored, but never imitated. A cast was offered in 1912 by some friends of Rodin to the French embassy in Rome and set up in the courtyard of the Farnese Palace. The ambassador rejected it: no headless statue to act as diplomatic agent for *his* country, even in a Rome full of beheaded antiques! As for Rodin, a pioneer in what was to become a dominant twentieth-century motif—the fragmented figure—he insisted that the body itself could express the noblest ideals. And even more than in the *St. John Baptist Preaching*, he achieved the nearly impossible: a walking figure that does not walk off its base. The more you study it the more you will discover departures from what would happen if a cast were taken from a living figure in this position. For a fuller account of this major work, the relevant pages of Albert E. Elsen, *Rodin* (New York: The Museum of Modern Art, 1963), are recommended.

Since the Baroque era of Bernini, no one had commanded the field of sculpture as Rodin did. An army of followers imitated him and many original talents who turned in new directions began their careers under his inspiration, among them Aristide Maillol and Constantin Brancusi (see CT 68). A brilliant younger German, Wilhelm Lehmbruck (1881–1919), arriving in Paris in 1910 for what turned out to be a four-year

190

stay, found the anti-Rodin movement toward greater simplification well under way. He was greatly attracted to Maillol (1861–1944), a painter who had turned to sculpture around 1900 and by 1905 had produced *La Méditerranée* (Paris, Tuileries Gardens), a masterpiece of serenity. Lehmbruck introduced a poignant inner feeling in his variations on Maillol's earthy classical nudes. Smith College's *Torso of the 'Pensive Woman,'*[191] cast in stone and reworked by the artist in 1913/14, superbly exemplifies Lehmbruck's early achievement. While the emphatic division of the body at the waist and the regularity of spherical and ovoid solids follow Maillol's lead, there is a new tenderness here, as well as an almost Gothic sense of vertical thrust. Note the hypersensitive flow of outline from thigh to waist. In sculpture, such an effect from one angle can result only from what, at another angle, is seen to be modeling. As you pass around the figure you will find that Lehmbruck's subtly molded surfaces produce similarly sensitive outlines from all views. The *Torso* was purchased in 1922, long before Lehmbruck became accepted in the United States, and, still more surprisingly, by that ardent Francophile, Alfred Vance Churchill.

Much attention in the foregoing has been paid to the two early directors of Smith College's museum. I am happy to add that succeeding ones have held to the high standard already set. Subsequent purchases already discussed include the Rodin, the Clodion, the Hassam, the McIlworth, the Rigaud, and the Greek *kylix*. There are many more for the visitor to discover.

191

Merrimack Valley Textile Museum

Location: 800 Massachusetts Ave., at exit 43 from Route 495
Hours: Tues.-Fri. 10-5; Sat., Sun. 1-5; closed New Year's Day, Easter, Thanksgiving, and Christmas
Admission: Charged, except on Sat. Ⓗ

This attractive and well-appointed museum developed from the energies of Samuel Dale Stevens (1859–1922), a wool manufacturer of North Andover who successfully promoted the establishment of the North Andover Historical Society in 1913. At his death he left a large collection of spinning wheels, reels, hand looms, warping frames, combs, tape looms, niddy noddies, and swifts. For readers needing further enlightenment on these terms, see Dr. Horatio Rogers's account of Stevens and his collection, published in January 1969 in the Essex Institute Historical Collections. Dr. Rogers, a retired surgeon, was the husband of Stevens's only daughter, who was determined to bring to fruition the original hopes of her father. In 1958, when Mrs. Rogers became president of the Historical Society, his collection was stored in a barn. With the enthusiastic support of Walter Muir Whitehill, director of the Boston Athenaeum, she laid plans to have the collection find its place in a museum that would give an account of the role of wool manufacturing in American history; and in 1959 a professional director was appointed. By this time some thousand cubic feet of the business records of M. T. Stevens & Sons Company had been added to her father's collection. With admirable vision the trustees decided against limiting the activities of the proposed museum by any regional or chronological restrictions. In 1964 the present building opened to the public; its eighteen thousand square feet of interior space was almost evenly divided among the exhibition area, the study collection, and administrative areas.

The exhibition, supplemented by photographic blowups, covers the development of American wool manufacturing from the seventeenth century to its modern industrialization, as well as the various processes required—from raw wool to finished product. Much of the time you may watch skilled craftspeople card, spin, and weave. Meanwhile, modern power machines hum and clatter. Examples of textiles are featured throughout.

A Conservation Center has also been added to the museum's facilities. Its extensive library is in constant use by scholars and other interested persons.

While this museum lies beyond the scope of the present book, a visit is such a delight that I have gladly made an exception. Furthermore, one of the exhibits, a loom of the type used in Holland since about 1700, brings a note of actuality to the Dutch Period painting of Vincent van Gogh discussed in the section on the Boston Museum of Fine Arts (MA 85).

Watson Gallery, Wheaton College

Location: Routes 123 and 140
Telephone: (617) 285-7722
Hours: Tues.-Sun. 1-5, Mon. 10-12 and 2-4; during summer and college vacations by appointment (phone ext. 428)
Admission: Free

The Watson Gallery, the gift of Mrs. Thomas J. Watson, is an attractively appointed modern space in the Fine Arts Center usually occupied by changing exhibitions organized by the gallery itself. An excellent reputation has been established for these exhibitions and their well-designed catalogues: a model for how to accomplish much on a very limited budget.

The permanent collection consists of the College Portraits, usually displayed in other buildings, and the gallery's modest but growing holdings. For the location of the portraits, inquire at the gallery. They include a series, painted mid-nineteenth century by Eunice M. Towle, of the Wheaton family. Judge Laban Wheaton (1754–1846) founded the college as a seminary for women in 1853 in memory of his daughter Eliza. He received the strong support of his wife and his daughter-in-law, Mrs. Laban Morey Wheaton. The last-named (1809–1905) appears, bespectacled, in a Towle portrait in her early maturity, and again, at the age of ninety-five, in a penetrating interpretation by John W. Alexander.

Among alumnae donors of art to the college was Eleanor Norcross (class of 1872), who founded the Fitchburg Art Museum. From c. 1890 to 1923 she was an expatriate artist living in Paris; there, at the height of enthusiasm for Japanese prints, she chose the fine collection given to the college by Mrs. Laban Morey Wheaton. They span the best period of such work, from Harunobu (1725–70) to Hiroshige (1797–1858).

The college's representation of nineteenth- and twentieth-century European and American prints is a good one, as is its collection of glass —from ancient examples to early and more recent American work. Among the paintings is *Audrey, the Shepherd Lass*, painted c. 1886/7 by Gari Melchers (1860–1932)—once owned by Potter Palmer of Chicago and before that widely exhibited in European cities. A George Inness, *Montclair: Meadow Scene*, dating from c. 1885, is in the misty late manner of this artist, whose stronger early work is discussed in examples at Orono (University of Maine), Andover, and Mount Holyoke College (MA 206). A strange but fetching little oil, *The Motherless*, painted c. 1865 by Elihu Vedder (1836–1923)—long before he turned muralist in Art Nouveau style—has a Dickensian sympathy for the orphaned.

The Berkshire Museum

Location: South Street (Route 7)

Hours: Tues.-Sat. 10-5, Sun. 2-5

Admission: Free. *For the Hancock Shaker Village (5 miles west on Route 20) see Hancock*

Founded in 1903 by Zenas Crane, the museum combines the functions of a museum of science and an art museum. The art collections are installed on the upper floor; in the basement is an interesting Historical Room with items of Berkshire interest. While two of the upstairs galleries are often occupied by temporary exhibitions, there are permanent installations of Old Master paintings, ancient decorative arts (fortified by a number of excellent plaster casts of major works of sculpture), and Far Eastern art. The Crane Room, at the head of the stairs, usually displays a very important group of large paintings by the Hudson River School.

The *Half-length Figure of a Priest*[192] is one of a series of six limestone sculptures from ancient Palmyra, an outpost of the Roman Empire in the Syrian desert. The date is about A.D. 150. These examples, particularly the one shown here, are among the finest in America of this phase of art history. Long before the formation of the Byzantine Empire, the elements of its art were so well established in Near Eastern art that it would be easy to imagine such a figure transformed into a gold-ground mosaic and looking very much like the representation of Justinian and his court at Ravenna. The priest, who holds an oil jar and incense bowl, is stiffly frontal, but by no means devoid of vitality. There is a wonderful play of three-dimensional forms, as in the chin, against the incised flat lines and ornaments. The eyes stare outward. Note that Boston's bust of the Emperor Elagabalus (MA 60), A.D. 219, though later and also Syrian, is much less Easternized; it originated in no desert outpost.

192

Two late medieval paintings in this museum are masterworks in any company of their peers. The first is an *Adoration of the Magi*[193] dated 1477 and signed in Latin by the north Spanish painter Juan Pons. It was presented to the museum in 1913, well in advance of the growth of interest in medieval Spanish art. (Mrs. Gardner, however, acquired the *St. Engracia* by Bermejo, M A 40, in 1904.) The life-size figures are compressed into the shallowest space, from which the only release is provided by a small marine landscape at the upper right. The painter combines a native delight in rich brocades, gold and Burgundy red, with a Flemish-inspired insistence on realistic detail. He leaves no doubt, for example, that Joseph was a carpenter. Joseph's halo, incidentally, is scalloped to indicate his lesser station in relation to the divine Virgin and Child. The ox and the ass are crammed into a sort of niche whose bow-shaped edge helps to centralize the action and unite the figures in this politely enacted scene.

Joachim Patinir (c. 1485–1524) is one of the links between Hieronymus Bosch and Pieter Brueghel in Flemish painting. In a later age he would have been a pure landscape painter; in his own day he selected religious themes, which gave him the greatest opportunity to exercise his remarkable gifts. Sometimes another painter executed his foreground figures. *The Flight to Egypt*,[194] and the related theme of the Rest on the Flight to Egypt, became one of his favorite subjects. It was also popular with Patinir's followers, of whom one of the most important was Adriaen Isenbrant, a Bruges master in the circle of Gerard David. Heartless recent connoisseurship has assigned the Pittsfield picture to Isenbrant rather than to Patinir himself. The distinction is a subtle one, but we must respect it. Beyond the foreground group, with their emphatic reds, we wind slowly toward the ice-blue distances of this landscape in much the same way that a Chinese painter invites us to join him in a contemplative journey through nature. Thus the element of time is added to visual art, as in a musical experience. For a total contrast, compare Hartford's *Return from the Flight to Egypt*, painted a century later at Antwerp by Peter Paul Rubens (C T 15).

194

193

A fine *Vision of St. Ignatius,* long attributed to Rubens, is now securely assessed as a school piece, though the design is possibly by Rubens. The forms are softer than those of the master and there is a greater sweetness in gesture and facial expression. Some Dutch pictures are under study to determine if they are replicas or variants by assistants. Several British portraits give a thoroughly autograph impression. A bust-length *Portrait of John Newton,* surveyor of His Majesty's Customs for Nova Scotia, is a work of John Singleton Copley not inferior to the great *Portrait of Thomas Flucker* at Bowdoin College (ME 12); it is on indefinite loan from the Berkshire Atheneum. The museum also owns one of many replicas of the bust of Hiram Powers's celebrated *Greek Slave* (see VT 9).

Valley of the Santa Ysabel,[195] an oil 40 by 60½ inches, is signed and dated 1875 (at the lower left) by Frederic E. Church (1826–1900). Discussing it in that year, Henry James wrote: ". . . a large and elaborate landscape at Goupil's—a certain 'Valley of Santa Isabel,' in New Granada. We know of nothing that is a better proof of the essential impotence of criticism, in the last resort, than Mr. Church's pictures. . . . If you praise them very highly, you say more than you mean; if you denounce them, if, in vulgar parlance, you sniff at them, you say less. . . . Why not accept this lovely tropic scene as a very pretty picture, and have done with it? A very pretty picture, surely, it was, and a very skilful, and laborious, and effective one . . . his brush is an extremely accomplished one, and we should be poorly set to work to quarrel with the very numerous persons who admire its brilliant feats" (*The Painter's Eye,* edited by John L. Sweeney; Cambridge: Harvard University Press, 1956, page 101).

Not my favorite art critic, but always provocative and interesting—even infuriating when he discusses Winslow Homer—James scored a near miss on Church's impressive panorama. What he missed, though he saw the "softest violet glow" and the level rays of the "yellow tropic sun" as they "come wandering forward down the mile-long gorges," was the poetic spell of the Luminism that connects Church with such earlier masters as Fitz Hugh Lane and Martin Johnson Heade. Such exotic visions as *Valley of the Santa Ysabel* are a very long way from Church's modest beginnings in New Haven a quarter-century before (CT 43). The road to New Granada began, soon after, in the Catskills section of the Hudson River. (See MA 210.)

195

The early residence of Alexander Calder, creator of mobile sculpture and later of "stabiles" (see CT 35), at Richmond, near Pittsfield, is signaled by works in the Berkshire Museum. Two small pre-mobile mechanisms, one worked by a hand crank, are in the starkly geometric vocabulary of the Bauhaus School. In the auditorium are two "mobiles," designed to flutter when the ventilation system is turned on; their gaily colored forms have the free shapes of the painting of Joan Miró (see CT 32) in the 1930s.

Pilgrim Hall

Location: 75 Court St. (take exit 38 from Route 3); Court St. is on Route 3A
Hours: 9:30-4:30 daily
Admission: Charged

Built in 1824 by the Pilgrim Society, Pilgrim Hall contains a library and collection of material bearing on the history of Plymouth Colony. In addition to architectural fragments, furniture, pewter, silver, and arms and armor, the collection contains several paintings of the seventeenth century.

Pilgrim Hall also contains a plaster death mask of Oliver Cromwell, whose connection with Pilgrim history came through his employment of Edward Winslow, governor of Plymouth Colony, on two diplomatic missions. Furthermore, Governor William Bradford hailed the English Commonwealth as establishing in England the principles for which the Pilgrims had been exiled.

As American painting prior to 1700 is exceedingly rare, almost any surviving example is worthy of note. While the three Winslow portraits (1651) seem to have been painted in London by Robert Walker, the *Portrait of Elizabeth Paddy Wensley* (1641–c. 1713), whose daughter married Isaac Winslow, is almost certainly an American work of about 1675. The painter is unknown, and any attribution is made more difficult by the poor condition of the picture. The colors run to a rather rich red-orange to brown scheme. The flat geometrical design with its tight details takes us back to traditional English painting of the Elizabethan era—here in a provincial echo. There are superficial resemblances to two works at the Worcester Art Museum (MA 303, 304): the *Self-Portrait* by Thomas Smith (c. 1680), and the highly accomplished *Elizabeth Freake and Baby Mary*, painted c. 1674 by an artist unknown, but not the same as the painter of Elizabeth Paddy Wensley.

Near Plymouth Rock a replica of the *Mayflower* is moored; and two miles south on Route 3A is Plimoth Plantation, a replica of the Pilgrim Colony (open daily mid-April through November; admission charged).

Essex Institute

Location: 132-134 Essex Street (parking garage on Liberty St. around the corner)
Hours: Tues.-Sat. 9-4:30, Sun. and holidays 1-5; open Mon. June 1-October 15; closed Thanksgiving, Christmas, New Year's Day
Admission: Charged

The institute was organized in 1848 by union of the Essex Historical Society and the Essex County Natural History Society. It operates some of Salem's most notable historic houses, including the John Ward House (seventeenth century, in the garden of the institute); the Gardner-Pingree House, designed in 1804 by Samuel McIntire (adjoining the institute at 128 Essex Street); and the Peirce-Nichols House, an earlier work of McIntire (at 80 Federal Street). The library of the institute is considered one of the finest in New England for historical research.

The museum, on the upper floor of the institute, contains a recently reconditioned picture gallery and a large collection of furniture, decorative arts, and miscellaneous historical items. The paintings, principally portraits of persons important in the life of Salem, include works by such leading artists as Badger, Greenwood, Smibert, Blackburn, Copley, Trumbull, Stuart, and Harding. Perhaps the most important example is Smibert's life-size *Sir William Pepperrell*,[196] inscribed "Lt. Gen. Sir Wm. Pepperrell, Bart. / The Victor of Louisbourg A.D. 1745." The portly hero indicated in no subtle manner the scene of his victory over the French land forces on Cape Breton Island. He was the first American to be created a baronet. Silver presented to him by the British is displayed at Saco, Maine (see page 455). His portrait, which came to the Essex Institute in 1821, must have been painted soon after Sir William (already knighted in 1745) returned in triumph in 1746, for Peter Pelham made a mezzotint of it in the following year. In style the paint-

196

ing contrasts considerably with the imported English fluency of Smibert's *Bishop Berkeley* group at Yale (CT 74), dating from more than fifteen years earlier. If the style is now "Americanized," it hardly rivals Robert Feke's attainments of about the same time (ME 10). The eighteen buttons down Sir William's endless scarlet coat exhibit patience, but not much painterly flair. Two cannon balls on their way to the French forces —with trajectory duly marked—hardly suggest imaginative subtlety. Some authorities have suggested the help of shop assistants, but there is little evidence in the artist's work of any real command of the human figure. For all that, the picture manages to convey an impressive physical presence.

Of the other portraits in this important collection, those by Joseph Blackburn and John Greenwood are especially memorable, and Trumbull's *Alexander Hamilton* is superb. An appealing *Nathaniel Hawthorne*, by Charles Osgood (1809–90), shows him young and handsome, with a kind of Byronic mien.

The startling scene of *Salem Common on Training Day, 1808*[197] is the work of George Ropes (1788–1819), a local Salem painter of marines, landscapes, signs, and carriages. If there is another instance of an artist who was deaf and dumb from birth, I am not aware of it. Ropes also painted a portrait of the fabulous *Cleopatra's Barge*, the personal yacht of Captain George Crowninshield (the picture privately owned, but published in *Antiques* for January 1930, together with an account of the splendid furniture with which the ship was equipped). *Salem Common* shows us the militia in formation before a considerable crowd of onlookers. Crowned by an arc of very tall and very stiff poplars, it is strangely similar to certain Paris scenes of Henri Rousseau (*le douanier*), and it could keep company with the finest Karolik-collection pictures by American primitives in the Boston Museum of Fine Arts. The former, however, were painted around 1900, while the Karolik pictures generally run toward the mid-nineteenth century.

A second Ropes painting in the institute, *Launching of the Ship "Fame" in Salem Harbor, 1802*, is enlivened by as many standees— ashore and aboard ship—as *Training Day*. If the enormous flags don't sink it, *Fame* will not founder. To whet the reader's appetite for the art of George Ropes, I suggest consulting the color plate of this picture in Priscilla Lord and Daniel Foley, *The Folk Arts and Crafts of New*

197

England (Radnor, Pa.: Chilton Book Co., 1975). Ropes should be much better known than he is at present. He should not be confused with Joseph Ropes (1812–85), also of Salem, whose four panoramic views of Hartford, each 18 by 62 inches and painted in 1855, describe the city's appearance from north, south, east, and west. They are owned by the Wadsworth Atheneum, Hartford.

Peabody Museum

Location: East India Square, 161 Essex Street (parking garage nearby on
Liberty St.)
Hours: Mon.-Sat. 9-5, Sun. and holidays 1-5; closed Thanksgiving,
Christmas, and New Year's Day
Admission: Charged. Ⓗ

East India Square, turned into a mall with attractive walkways, plant-
ing, and restored fine buildings, must rank as one of the most successful
examples of urban redevelopment. The Peabody Museum is at its entrance from the end of Essex Street. A superb modern addition, providing a corner entrance, has more than doubled the exhibition space.
Built in 1976, it is sensitively related to the original building (facing
the square), erected in 1824 by the East India Marine Society. The
society was founded in 1799. The ground floor of the old building was
once occupied by the Asiatic Bank, the Oriental Insurance Office, and
the U.S. Post Office, while the large hall above was devoted to the
museum and to the meetings of the society. At the dedication exercises
President John Quincy Adams delivered the main address. Apart from
the recent expansion, additions were built in 1885, 1906, and 1952 to
provide for the growing collections amassed by the society in its worldwide activities.

This museum is of unique importance in America, for its collections
long predated the modern interest in primitive art and anthropological
research. As a historical display of American maritime commerce it is
unrivaled. Its name comes from George Peabody, born near Salem in
1795, died in London in 1869, who in 1867 gave funds to combine the
museum of the society with the natural-history collections of the Essex
Institute for the promotion of "Science and Useful Knowledge in the
County of Essex." Membership in the society was open to "any persons
who shall have navigated the seas near the Cape of Good Hope or Cape
Horn, either as Masters or Commanders or (being of the age of twenty-
one years) as Factors or Supercargoes of any vessels belonging to Salem."

Comment on the fine assortment of ships' figureheads in the Marine
Hall is reluctantly omitted, and the reader is referred to the discussion
of similar work at Mystic Seaport (p. oo). Our illustrations of the ethnological collections can give only the merest suggestion of the fabulous
wealth of material on display. Although the Peabody Museum was never
intended to be an art museum, its contents often command respect on
aesthetic grounds. There are many thousands of exhibits, covering all
the non-European world, with emphasis on the Pacific Islands and Japan.
Catalogues and a useful *Visitor's Guide to Salem* are available.

East Hall, entered from the Marine Hall, is dominated by a 6-foot *Wooden Idol*[198] from the Hawaiian Islands. Coming from a *morai*, or cemetery, it was given to the society in 1846. It is thought to have been the temporary resting place of a particular god during ceremonies at a temple, and not an actual object of worship. The powerful forms speak their own language of warlike grandeur. One cannot help wondering what the outcome would have been if the accidents of history had brought such "idols" to the attention of Picasso and other modern artists instead of those much tamer African Negro sculptures which they "discovered" in Paris art shops about 1905.

The Maori civilization of New Zealand is abundantly represented in the same gallery. The so-called *Short Club*[199] (Number 144) was used as a thrusting weapon somewhat in the manner of fencing, not as a club. It is beautifully ornamented with curvilinear interlacement, a more elaborate example of which may be seen on a *Door Lintel* (Number 559).[200] If such ornament reminds us of Scandinavian woodcarving of the ninth century (the Osberg Ship at Oslo) and later, or of Irish manuscript illumination, or of very ancient Chinese bronzes, we should not be altogether surprised. While the explanation may lie purely in the realm of coincidence, there is much credibility in the theory of the migration of cultures.

The visitor interested in the art of the Pacific Islands should consult the books of Hooper, Borland, Tichnor, and Linton. The ethnological background is covered in Elsdon Best, *The Maori as He Was*, in Sir Peter Buck, *The Coming of the Maori*, and in David Malo, *Hawaiian Antiquities*.

199

198

200

The representation of objects brought in through the China Trade (discussed in the section on the museum devoted to that field at Milton, page 244) is one of the most important in existence; and the same can be said of the scrimshaw collection, which has unusually large examples. Ship models trace the full range from the age of sailing to the present, including the *Bremen,* the *Queen Mary,* and the *Queen Elizabeth II.* Ship paintings, also in abundance, include several by Fitz Hugh Lane (see MA 155), one of them the *Brittania* in a bad storm. Ships' figureheads include a surprise: the *Rembrandt* (built in Kennebunkport, 1876), showing the artist young, in a red tam-o'-shanter and a red cape falling all the way to his feet. This figure is nearly twice life-size. It is so memorable that I gladly contradict an earlier statement that comment on these carvings would be omitted.

Heritage Plantation of Sandwich

Location: Pine St., 1 mile from the center of the village. From Sagamore Bridge follow Route 6A; from the village center take Route 130 *north* for ½ mile, turn left on Pine St. and follow it to the plantation
Hours: 10-5 daily from mid-May to mid-October
Admission: Charged. Ⓗ

Located outside Cape Cod's oldest town, the plantation consists of seventy-six acres of gardens and woodlands—a delight in their own right—and several museums of Americana. Flatcar buses take you easily from spot to spot.

The ensemble was founded in 1969 by Mr. and Mrs. J. K. Lilly, in memory of Mr. Lilly's father, an enthusiastic collector of many phases of popular and utilitarian American art, including automobiles. These are superbly shown on two levels of a replica of the celebrated Shaker Round Barn at Hancock (see page 230). The 1912 *Mercer Raceabout,*[201] gleaming yellow and black, and in perfect condition, is one of the most spectacular of these machines. Its four-cylinder, fifty-eight-horsepower engine drove it slightly faster than its legendary competitor, the Stutz Bearcat (also seen here in yellow and black). A small circular windshield provided the only protection; goggles, caps, veils, and dusters were *de rigueur.* The 1912 cost was twenty-five hundred dollars. The svelte lines and shapes proclaim this two-seater a work of art appropriate for inclusion in this book. On a plane of high luxury, however, consider the thirty-eight-hundred-dollar red Oldsmobile of 1912, with its brasses and mahogany floorboards, and the forty-thousand-dollar Duesenberg touring car built in the 1930s for Gary Cooper. A 1906 Stanley Steamer like the 1911 example here had the distinction of achieving a speed of 197 miles per hour—before it became airborne and disintegrated.

The Military Museum houses firearms—including a model of the great German gun that bombarded Paris in the First World War from a distance of seventy-five miles—and some two thousand hand-painted military miniature figures arranged in historical settings. Attached to the Arts and Crafts Museum is a complete and functioning carousel (with

201

calliope) built about 1912 in Riverside, R.I. Within are extensive collections of Currier & Ives lithographs, early American tools (the fish spears are of especially beautiful design), and American folk art. Here you may see a smaller variant of the *Grasshopper Weather Vane* that surmounts Boston's Faneuil Hall (see page 133), made of copper about 1882, probably at Waltham, Mass. Note the spikes on the back legs, and note too how the designer has given this creature a sense of potential speed. Up to life-size painted wood figures, not all of them commercial, attain a considerable degree of vitality. I particularly enjoyed a batsman, rather like the figure in Eakins's *Baseball Players* at Providence (RI 17). Much more sophisticated, but overloaded with descriptive detail, is the bronze *Mountain Man* by Frederic Remington (1861–1909) of 1902/3, with the horse inclined downhill at a dizzying angle. The small but choice scrimshaw collection includes finely designed knitting needles and swifts (to hold yarn). The paintings are best described as good period pieces. There is some artistic merit, as well as accuracy, in the collection of carved and painted birds, many of them by Anthony Elmer Crowell (1862–1951) of East Harwich.

A leisurely visit to the Heritage Plantation, especially on a fine day, will be well rewarded.

Art Museum, Mount Holyoke College

Location: Route 116, near the intersection of Route 47
Hours: Academic year: Mon.-Fri. 11-5, Sat., Sun. 1-5; closed academic holidays. Summer: Mon.-Fri. 1-4. Parking provided
Admission: Free. Ⓗ

In 1976 the museum celebrated with an exhibition the one-hundredth anniversary of the housing of the college's art collection in a permanent home on the campus. "College Collections, 1776–1876" traced the history of art collecting by American colleges in that period. As the list is both short and of some interest, we mention the colleges included: Amherst, Bowdoin, Dartmouth, United States Military Academy, Vassar, and Mount Holyoke. Not included, but listed with a historical summary, were: University of Michigan, University of Notre Dame, University of Vermont, Syracuse University, Harvard University (but the collections were for the most part kept at the Boston Athenaeum and the Museum of Fine Arts until 1895), and Cornell University (a hope at its founding in 1865, but not fulfilled until 1953).

The present building, which opened in 1971, provides well-appointed facilities for the art department, its library, and the collections—now fast growing since their move from the rugged old Dwight Art Memorial of 1902. Extension of the museum space is already anticipated. Modest purchase funds were augmented by gifts and by an unusually dedicated and active Friends of Art organization; special funds donated by Mrs. John M. Warbeke in memory of her husband have made possible the acquisition of an impressive Far Eastern collection. Continued interest of the department of classics, especially in excavations, has made possible a fine small collection of Greek and Roman art. The print collection is large, broadly ranged, and well selected. A special bequest brought in a small group of early Italian paintings of quality. In the contemporary field, acquisitions have emphasized, but not excessively, work by women artists.

To our survey of Greek vase painting, notably in the entry on Bowdoin College (ME 1–3), we now add a fine example of the Geometric Period, eighth century B.C. This *Low-handled Bowl*,**202** or *skyphos*, is covered with abstract motifs typical in such ware. The repetitive figures of women spinning, like the ornament, are applied flat on the surface.

202

Unlike sixth-century black-figure ware, these have no engraved interior lines. The shape of the vase, squat but capacious, suggests utility without concern for elegance.

The prize of the Classical collection is a Greek bronze statuette, under 9 inches high, of a *Standing Youth with Right Arm Extended*,[203] closely related in style to the famous *Charioteer* of Delphi (c. 475 B.C.). From every angle, but especially from the back, this small masterpiece conveys the sense of excitement that the sculptor must have felt in liberating the human body, as he surely did, from the confines of inorganic material. In this unique gift of the Greeks to human self-understanding, bronze led monumental sculpture; thus not even the magnificent marble sculptures of the Temple of Zeus at Olympia, dating from c. 460, match the little bronze in resilience and freedom of movement. (That is no criticism of the Olympia sculptures, for their more rigid and formal character is exactly right in their architectural context.) In the Mount Holyoke bronze, acquired near Athens in 1926 by Professor Caroline Galt of the classics department, there is prodigious energy in the rounded planes and contours; prodigious too is the inner restraint. An article in the fall 1977 issue of the museum's *Newsletter* reported on a thorough laboratory examination of the *Standing Youth*. If you have been disturbed by the right arm, you will be glad to learn that it has been bent. (Much of the hand is obviously missing.) Less disturbing is the right leg, newly bent from the knee down, with resulting displacement of the foot. The nipples have been gouged, perhaps to extract small gold inlays. The head has fortunately escaped the breaks and patchings apparent in the neck area. Fears that these might mean the head did not belong to the body were allayed when radiography demonstrated that the two were never completely separated. Possibly the original casting was defective in this area. Very likely the youth was shown pouring a libation from a cup of gold; and there is some slight evidence that the whole figure was gilded. My unusually detailed discussion of this marvelous piece is surely appropriate to its quality and importance in Greek sculpture of perhaps its greatest period.

In the exquisite field of fourteenth-century Sienese painting, Mount Holyoke boasts a small panel from the great *Maestà* painted in 1308–11 by Duccio di Buoninsegna (active 1278–1315). The *Bust of an Angel*[204] served as one of the small pinnacle elements atop the frame

203

204

of the elaborate altarpiece, painted for the high altar of Siena Cathedral, and now shown in the adjacent Opera del Duomo. In a work of such complexity and magnitude, it is not unlikely that auxiliary parts like this were assigned to an assistant, but if so the painter worked faithfully in the master's style. The *Angel* was once in the collection of the Kaiser Friedrich Museum in Berlin. It was acquired by gift to Mount Holyoke in 1965. Panels from the predella below the central Madonna and Saints are in the Frick Collection, New York, and the National Gallery, Washington.

A pen drawing of *Christ among the Doctors*[205] is attributed to the Italian Baroque painter Guercino (1591–1666). This master worked primarily in the region of Bologna, but in the early 1620s he was in Rome, where he painted his famous *Aurora* for the ceiling of the Casino Ludovisi (not to be confused with Guido Reni's tamer version of the same subject in the Casino Rospigliosi). This drawing seems to have been made during Guercino's stay in Rome. While it is more conservative than the art of Bernini, its Baroque character is clear. Observe the breadth of Guercino's forms, and the freedom of their diagonal movement forward and back in space. For Guercino, line was movement, texture, shadow, and volume, all merged inseparably. On the reverse, a slightly later drawing by Guercino in a tamer technique, representing *Christ among the Doctors*, shows us, first, that paper was expensive and, second, that Guercino was not always at top form.

Acquired in 1981 is an impressive oil, nearly six feet high, *St. Sebastian Attended by St. Irene*, Italian work of the later seventeenth century. The artist, not as yet identified, is clearly one of consequence.

Not illustrated here—only because of generous coverage of the artist in other museums—is a fine landscape by Albert Bierstadt (1830–1902), *Hetch Hetchy Canyon* (some fifty miles from the Yosemite). It was painted in 1875 and the following year purchased from Bierstadt himself and presented to the college on the opening of its first museum building. (See VT 14.)

The Conway Meadows,[206] an oil more than 3 by 5 feet, is a brilliant example of the work of George Inness (1825–94). Painted in the White Mountains in 1876, it departs significantly from Hudson River School approaches to landscape, to which Inness twelve years earlier, in *The Elm* (ME 23), had been so faithful. It is equally different from his brooding, perhaps symbolic *White Monk* of 1873 (MA 16), painted

205

206

during his four-year stay in Europe. On his return, in 1875, he developed from sketches made on the spot the brightly luminous *Etretat* (Wadsworth Atheneum, Hartford) in a style clearly affected by the work of the Impressionists. Yet the texture, even on these great white cliffs of the Normandy seacoast, is furry rather than dappled, and the color is more local than broken up into prismatic glints. *The Conway Meadows* came in the following year. It carries still further, into a composition of size, the freedom of Inness's oil sketches. With extraordinary consistency it maintains the broad sweep of cloud-covered land while at the same time all the details sparkle as in an early morning dew. The greens are wonderfully varied and fresh. In all respects the picture surpasses the oil study of the same subject owned by the Fort Worth Art Association. Late in his life Inness moved into an atmospheric-mystical vein based on the late phases of Whistler and Corot. (Two examples from 1891/2 are in the Clark Art Institute, Williamstown.) His earlier work seems much more inspired, perhaps because in the nineteenth century the American imagination functioned best on a basis of meticulous observation, whether in painting or in literature.

The *Portrait of Annie Lavelle*,[207] by Robert Henri (1865–1929), the leading figure in the so-called Ashcan School of the early 1900s, indicates his winning informality, sharp eye, and deft brushwork. Henri's portraits should be contrasted with the more elegant and much more thoughtful ones of his exact contemporary, John Singer Sargent (CT 45 and MA 84). In his reaction against Sargent's high-toned posture, Henri sought out the life of city streets, and he resisted European influences. Nevertheless, his technique owed something to that of Edouard Manet, but coarsened to a point just short of commercial painting. This charming study of a child, however, rings true, and the range of reds and pinks produces its own visual delight.

From the college's Far Eastern collection we have selected a Chinese hand scroll, here illustrated by a detail. *Spring Morning at Yen-Chi*,[208] in ink and colors on silk, is the work of Wang Hui (1632–1717), a major painter of the Ch'ing dynasty. To judge from Laurence Sickman's account of him in the Pelican History of Art volume (*The Art and Architecture of China*, pages 191–92), he had such varied talent that he

207

208

could "paint successfully in a number of different ways and yet assert his own individuality." The Mount Holyoke scroll strongly resembles an album leaf, dated 1677, in the Musée Guimet, Paris; thus, it appears to be a personal variant of the style of Wang Mên (died 1385), an outstanding artist of the Yüan dynasty (1260–1368). Worthy of note in the Mount Holyoke scroll are the tender washes laid in strips horizontally across the top, where mists cut off the summits of the highest hills.

Had there been more space in this limited survey of an excellent small museum, I should like to have discussed a superb Maurice Prendergast watercolor, *Festival, St. Mark's Venice*, c. 1898/9; *Lurid Sky*, an oil of 1929 by Yves Tanguy (see MA 227); Dmitri Hadzi's *Floating Helmets*, a bronze study for the large version of 1965 at Yale University; and a precious late Gothic statuette of polychromed wood representing *St. Anne with the Virgin and Child*.

On the Quadrangle

Location: For directions, see Museum of Fine Arts, Springfield

Before or after visiting Springfield's two art museums, which we are about to discuss, be sure not to miss the monumental bronze figure of *The Puritan*[209] by Augustus Saint-Gaudens (1848–1907), which commands the slope at the open northern angle of the Quadrangle—on which both museums face. Saint-Gaudens was the leading American sculptor of the nineteenth century. Erected in 1899 on a well-designed circular granite base, it is a theoretical portrait of Deacon William Chapin, one of the founders of Springfield. A variant, with a different base, is in Fairmount Park, Philadelphia; and small castings of this variant exist in some quantity (examples are at the Addison Gallery, Andover, Mass.; the Williams College Museum of Art; and at the Saint-Gaudens Memorial, Cornish, N.H.). The rear view is especially powerful, with the flowing cape masking what may seem excessive detail from the front. At his best, Saint-Gaudens achieved much of the breadth and energy we find in the architecture of his great contemporary H. H. Richardson.

The Puritan was presented to the city of Springfield by Chester William Chapin, banker, railroad president, and descendant of Deacon Samuel Chapin (1595–1675), one of the city's founders. No visual record of the deacon being available, Saint-Gaudens modeled the head from the donor's son, whom he had met in Paris. He theorized that the deacon must have had the same square jaw and beetling brows. The statue, 12 feet high, was unveiled in Sterns Park in 1887, but in 1899 it was moved to its present position.

For further discussion of the artist, see the entry on the Saint-Gaudens National Historic Site, Cornish, N.H.

209

George Walter Vincent Smith
Art Museum

Location: On the Quadrangle. For directions, see Museum of Fine Arts, Springfield

Hours: Tues. 12-9, Wed.-Sun. 12-5; closed New Year's Day, July 4, Thanksgiving, and Christmas

Admission: Free

The George Walter Vincent and Belle Townsley Smith collections were installed in an Italianate villa designed by the firm of Renwick, Aspinwall and Renwick, and Walter Tallant Owen of that firm, in the year 1890, opened to the public in 1895 and deeded to the city of Springfield in 1914. This is the oldest of the four museums on the Quadrangle and was originally called the Springfield Art Museum, although it then also housed the Museum of Natural History.

There had been a Museum of Natural Science, Art, and Curiosities established in 1859, which shared with the city library two small rooms in the old city hall. By 1889 a number of prominent citizens began plans to move the museum to its present location. The property was secured through the bequest of Horace Smith, and many other Springfielders contributed to the building fund.

The architecture and collections of the museum have remained intact since the death of the Smiths, George Walter in 1923 and Belle Townsley in 1928, giving the historian and the museum visitor a clear picture of the tastes and aesthetic sensibilities of a bygone era. Nine elegantly arranged galleries present a treasure trove of decorative arts and paintings from Europe, Asia, and America. The Oriental collections of jade, cloisonné, ceramics, armor, and rugs are among the finest in America. There is a large collection of plaster casts of famous sculpture and a gallery devoted to changing exhibitions in which the work of many artists and craftsmen have received their first public exposure. The museum's lively program of classes for children and adults makes it one of the region's leading centers for the study of the visual arts.

The collection of American paintings is strong in its representation of artists of the Hudson River School, especially Sanford R. Gifford (see VT 16) and Frederic E. Church (1825–75), whose *Scene in the Catskills*,[210] some 3 by 4½ feet in size, dominates one of the galleries. Painted in 1851, it greatly expands the scope of Church's modest but winsome beginnings seen in the New Britain Museum's *Haying near New Haven* (CT 43), painted two years earlier. Indeed, the Catskills picture may be taken as an absolutely typical Hudson River landscape, and one of highest quality. Later, Church was to venture afar in search of more spectacular subjects, as in *Icebergs*, in the museum at Waterbury (CT 102), and the *Valley of the Santa Ysabel*, at Pittsfield (MA 195).

Other memorable paintings are by George Inness and by Alfred Bricher, whom we discuss in the entry on the Holyoke Public Library (MA 161). The stained-glass window at the head of the stairs was made by Louis Tiffany Studios from a design by Edward Simmons.

The collection of casts, recently refreshed and now superbly exhibited, rivals that at Norwich (CT 94). An attractive illustrated brochure is available. As with the Norwich collection, Ancient Greek and Roman and Italian Renaissance examples are included—nearly fifty of them— but the Middle Ages are skipped. Such was the force of classical taste prevalent around 1900. Greek works seen here in replica begin with Myron's *Discobolus* (Roman copy) and the lovely fifth-century Eleusinian relief; and Hellenistic ones include the *Laocöon* and the *Venus of Melos*. *Hermes Resting* is a notable Roman bronze. From the Florentine Renaissance are major works by Donatello, Luca della Robbia, and Jacopo della Quercia; and Michelangelo dominates with the Louvre's *Bound Slave* and three figures from the *Tomb of Lorenzo, Duke of Urbino*, in the Medici Chapel, Florence.

210

Museum of Fine Arts

Location: 49 Chestnut St. Follow these directions carefully! Take Springfield Center exit from I-91; turn east onto State St. Continue on State St. for two blocks; turn right onto Dwight St. Extension. Follow arrows and bear left onto Chestnut St. Entrance to the Quadrangle is the first driveway on right

Hours: Tues. 12-9, Wed-Sun. 12-5; closed New Year's Day, July 4, Thanksgiving, and Christmas

Admission: Free. Ⓗ by prior arrangement

The Springfield Museum of Fine Arts was founded in 1933, when the present building was constructed. Growth of the collections has been rapid, thanks especially to an endowment by James Philip Gray for the purchase of paintings. Dutch paintings of the seventeenth century, French and Italian of the eighteenth, French of the nineteenth, and American paintings form the main strength of the museum's holdings. There is also an extensive collection of Far Eastern art, including more than three thousand Japanese prints, and Western printmaking is well represented. The museum is rich in decorative arts, and there is a special collection of "Art Deco." An excellent handbook is available.

An adroit system of labeling has been initiated here. Happily, the museum believes in giving the visitor background information about the works of art on display. This function is accomplished by an illustrated leaflet available in each of several galleries. The leaflets are well written and no charge is made. The usual solution—extensive labels attached to the wall—can interfere with the visual effect of a gallery, and they are hard to read with any comfort.

Outstanding among the fine Dutch pictures here is a foot-high *Landscape near Dordrecht*[211] by Jacob van Ruisdael (1628/9–1682), the leading figure among many Dutch specialists in this field. It is signed and dated 1649, a year later than the *View of Egmond* at the Currier Gallery of Art, Manchester (NH 24). This "little giant of a picture" (a phrase reserved for such occasions by Professor Frank J. Mather, Jr.) manages to embrace most of what is important in Dutch painting of this sort: land, sea, clouds, trees, human interest, all constituting a voyage into infinite distances. This effect, achieved by diagonal and serpentine movement and by rich contrasts of dark and light, connects Dutch landscape painting with the prevailing trends of seventeenth-

211

century Baroque art. Ruisdael was probably influenced by Rembrandt's famous etching *The Three Trees* (1643), which it superficially resembles.

Ruisdel painted a number of superb marines (for example, MA 74) in addition to his landscapes, but Willem van de Velde the Younger (1633–1707) devoted a career to them. *Fishing Boats Offshore in a Calm*[212] (28 by 34 inches) is a typical example. Employing a horizon line hardly a seventh of the height of the whole composition, he enveloped the scene in a vast space flooded with light. Working first in Amsterdam, he spent the last thirty years of his life in London and Greenwich. The National Maritime Museum at Greenwich preserves his many pen drawings and grisaille studies of English ships, which set high standards for later ship painting in England and America. The Springfield picture, monogrammed at the lower left, is not dated; it appears to have been painted c. 1690, and thus during his English period. It passed through several distinguished English collections and was exhibited at the Royal Academy in 1871.

Alessandro Magnasco (1677–1749) was a prolific Genoese painter whose mannerisms and bravura often became a substitute for artistic creativeness. His forms stand midway between Baroque drama and the more intimate and small-scale art of the Rococo. *Monastery Interior*,[213] an oil more than 3 feet high, shows him at his best and in his specially favored subject. This is certainly no scene of cloistered medieval piety; indeed, these frantic monks seem attacked by St. Vitus's dance. In an

212

213

interesting article in *Apollo* magazine (1938, pages 69ff.) E. Scheyer
dates the picture about 1712 and discusses it in connection with the
monastic decline of the time in Italy. The possibility of satire in
Magnasco's paintings of this sort should not be discounted. His technical
procedure consisted of first painting the canvas a rich dark brown and
then brushing on warm and cool bluish tones for a nearly monochromatic
effect.

The Arch of Titus[214] gives us an impression of the art of Giovanni
Paolo Panini (1691–1764) very different from his vast *Interior of St.
Peter's* at the Boston Athenaeum (MA 26). Signed and dated 1754, and
only 29 inches high, it appears to have been made on order for the two
English students who take in the spectacle of past Roman glory under
the guidance of their dark-garbed tutor. Note the picturesque condition
of the Roman Forum as it existed over two centuries ago. While many
works of this Venetian-born painter who made a career of view painting
in Rome run to archaeological tedium, here a limpid light envelops the
scene and little vignettes of contemporary Roman life enliven it—while
at the same time helping establish the measured recession toward the
Colosseum in the far distance.

The Fortress Königstein, near Pirna[215] is a masterwork of an itinerant
Venetian landscapist named Bernardo Bellotto (c. 1720–80). The
nephew and pupil of Canaletto (see MA 76), he is also known by his
uncle's name. He worked in Germany—Pirna lies on the Elbe not far
from Dresden—Austria, Poland, and Russia. While his art followed
eighteenth-century fashion in its small scale and animated surfaces,
Bellotto displays his Baroque inheritance in his dark foreground and in
the forceful way he pulls us down this serpentining prospect. His detail
is both painstaking and insistent, but everything falls magically into
place in this highly ordered design.

In the memorable 1979 retrospective exhibition of the work of Jean
Baptiste Siméon Chardin (1699–1779) held at the Boston Museum of

214

215

Fine Arts, Springfield's oval still life, subtitled *Rafraîchissements*,[216] held its own in competition with celebrated works lent by the Louvre and other great museums of the world. Many thought it one of the finest pictures on display. The oval format, popular in eighteenth-century portraits and other compositions, is unusual in Chardin, but the design sensitively accords with it, and the position of Chardin's dated signature (1764) helps confirm the impossibility that the picture was cut from an originally rectangular frame. Its 5-foot height is also unusual in the work of this modest master, but since even his smallest works have a way of seeming much bigger than they are, it is not surprising that he could manage the large canvas as well. In an age of Rococo frivolity in court circles, Chardin stands out as a disciplined forebear of the still-life paintings of Paul Cézanne. To their credit, Rococo patrons recognized his merit. It seems fortunate that Chardin died before the Revolution. There would have been no place for him in a world dominated by the marbleized art of Neoclassicism.

Judge Suetonius Grant Heatly with His Sister, Temperance[217] is the hefty title of a charming "conversation piece" by the German-born English painter Johann Zoffany (1735–1810). Approximately 40 inches high, it was painted in India during the 1780s. Exquisite in color and workmanship, its crisp outlines and smooth surfaces echo the gradual shift that was taking place in European art from the painterly Rococo style (as in the museum's *Journey to Market* by François Boucher) toward Neoclassicism. Zoffany's meticulous detail, however, is part of his German inheritance that in turn runs all the way back to the Flemish fifteenth-century masters. The relaxed atmosphere of the conversation piece—of which Zoffany is one of the acknowledged masters —is indicative of eighteenth-century reaction against the stiff etiquette and high ceremony of the Baroque courts. Zoffany visited India from 1783 to 1789, but it would be pointless to look for overtones of Indian art in his work of those years. He was as much the Britisher abroad as Judge Heatly and his sister—and as satisfied about it. Nevertheless, the

216

217

Indian at the left caught his interest, even to the extent of unbalancing a rather sloppily composed arrangement.

Although the large white-gowned portrait of *Madame de Servan* (not illustrated) is no longer considered to be the work of Jacques Louis David, but of a follower, it is a fine period piece, c. 1800; and it well exemplifies what has been said above about Neoclassicism. More than period interest, however, can be gained from the *Portrait Head of a Young Man*, formerly attributed to Eugène Delacroix. The intense, brooding gaze, reinforced by a smashing contrast of black hair and yellow coat, are Romantic to the core—a Heathcliff, as it were, out of *Wuthering Heights*.

When we come to the *Madman-Kidnaper*,[218] we are confronted by an authentic work of that inspirer of Delacroix, Théodore Géricault (1791–1824). This great initiator of French Romanticism not only unleashed the passions but he literally carried these forces beyond reason's control. One of Géricault's intimates, a doctor turned psychiatrist, commissioned him to make a series of portraits of mad persons, of which the *Kidnaper* is one. It rivals the most famous of them all, the old woman known as *The Hyena* (in the Lyons Museum). Both in subject and in painterly technique Géricault broke with David, as we have seen before in the Fogg Museum's wash drawing of a *Negro Soldier* (MA 127) and Hartford's watercolor of *The Coal Wagon* (CT 19). In so doing he managed to usher in both of the main streams of French nineteenth-century painting before the Impressionists: Romanticism and Realism. All of this, and dead at thirty-three!

Other French pictures not to be missed are Jean François Millet's sketch for the celebrated *Gleaners* (in the Louvre) and his sensitive early *Portrait of Virginie Roumy*, and Gustave Courbet's *Château de Chillon*, painted in Switzerland in 1873, when he was in exile for his participation in the pulling down of the Vendôme Column in Paris, during the Commune. The rise of Impressionism can be traced in the sequence from Eugène Boudin's three small landscapes to Gustave Caillebotte's *Game Birds and Lemons* (1883). Boudin was Claude Monet's mentor at Honfleur. Caillebotte, a member of the Impressionist circle, has received critical attention for his innovative treatment of space (see the catalogue of a major retrospective at the Brooklyn Museum, organized in 1976/7 by J. Kirk T. Varnedoe).

Early American painting is well represented at the museum by

218

Raphaelle Peale's *Still Life with Watermelon* and by a glossy *Portrait of Nymphas Marston*, a Boston work of John Singleton Copley. The latter somewhat resembles the magnificent *John Erving* at Smith College (MA 175), but without its intensity or flair.

The American gallery is dominated by an enormous canvas, *Historical Monument of the American Republic*,[219] 9 by 13 feet, painted c. 1876 by Erastus Salisbury Field (1805–1900). Field, who had studied with Samuel F. B. Morse (see CT 6), painted adequate portraits for some thirty years before suddenly launching into this strange, but impressive, manifestation. In his excellent *American Painting: History and Interpretation* (New York: Bonanza Books, 1960, page 571), Virgil Barker introduces Field with the following comment: ". . . a workman in possession of a technique adequate for his ordinary purposes may venture into unfamiliar territory of the mind with a bland unawareness that he needs a different technique. He may be ignorant of what he needs, but his self-forgetful confidence in what he wants to say transforms his ignorance into an innocence fresh enough to bring him easily through." What a Babel of towered fantasy Field has given us! I shall not try to compete with Barker's description: ". . . multiplied masses of Sumerian ziggurats rounded into dwindling Tombs of Hadrian and walled with Romanesque arched galleries so maze-like that the total effect approaches the Gothic."

We return abruptly to reality with *Emblems of Peace*,[220] an unusually large and sumptuous fool-the-eye composition by William M. Harnett (1848–92). Measuring 28 by 34 inches, it is signed and dated 1890 at the lower left. Reference to Harnett's *Still Life with a Bottle of Olives* at Fitchburg Museum (MA 153), painted in 1877, will quickly indicate his extraordinary development—without, however, denigrating the

219

220

quality of the earlier work. In discussing J. F. Peto's *Discarded Treasures* at Smith College (MA 187) we have rehearsed the story of how some of Peto's work was, for a time, sold with forged Harnett signatures. Comparison with the Springfield picture will immediately show how different they were. The museum acquired its Harnett from a Springfield hotel owner-manager who had bought it from a Springfield dealer for ten thousand dollars in the year after Harnett's death—well before the twentieth-century revival of interest in such pictures sparked the forging activity.

Harnett, a Philadelphia painter, was an ardent student of Dutch art, but his infinitely painstaking detail puts us more in mind of Flemish art in the tradition of Jan van Eyck. *Emblems of Peace* is perhaps more like the skin of a van Eyck than its substance, because there is no hidden significance in this patient inventory. Unlike Chardin (see MA 216), Harnett is not concerned with formal relations between objects in space. Every inch of his surfaces claims the same attention, and their accentuation denies all consideration of spatial position. When the picture was once exhibited at Smith College, a professor of music had a moment of triumph on discovering that Harnett had omitted the dot of a quarter-note on the score.

Like several other New England museums, Springfield is fortunate in possessing a pair of portraits by William Jennys (active 1795–1805), whose work we have discussed at New London (CT 87). Its oil by Winslow Homer, *Promenade on the Beach*, is one of only two known works of his in this medium from the year 1880—a year of great progress in his watercolors toward his later style, darker and soberer than before (see the example at Rockland, ME 31).

We conclude this too brief survey of a fine collection of paintings with two large twentieth-century canvases. George Bellows (1882–1925) painted *Edith Cavell*[221] in 1918, three years after the English nurse was shot as a spy by a German firing squad. It is worth remembering that Goya's great picture of the *Massacre of Madrileños* on May 3, 1808, was not painted until 1815. Like Goya, Bellows had time to contemplate—and to raise propaganda to the level of considered artistic expression. Perhaps, in Bellows's case, the picture was a bit too carefully planned as a composition and too much loaded with ancillary detail to achieve Goya's shock impact. However that may be, the light is eerie, the darks portend the coming tragedy, and the white figure of Edith Cavell stands out effectively. Personally, I could do without the stacked

221

rifles and spiked helmet, though it was necessary to emphasize the foreground plane at that point and lead the spectator's attention to the firing squad, dimly suggested at the extreme right.

Helen Frankenthaler (born 1928) is the author of an abstract image, 10 feet high, painted in acrylic in 1969. It bears the mysterious title *Cave*.[222] This afterthought may have been a purely associative reminiscence, but as a cave the picture could be read as either looking in or looking out. Such ambiguity is intrinsic to Surrealism, and as well to such older masters as Paul Klee and Pablo Picasso; but Frankenthaler's connection with these currents of modern art is at best tenuous. What counts here is the impact of pure shape and of pure color: from left to right, olive green, raw canvas, cinnamon orange, deep purple, and sky blue. It is remarkable how well these colors carry in the black-and-white photograph. That suggests a rare perception of color value, of the sort that is so extraordinary in the painting of Edouard Manet (for example, in Hartford's *Beach at Berck*, CT 23). As for shape, observe the power of the dominant purple area, forming a kind of 7; and observe, too, how the other colors set it off. The effect is of something colossal; thereby, it seems to me, the great size of the picture is justified. At such a scale straight edges and flat painting would produce boredom: hence the careful modulations of texture through brushwork, particularly in the purple and "orange" areas; and hence the ragged edges, as of torn papers, suggesting a collage that does not exist. Finally, a strange light seems to seep forward through the screen of purple. This picture can be passed by as formalism without content—or in Mark Rothko's phrase ("a painting does not *represent* an experience, it *is* an experience") it can be an experience of envelopment, as in a dream.

222

Chesterwood, the Studio
of Daniel Chester French

Location: Two miles west of Stockbridge, off Route 183; follow the signs at Glendale. If arriving by the Mass. Tpke., use exit 1
Hours: 10-5 daily, from May 1 to October 31 or early November
Admission: Charged

Owned and operated by the National Trust for Historic Preservation in the United States, Chesterwood, with the Saint-Gaudens National Historic Site at Cornish, N.H., makes available to the public the life and work of one of New England's—and America's—two most prominent sculptors of the late nineteenth and early twentieth centuries. They were almost exact contemporaries: Augustus Saint-Gaudens (1848–1907) and Daniel Chester French (1850–1931).

Chesterwood opened in 1955. It contains models, casts, and photographs of the work of a prolific career, and a large collection of personal mementos. In the studio itself the most important piece is the 6-foot-high *Plaster Study*[223] for the 20-foot marble statue of *Abraham Lincoln* in the Lincoln Memorial, Washington, D.C. This commission came near the end of French's career, almost fifty years after his figure of the *Minute Man* was unveiled by Ralph Waldo Emerson at Concord, Mass., in 1875. The Concord commission had come to him when he was only twenty-two, and it was his first statue. Other notable works by French include the *Alma Mater* for Low Library at Columbia University, *John Harvard* in Harvard Yard, the equestrian *George Washington* in the Place d'Iéna, Paris, and the standing *Lincoln* for the statehouse at Lincoln, Nebraska. To this list of widely familiar monuments I would add one admired locally, but too little recognized for its surpassing quality, the *General Oglethorpe*, on one of the main downtown squares of Savannah, Georgia.

In *Memories of a Sculptor's Wife*, Mrs. Daniel Chester French describes the difficulties encountered in erecting the huge marble *Lincoln* within the Lincoln Memorial. When it was finished in 1920, the architect, Henry Bacon, French's close friend, had died and his original plan for a glass ceiling had been changed to one of translucent marble. Though the interior had a beautiful glow, the lighting of the statue was disastrous. French had, of course, expected a lighting identical to that in the Chesterwood studio. Eventually Congress appropriated the money required to effect the present system of indirect lighting in the memorial. An interesting comparison of two photographs of the face (page 262 in Mrs. French's account), one lighted from above, as intended by the artist, the other from the front and below, graphically illustrates what is perhaps sculpture's most crucial problem. Today in Washington as well as at Chesterwood this noble image achieves the effect its maker desired.

In addition to the studio, one may visit the adjacent house and the Barn Gallery, which is attractively appointed to serve permanent and temporary exhibitions dealing with French's life and career, the Berkshire milieu, historic preservation, and local history. You will also enjoy walking through the beautiful wooded areas of the 120-acre estate, with their fine views of the surrounding Berkshires.

Until 1969, when Chesterwood passed to the National Trust by gift of French's daughter, Margaret French Cresson, Mrs. Cresson devoted over thirty years to preserving the estate with its studio, working toward opening it to the public and (after 1955, when this was accomplished) to presiding over its activities. The remodeling of the barn in 1962 was designed by Helen D. French, A.I.A., and the grounds were landscaped by her husband, Prentiss French, F.A.S.L.A., newphew of the sculptor.

223

The Old Corner House

Location: Main Street (Route 7), corner of Elm Street
Hours: Open daily 10-5, except Tues.; closed Thanksgiving, Christmas, New Year's Day, and the latter two weeks of January
Admission: Charged

Since this book is not concerned with architecture, we pass over the beautiful house itself, of late eighteenth-century design and formerly the home of James Fowler Dwight, a descendant of Joseph Dwight of Stockbridge, a general in the French and Indian War. Saved from demolition in 1967 by the activity of concerned Stockbridgians, it was restored and soon put to use as a home for the works of the town's most famous citizen.

This display is the only significant collection of paintings by Norman Rockwell (1894–1978) in existence. Most of these are owned by the Norman Rockwell Foundation, on loan as long as the Corner House shall exist, but some are borrowed from private collections, and others have been acquired as permanent possessions by the museum itself. Since we have discussed and illustrated at the New Britain Museum of American Art one of Rockwell's finest humorous illustrations (*Weighing In,* CT 51, for which the redoubtable Eddie Arcaro posed), our selection from the Old Corner House collection presents Rockwell's serious side. *The Problem We All Live With*,[224] an oil 36 by 58 inches, was painted on commission for *Look* magazine, which reproduced it in the issue of January 14, 1964. Centered between the towering legs of two pairs of U.S. marshals, a little black girl neatly dressed in purest white marches bravely forward. A ripe tomato, smashed against the leaden gray wall, lies on the ground. Graffiti on the wall tell the rest of the terrible story. Norman Rockwell invariably insisted, with characteristic modesty, that he was an illustrator, not an artist. This painting, however, rivets the attention not only by its message, nor even only by its realism, but by its shapes *as such*, by its sequence of darks and lights, and by the dread rhythm of its march.

224

Old Sturbridge Village

Location: On Route 20, ½ mile west of junction of Mass. Tpke. (exit 9) and I-86 (exit 3). Parking provided
Hours: April-October: 9:30-5:30 daily; November-March: 10-4 daily, except closed Mon. December-March; closed Christmas and New Year's Day
Admission: Charged. Ⓗ

One of our largest "outdoor" museums, Old Sturbridge Village tells the story of inland New England life during the eighteenth century and up to about 1840. On a two-hundred-acre tract bordering the Quinebaug River, the more than thirty buildings brought from nearby towns in Massachusetts and Connecticut have been sited to form a typical village and neighboring farm area. A separate formal-exhibits and demonstration area concentrates on the vast collections of arts and crafts and offers living demonstrations of the processes and techniques involved. Entrance is through the well-appointed modern Visitor Center.

Except for its many paintings and occasional examples of sculpture, Old Sturbridge Village lies outside the scope of this book. For further information see the forthcoming volume on *Historic Houses of New England* (in the David Godine series) by Margaret Supplee Smith.

Like the other collections here, the paintings owned by the village are generally limited to the cutoff date of 1840 and to what might have been seen in village establishments of the period. As of this writing, there is no special building for their display, and for security reasons the most valuable ones cannot be shown as incidental ornaments in the various houses. The Visitor Center, however, mounts changing exhibitions that often include selections of them. Visitors who have a particular interest in works and artists in the following list should make special arrangements in order to be sure to see them. Artists of unusual quality represented here are Mrs. Shute, Ethan Allen Greenwood, Erasmus Salisbury Field, and Matthew Prior. Most of the artists are anonymous. One of them painted a terrifying child in blue with a woolly dog; this picture reminded me of the rubbery, inflated humans of the contemporary Colombian painter Fernando Botero.

A rare example of wall painting will be found in the large room upstairs in the Salem Towne residence. These decorations (c. 1796), probably representing cedars of Lebanon, are original with the house, and were moved with it. In that year the Fayette Lodge of the Masonic Order was founded in the Charlton-Dudley-Sturbridge area, and for the first ten years of its existence it met in this room. The lodge was named for General Lafayette. Some of the paintings have been restored.

Overmantel paintings are an especially interesting branch of Early American art. The format calls for decoration on a wood panel and it offers an opportunity for a background of landscape. The village owns an unusual example depicting Moses Marcy of Sturbridge. As Marcy died in 1777, the painting is presumably pre-Revolutionary and thus one of the earliest such panels in existence. The subject was a merchant. In eternally fixed pose he invites us to survey his world. His house, rather startlingly located in this strange scene, is not unlike Publick House, a famous coaching inn built in 1771 in Sturbridge itself, about a mile from Old Sturbridge Village.

Rose Art Museum, Brandeis University

Location: From the Mass. Tpke. take exit 14 (coming from the west) or exit 15 (from Boston), onto Route 128 North; exit on Route 30 West, turn right (just before the stoplight) onto South St., which leads to the campus. The university is located east of Route 128 midway between Routes 30 and 20. Parking nearby

Telephone: (617) 647-2402

Hours: Tues.-Sun. 1-5; closed holidays

Admission: Free

The gift of Mr. and Mrs. Edward Rose of Boston, the well-designed building by Max Abramovitz dates from 1961, only thirteen years after the establishment of the university. A major addition was completed in 1974. The museum specializes in American and European art of the twentieth century. In the field of painting and sculpture since the Second World War it shares leadership in the Boston area with the Massachusetts Institute of Technology. The print collection, both in this field and in Japanese Ukiyo-e prints, is large; and the photograph collection is fast growing. Other collections include Tibetan, Oceanic, American Indian, and Pre-Columbian art, and the Rose collection of ceramics.

Because much of the available space is often filled by temporary exhibitions, it is advisable to call ahead about seeing the permanent collections. When you arrive at the university's information booth, ask directions to the museum and follow them carefully!

While the collection of modern art well represents the Post-Impressionists, the School of Paris, the Cubists, and early twentieth-century Americans, it is strongest in Abstract Expressionism, Pop Art, Color Field painting, and more recent developments.

Suspended appropriately in a network of rods set in the center of a reflecting pool is *Figure in Space*[225] (1958/9, total height 56 inches), a bronze by the English sculptor Reg Butler (born 1913). If you are familiar with the paintings of the same decade by Butler's compatriot

225

and contemporary Francis Bacon—smeared figures similarly imprisoned —you will sense a mutual affinity. Expressive of the tenuousness of the human condition, Bacon's figures are regularly detached from earthly support. Like many modern sculptors, Butler evades gravity, traditionally respected since Graeco-Roman times in the sitting, kneeling, standing, or walking figure. The tensile properties of metal, rather than the static ones of stone, are exploited to make this departure possible. It was a brilliant idea to set Butler's piece over water; the reflection accentuates its lift.

A remarkable oil by the Belgian Surrealist René Magritte (born 1898), provides an earlier analogy for Butler's topsy-turvy world. *L'Atlantide*[226] (also called *The Reflection*), 40 inches high, was painted in 1927. This was the year of his first exhibition, at Brussels; and the unfavorable response stimulated a move to Paris, where Magritte was quickly taken up by the newly founded Surrealist group. Against a black so deep as to suggest the space of a dream, a masonry-veneered tub establishes an abrupt and stark foreground. At its left end what seems like a curtain rises diagonally to top center—a curtain until you discover the upside-down corridor leading up a flight of stairs to a closed chapel in a rocky cliff. In the following year, 1928, Magritte painted a kind of manifesto: a meticulous fool-the-eye smoking-pipe. But under it he carefully lettered the following inscription: *Ceci n'est pas une pipe.* Not a pipe, that is, but a painting. Reality, as certain of the ancients insisted, lies not in appearance.

Another Surrealist painter of the dream world represented here is Yves Tanguy (1900–55), who lived and worked in Connecticut after leaving Paris in 1940. He married the American Surrealist painter Kay Sage (see CT 103), and it was from her estate that *Terre des Dormeuses*[227] came to the Rose Museum. All Tanguys evoke dreams,

226

227

and their titles—often more oblique than this one—direct us to the subconscious. While Magritte exploits the paradox of realism transformed, Tanguy fills his dream space with bonelike shapes, some soft, some brittle and piercing, and with Miró-like shadows cast by yet others not seen. The Brandeis example was painted in the same year, 1927, as Magritte's *L'Atlantide*.

Still Life: Radio Tube,[228] by Stuart Davis (1894–1964), is a companion piece to *Salt Shaker* (1931) in the Museum of Modern Art, New York. These and the work of the same year discussed at the Portland Museum of Art (*New York–Paris Number 2*, ME 25) are the fruit of an eighteen-month exposure to Cubist art in Paris. It is true that Davis had already worked out of illustrative painting into Cubist forms prior to his Paris sojourn, but that experience gave him the confidence he needed to move ahead in a direction that culminated in his magnificent canvases of the 1950s and early 1960s. At the ambitious size (for Davis at the time) of 50 by 32 inches, *Radio Tube* combines abstract Cubist forms with Fernand Léger's interest in those of modern industrial machinery; and in a characteristically brusque American way it adapts the amalgam to a specifically American subject, diminutive by the tape measure, explored and then enlarged. Through the art of Stuart Davis a radio tube and a saltshaker somehow become symbols of the American scene. Not surprisingly, he later influenced the development of Pop Art in the United States. In *Radio Tube* the restricted color—cleanly defined small areas of intense red, yellow, blue, and green spotted against much larger areas of black and white—indicates that the work of Piet Mondrian was yet another ingredient in the Davis mix. For this American, however, it was impossible to stay within Mondrian's ascetic limits, or within Léger's formal language of planes and cylinders. Furthermore, his American pragmatism barred Davis from Picasso's wild flights of imagination. He had permanently eliminated the human figure as his vehicle of expression. From now on he would find human interest in the colors, rhythms, half-read advertising slogans, and the overall excitement of life in a modern American city.

The inspiration for *Elegy to the Spanish Republic, Number 58*,[229] measuring 7 by 9 feet, by Robert Motherwell (born 1915) may date

228

229

from 1937, when the very young art student, graduated only a year before from Stanford University with a bachelor's degree in philosophy, heard André Malraux speak on the Spanish civil war at a San Francisco rally. Such a statement is simplistic, for it skips eleven formative years of Motherwell's artistic and intellectual life. However that may be, the motif first emerged in 1948; *Number 34* of 1953/4 is a major masterpiece of Abstract Expressionist painting (Albright-Knox Gallery, Buffalo: see my *Art Tours and Detours in New York State*; New York: Random House, 1964, page 23); *Number 54* (Museum of Modern Art) differs greatly from the Rose Museum's *Number 58* of the same period, 1957–61; and as late as 1978, in *Reconciliation Elegy*, the motif finds a tenuous resolution in stability in an enormous friezelike canvas in the new East Wing of the National Gallery of Art, Washington. Motherwell has said that his Elegies are not specifically political, but are "general metaphors of the contrast between life and death, and their interrelation." They are his personal *Guernica*. Many of them, including the Brandeis example, were shown in a major retrospective exhibition of the artist's work at the Museum of Modern Art in 1965, and illustrated in the catalogue. Such a decades-long series, always varied, always evolving, is a sure sign of a talent in depth. It is a modern equivalent of Cézanne's Mont-Ste-Victoires, of Monet's Water Lilies, and—to take the artist above all revered by Motherwell—of the Bathers of Matisse.

In the Buffalo *Elegy* of 1953/4, the motif is a relatively clean "7070" hanging free at the base, the menacing black 7's crushing the o's into vertical ovals held precariously; and the dominating blacks are relieved by small touches of intense color. By the time of the Brandeis example, black and ashen white bring the tonality closer to that of Picasso's *Guernica*, and the forms are looser. The direction of change is much like that which led to the latest Mont-Ste-Victoires of Cézanne and to Matisse's murals of cutout papers. A final suggestion to the reader: turn our illustration upside down and note how much is lost when the forms are no longer in suspension; note too that the deceptively slipshod drips and the downward pulls of the brush no longer have a gravitational reference.

The expressiveness and power of our next painting, appropriately titled *Untitled*,[230] cannot begin to be conveyed in a black-and-white

230

photograph. The picture itself makes its statement exclusively through color and brushwork. Willem de Kooning (born 1904) is a leading figure in the first generation of Abstract Expressionist painters that emerged—one might say exploded—on the New York scene in the 1940s and 1950s, soon to be joined by such younger artists as Jackson Pollock and Robert Motherwell. The Rose Museum's *Untitled* (80 by 70 inches) dates from 1961, and is thus a latish example of de Kooning's vigorous shorthand transcription of landscape. (The pictures in his celebrated Woman series of the 1950s—for all their savage reference to billboard sex symbols—have been described as female landscapes.) If *Untitled* moves you, dear reader, skip to the next paragraph. If it does not, look through Thomas Hess's catalogue for the Museum of Modern Art's major retrospective (1968). The following quotation from the artist may be obliquely helpful. It comes from the year of *Untitled*, when the artist found his image not in the clamorous metropolis but in farthest east Long Island. "I am very happy to see that grass is green. At one time, it was very daring to make a figure red or blue—I think now that it is just as daring to make it flesh-colored." Flesh-color finds its way into this landscape too, in a heady admixture with the greens, yellows, blues, and earth browns that animate it.

Just as post–Second World War Abstract Expressionism (also called, perhaps preferably, Action Painting) was a revolt against the meticulous detail and the storytelling art of the Regionalist painters of the 1930s (see Grant Wood's drawing in the Rose Museum for his well-known *American Gothic*), so Action Painting gave rise to a countermovement in the early 1960s. Pop Art was no return to the art of Wood, Benton, and Curry; but it did involve a return to elements of everyday life, and it eschewed the deeply personal flavor of the frenetic brushwork of de Kooning, Kline, and Pollock. Andy Warhol and Roy Lichtenstein are the most prominent names here, but in my opinion James Rosenquist (born 1933) is the major talent. The museum's *Two People*[231] (also called *Fishpole*) was purchased in the year of its execution, 1963. An oil and assemblage on canvas measuring 72 by 93 inches, it compacts disassociated fragments of leering billboards, food, common textiles, a license plate (full of nothings), and come-ons for a summer vacation into a closely knit, powerful design. Rosenquist's paintings have been described as floating like giant clouds. Cacophonous and disquieting, their impact is ironically not unrelated to that of the very art the Pop artists rejected: the harsh clang of a Franz Kline (MA 162) and the wild frenzy of a late Pollock (CT 34).

231

Wellesley College Museum

Location: In the Jewett Arts Center, between Routes 16 and 135; from Route 128 take exit 54 onto Route 16. Parking available

Hours: Mon.-Sat. 10-5, Sun. 2-5; closed Easter Sunday, mid-June through August, Thanksgiving, December 24, 25, and 26, New Year's Day

Admission: Free. Ⓗ

A brilliant new chapter opened for the museum in 1958, when it moved from a venerable building given by Isaac Farnsworth in 1883. Nevertheless, the old quarters had hospitably housed a long-distinguished art-history department and a collection that took on new life in 1944 with the appointment of Professor John McAndrew as its director. Sophisticated, scholarly, and endowed with taste and enormous enthusiasm, McAndrew quietly performed a miracle in the years of his stewardship. When the collection was unveiled in its wing of the spacious new Jewett Arts Center, it was quickly recognized as one of the best in the nation's smaller colleges. In the year following McAndrew's retirement from teaching in 1968, the museum mounted an exhibition of some forty works selected from the great many more that he had given, or persuaded others to give (in his time there were no purchase funds of consequence), as well as other works presented for the occasion in his honor. Few directors have done so much with so little.

Sad to relate, the construction of the new museum was accompanied by McAndrew's resignation as its director. Opposition by the administration on certain critical issues produced a deadlock; but the museum's loss was teaching's gain for another decade. McAndrew's final years were devoted to Venice, where he died, much honored for his untiring efforts in organizing support for conservation of Venice's deteriorating buildings and works of art.

John McAndrew's interests were wide-ranging. He took advantage of the then low prices for sculpture (which is particularly difficult to teach through slides and photographs). He assembled a rich array of Baroque painting and of modern art in all media—areas that had been sadly neglected. Virtually every important twentieth-century artist is represented in at least one medium.

Today, the collections, enriched by further gifts and purchases, are extensive in sculpture, painting, drawings, and prints. Since 1971, with the gift of twenty examples of the work of Eugène Atget (1857–1927), the photograph collection has also forged ahead. Attention is currently being paid to developing the representation of nineteenth-century American art.

An active Friends of Art organization issues a *Newsletter*, but no catalogue has appeared since *European and American Sculpture, Paintings, and Drawings*, published on the occasion of the opening of the new museum in 1958. A new catalogue, however, is projected.

The Jewett Arts Center, the gift of the family of George Frederick

Jewett, was designed by Paul Rudolph. Elaborate and interesting in plan, elevation, and interior spaces, and fitting harmoniously with the brick-and-stone College Gothic of the surrounding buildings, it received considerable critical acclaim; but there are some who wish it had the simplicity of a Mies van der Rohe design or the substance of one by Louis Kahn. As you arrive you are confronted by a handsome bridge connecting two major wings set at a comfortably enclosing angle. The left wing provides facilities for music and drama; the right one contains the museum, the art department, and its fine library; and the bridge, under which you pass, is the main gallery of the museum—also serving as the foyer for concerts and theater productions.

Although our first piece, the life-size marble *Torso of an Athlete,*[232] is an ancient Roman copy of an original work by Polykleitos, it gives an excellent impression of later fifth-century Greek sculpture. Comparison with the contemporary grave stele of a *Warrior* at Worcester (MA 289) is helpful, both to complete the action of the Wellesley figure and to clarify the original strength of the badly eroded surfaces of the Worcester example. While the body twists freely on its axis, the frontal plane is strongly emphasized, and a similar planar effect will be gained from observing the magnificent back. Thus Polykleitos tempered his daring innovations with the discipline of earlier Greek tradition. How taut this figure is may be quickly discovered by comparing it with the *Meleager* at the Fogg Museum (MA 111), a work marked by the Baroque trends of the next century. The Wellesley statue is the finest of some nine known copies of Polykleitos's *Discophoros* (the figure once held a discus in his left hand; the right arm was extended). It long stood in the Palazzo Odescalchi in Rome, embellished by fanciful restorations that were removed when it was sold and soon afterward given to Wellesley in 1905. It is not at all certain that the head belongs to the torso. What is very certain, however, is that it was attached erroneously—the two breaks do not coincide and a neck connection was invented—with the result that the head does not have its proper downward turn to the right, visible in other copies. This has the further disadvantage of disrupting the rhythmic curve from bottom to top in the otherwise superb rear view.

232

Not a capital like the somewhat related Burgundian example in the Fogg Art Museum (MA 112), but a corbel support, is the late twelfth-century Romanesque *Musician Playing a Viol*.[233] This sensitive carving in limestone, a foot high, comes from Provence; and because of its close similarity to a corbel in the Cloisters, New York, showing a dancer or acrobat, it appears to have come from the neighborhood of Saint-Gilles, not far from Arles.

The profile *Portrait of Estienne Menessarre*, a 5-inch roundel relief of sparkling marble, is a superb example of French sculpture of c. 1500, subtly balancing late Gothic realism with Italianate formal clarity. It was acquired in 1980.

The polychromed terra-cotta statue of the *Madonna and Child*,[234] 3 feet high, is attributed to Jacopo Sansovino (1486–1570) because of its relationship to his bronze figures and his terra-cotta *Madonna and Child* on the Loggetta in Venice, at the base of the great bell tower of the Piazza San Marco. The possibility of an atelier variant is not eliminated, but the piece is faithful to the master's subtle style of the 1540s. Trained in Florence in the purest traditions of ancient art then known to the Western world, Sansovino moved to Venice in 1527. Because of the higher polish of the Wellesley statue near its base, it is thought that the figure was designed to be seen high up, and presumably in a niche, since the rear is unfinished. Despite its Mannerist elongation, it preserves something of the sturdiness of Donatello (for example, in the pressure exerted by the Virgin's hands) and of the vigor of Michelangelo, who was only ten years Sansovino's senior. Purchased for a former owner by Wilhelm von Bode, the great German connoisseur of Renaissance sculpture, it was for some time on loan to the Kaiser Friedrich Museum in Berlin. Sansovino's sweetness and serenity require no special comment.

Wellesley owns a 2-foot bronze version of the famous marble of *The Rape of the Sabine Women* by Giovanni Bologna (1529–1608) in the Loggia dei Lanzi, Florence. Bologna's marble (1579–83) won him such fame that there developed a wide demand for small bronze replicas, turned out by highly trained assistants. Whoever made this

233

234

one—not excluding Giovanni Bologna himself—it is of very high quality. The whirling action is contained within an invisible cylinder, and only to this extent is it more restrained than the fully centrifugal explosions of Baroque sculpture of the seventeenth century.

An *Angel*,[235] only a foot high but seemingly larger, of gilded and polychromed wood, is the work of Meinrad Guggenbichler (1649–1723). It came from a side altar erected in 1706 in the celebrated little parish church in St. Wolfgang, on a beautiful lake in the mountains east of Salzburg. Wonderfully tender in feeling, somehow floating instead of standing on its pedestal, and with outstretched arms that once held a swinging censer, it is typical of those Austrian and German variations on Italian Baroque forms—Bernini's Angels on the bridge leading to the Castel Sant'Angelo in Rome may be a source of inspiration here—that marked the first half of the eighteenth century. Where Bernini is heroic and operatic, the Austro-German sculptors are spiritual and tremulous. Bernini is grandiloquent like Rubens; Guggenbichler, lyrical like Botticelli. The fluttering wing of the *Angel* is as expressive as the face and hands. Such works are rare outside the region of their origin. They are as much beloved by Austrians and Germans today as when they were made. In our discussion of the Busch-Reisinger Museum at Cambridge, we mentioned a larger group of Guggenbichler's, *The Return from the Flight to Egypt*. A delicate little half-length *St. Joachim*, perhaps by his school, is in the Williams College Museum of Art.

Only in Austria and Germany, and in Spain, did the medieval tradition of polychromed and gilded wood sculpture continue in popularity through the Baroque era. This reflects the deep piety of those Catholic areas—a piety not notable in eighteenth-century Italy. One of the most remarkable Spanish sculptors of the time was Francisco Antonio Salzillo (or Zarcillo), whose career was restricted to the provincial region of Murcia, back from Spain's southeast coast. He lived from 1707 to 1783. The attribution to him of Wellesley's *St. Teresa of Avila*[236] has strong scholarly support. Salzillo's reputation is based primarily on his painted wooden *pasos*: life-size scenes from the Passion wheeled through the streets in Holy Week. In his lifetime they were thought to have been

235

236

made with divine assistance. The *St. Teresa*, about 2 feet high, may well
be the work of assistants, at least in part, because Salzillo employed a
great many, apportioning them specialized tasks, such as flesh painting
and drapery painting. With some eighteen hundred works assigned to
him, caution must be one's guide. However that may be, the combination
of strong sentiment and intense realism comes through here as profoundly Spanish. That and, as well, great reserve: the most fleeting
memory of Bernini's ecstatic marble altar of St. Teresa in Rome will
indicate how far Salzillo's art strayed from normal Baroque canons
of religious representation. Bernini, the pure sculptor, got his color from
concealed amber glass lights; Salzillo liked the contrast between a black
robe and a flowered silk cape, and between highly polished flesh tones
and eyes of glass. A folk-art votive element here is a panel in the drapery
that opens to reveal a startling illusion of the saint's heart.

We continue our selections from Wellesley's sculpture with two very
different heads of women by French contemporaries active during the
second half of the nineteenth century. The terra-cotta *Head of Anne
Foucart at Age Sixteen*[237] was modeled by Jean-Baptiste Carpeaux
(1827–75); that of *Diana Huntress*,[238] carved in marble, is a replica
of the full-length nude figure by Jean-Alexandre-Joseph Falguière
(1831–1900). The contrast is absolute. The Carpeaux shows painterly
modeling in the tradition of Bernini (see MA 121) and Houdon (see
CT 67): animated psychology, flying hair, a twisting neck, a deftly
raised shoulder. The Falguière has the process of carving concealed under a veneer of pure white surfaces, a minimum of light and shade oppo-
sitions, a closed psychology, smoothed hair, a little animation suggested

237

238

by a turn of the head and the stump of a raised arm. The lives of the two sculptors differed in ways we should expect. Carpeaux's beginnings were marked by suffering and discouragement until at age twenty-seven he won the Prix de Rome; yet there was the fond memory of having been received at age eighteen by the great François Rude (see VT 10) and instructed by him for a year and a half. Important commissions came his way during the Second Empire (pediments of the Louvre, *La Danse* for the facade of the Opéra), but always marked by bitter controversy. Carpeaux died in his late forties at the height of his powers. Falguière had, on the other hand, favorable acceptance at the Ecole des Beaux-Arts; dutiful Academic training; the Prix de Rome and eventually the medal of the Légion d'Honneur; a long and untroubled life. In painting, the best parallel for Carpeaux is Gustave Courbet (that is, in Courbet's frank nudes and vigorous portraits). It would be unfair to call Falguière the Bouguereau of sculpture (see MA 257), for his *Diana* exudes a purity that Bouguereau never expressed. Furthermore, it should be said that Falguière transcended the limitations of those pale remnants of Neo-classicism that many other Academic sculptors clung to. The reader will easily guess how my choice lies, but I urge a careful look at the *Diana* for its lack of affectation and its very high order of craftsman-ship. As for the *Anne Foucart*, I reproduce the back view[237A] as well as the front, to show how the movement is generated at the lower left and never loses its momentum. You can see the mark of the tools on it, and may even expect to find the sculptor's fingerprints, so much are you caught up (I hope) in the excitement of witnessing the creative act. Many Carpeaux heads exist in terra-cotta replicas, but they generally lack the all-important personal touch of a sculptor whom Rodin was proud to call his master.

The work of the somewhat younger Aimé-Jules Dalou (1838–1900), who studied for a time with Carpeaux, has received considerable critical notice in recent years. Like Gustave Courbet, he became involved with the Commune in 1870/1 and was forced into exile. Unlike Courbet, he later returned to Paris, received major commissions for bronze monu-ments, and was awarded the exalted title of Officer of the Légion d'Hon-neur. It is his smaller works and studies that are especially admired today. Those familiar with Dalou's vast, heaving *Triumph of the Re-public*, in the Place de la Nation, may be surprised by the poignant real-ism of his bronze *Lavoisier*[239] and its compact design. This fine piece,

239

acquired by purchase in 1977, is a reduction of Dalou's 1892 monument (in the Sorbonne) to the great scientist who was guillotined in
the Revolution. At a height of only 20 inches it suggests much larger
forms. The rare malachite green patina is only one of many indications
of refinement in this penetrating work. The original plaster is in the
Petit Palais, Paris.

Other fine bronzes in the collection are by Giuseppe Piemonte (1664–
1742) and Renoir in his final years.

Two superb heads, by the German Wilhelm Lehmbruck (1881–1919)
and by Marcel Duchamp's brother, Raymond Duchamp-Villon (1876–
1918), take us into the twentieth century. Both works date from 1911
and both loom large in the artists' careers. Lehmbruck's *Head of the
Kneeling Woman*,[240] 20 inches high, is a cast stone replica, patinated
by the master himself to resemble terra-cotta, of the upper part of his
celebrated 70-inch 1911 figure in the Museum of Modern Art. A second
cast stone version of the *Kneeling Woman*, purchased in 1938 by the
Albright-Knox Gallery, Buffalo, was exhibited at the famous Armory
Show in New York, in 1913. Buffalo already owned the Wellesley head
(a gift in 1927), but the acquisition of the complete figure resulted in
the sale of the head, which Wellesley was most fortunate in acquiring
through a generous gift. For further discussion of Lehmbruck, a suicide
at thirty-eight and generally acclaimed as Germany's finest twentieth-
century sculptor, see the entry on his *Torso of the "Pensive Woman"*
at Smith College (MA 191). Although it is two or three years later than
the *Kneeling Woman*, the Smith example is more conservative and less
typical of the artist's expressive attenuation of forms.

Duchamp-Villon's *Bust of Baudelaire*[241] is a painted plaster version
of a work ordinarily seen in bronze. This somber head, with its haunting eyeless gaze, became the subject of two Cubist etchings by Jacques
Villon, the artist's older brother. Such a development is of itself evidence of the formal purity of the work. (One can hardly imagine a
Cubist version of a Rodin.) Duchamp-Villon was a leader in the reaction against Rodin's scarified and deeply penetrated surfaces. As a
characterization, the head has little of the morbid overtones of Baude-

240

241

laire's nineteenth-century verse; but it conveys much about his great critical intelligence and perceptiveness.

A fine selection of African sculpture includes a superb Benin bronze *Warrior* of the seventeenth century (compare MA 143) once owned by the painter André Derain, a leader in the modern interest in "primitive" art. It is one of many gifts from Mr. McAndrew. Of the ten sculptures already illustrated and two others mentioned, eight came to the museum through the generosity or the persuasiveness of the former director.

The oldest painting in the museum is also one of its earliest acquisitions. Purchased in 1905 from a fund given by President Hazard, *Christ Mounting the Cross and the Burial of St. Clara*, tempera on panel 31 by 21 inches, is the work of a follower of Guido da Siena, the late thirteenth-century initiator of Sienese painting and predecessor of the great Duccio (see MA 204). Strongly influenced by Byzantine traditions, it breaks with them in its linear swing, an element fundamental to the art of Duccio and Simone Martini (see MA 115).

The *Holy Family with Saints Francis and John the Baptist*,[242] by the Florentine painter and biographer Giorgio Vasari (1511–74), is the museum's most impressive pre-Baroque painting. Oil on panel 41 inches high, it is in mint condition, and its harsh pink reds, ice blues, greens, and apricot oranges make a strong foil for the enameled flesh tones. The date is c. 1544, soon after the artist received his first important commissions. Other versions of this work exist in the museums of Bordeaux and San Francisco (De Young Museum), but Wellesley's is the finest. Vasari drew from many sources, and never managed to achieve a unique style; but his sources were admirable and he combined them with great skill. Echoes of Andrea del Sarto appear in the elderly saints, of Michelangelo in the heroic Madonna, and of Parmigianino in her long neck and attenuated right hand. The hardness that gave a nickname to the painter Bronzino (1503–72) is also in evidence here. The general format, with its vertical axes climbing up symmetrically across a central one, and the twisting of forms to bring them parallel to the picture plane, suggests Il Rosso's *Dead Christ with Angels* (c. 1525/6) in the Boston Museum of Fine Arts (MA 70).

Limitations of space and the discussion of many fine examples in other museums force me to summarize Wellesley's fine display of seventeenth-century painting. Not to be missed are a *Youth in a Plumed Hat* by a

242

follower of Caravaggio, *Christ and the Woman of Samaria* by Domenichino (with an early appearance of modern landscape), and religious paintings by Crespi, Dolci, Furini, Giordano, and especially the *St. Francis in Ecstasy* by Bernardo Strozzi (see CT 14). Many of these Italian pictures were the gift of Dr. and Mrs. Arthur K. Solomon, of Cambridge, as was a large, Italian-inspired mythological picture by the Flemish painter Abraham Janssens the Elder (c. 1574–1632), a contemporary of Rubens. Dutch marine painting is well represented in a battle piece by Willem van de Velde the Younger (see MA 212); Dutch church interiors in an example by Emanuel de Witte; and Dutch genre painting in the remarkable *Soldiers Playing Cards*, by Gerard Ter Borch (1617–81), of which other versions exist.

Landscape with Approaching Storm, by the Venetian Marco Ricci (1676–1729), takes us into the early eighteenth century. A similar verve animates the brush of the Genoese painter Alessandro Magnasco, whose small *St. Bruno in Ecstasy* recalls the agitated monks in his painting at Springfield (MA 213). Evidence of the spread of Parisian Rococo style is seen in the fresh and charming *Perseus and Andromeda* by the Venetian-born Jacopo Amigoni (1675–1752), who worked in Bavaria, England, and Spain, as well as in his native city.

During the 1970s two important gifts from alumnae strengthened the representation of American painting: J. S. Copley's Boston-period *Portrait of Mrs. Roland Cotton* (c. 1763) and a 40-by-60-inch canvas, *The White Mountains: Mt. Washington*, by John Frederick Kensett (1816–72).[243] The latter is an absolutely superb example of art in the Hudson Riven vein, comparable to such works we have discussed as the early Bierstadts at Framingham and the Fruitlands Museums at Harvard, and Frederic Church's *Scene in the Catskills* (1851) in the George Walter Vincent Smith Museum at Springfield. The Kensett panorama dates from toward the end of the 1860s. It has his typical low-intensity colors. He once explained that "bright colors are sparingly distributed throughout the natural world . . . the main masses are made up of cool greens, grays, drabs and browns intermingled, and are always harmonious and agreeable."

An unexpected introduction to the modern movement in painting is provided by a brashly stroked, primarily black-and-white *Portrait Romantique*[244] of c. 1868–70. I suspect you will have trouble guessing which

243

244

celebrated artist painted it, even after being told that it is an early work. Early works can be deceptive, and this one is further offbeat because the artist was not often given to Romantic overtones—though there are other examples of the same period. His technical source here is the "black" works of Edouard Manet of the 1860s with their revolutionary emphasis on painting by flat tones; but this artist laid them on heavily in a near frenzy, that is, in a spirit totally different from Manet's judicious strokes. Instead of Manet's elegant aloofness we find here a devil-may-care explosion of energy. Should you need further identification, illustration MA 82 will show you a portrait of 1877, and illustration RI 21 another of c. 1890–92—by the same master.

Head of a Man by Pablo Picasso is only a small gouache sketch, but it has the force and the nascent Cubist character of his large *Standing Figure* of the same year (1908) in Boston (MA 87). It is thought that the relative calm seen in Picasso's work of 1908, following the violence of his 1907 *Demoiselles d'Avignon*, resulted from the influence of the memorial exhibition in Paris of the work of Paul Cézanne, who had died in 1906.

Mother and Child,[245] a Cubist composition measuring 26 by 21 inches, was painted in 1921 by Fernand Léger (1881–1955). It was given in honor of Alfred H. Barr, who introduced at Wellesley the first course in America on contemporary painting. Léger's cylindrical and spherical forms have been called "Tubist." Set against an emphatic vertical and horizontal grid in a compressed space, they give a feeling of three-dimensional sculpture. Color, which runs to primaries and high intensities, adds another note of formal purity. The restraint and equilibrium of Léger's geometric world is thoroughly French, in the tradition of Seurat and Cézanne. An affinity with the Classicism of Poussin (1594–1665) becomes most striking when the picture is compared with Poussin's *Holy Family* at the Fogg Museum (MA 123). A sharp contrast, however, emerges on comparison with Picasso's *Table* of 1919/20 at Smith College (MA 185), even though the two artists were born in the same year and Léger's Cubism owed its origin to Picasso's pioneering inventions. Neither picture makes much of its apparent subject.

245

Both depart from it to achieve other artistic goals. Picasso sought a symbol of modern anxiety; Léger, a symbol of the power of modern machinery.

Noir et Rouge,[246] a collage of cutout colored papers by Henri Matisse (1869–1954), measures only 17 by 21 inches, but it could easily be enlarged to mural dimensions. The date is 1950, before Matisse did in fact expand his new technique into vast decorative schemes such as the *Swimming Pool* (Museum of Modern Art, 1952). Beset by infirmities of old age, the great painter could no longer manipulate a brush. With a long stick he traced these biomorphic shapes on sheets of paper already colored in gouache and on contrasting black ones. Assistants performed the cutting operation for him. "To cut to the quick in color," he once said, "reminds me of direct cutting in sculpture." Reference to the bronze nude *Seated Woman* at Manchester (NH 30)—fashioned, of course, in clay before it was cast—will not only clarify Matisse's statement; it will suggest that his collage shapes are not as flat as they at first appear to be.

We have discussed in some detail an untitled composition of 1961 by Willem de Kooning (born 1904) at the Rose Museum in Waltham (MA 230). Wellesley's *Woman Springs*,[247] painted on a door panel 80 by 36 inches, is signed and dated 1966. It was given in 1978 in memory of Professor McAndrew. The title may well have a double meaning. This woman indeed springs, as in a wild dance; but Springs is the name of the eastern Long Island village where de Kooning and other artists of his circle have enjoyed a retreat from New York City. This sea of flesh-colored oil is a kind of Soutine landscape or marine extracted from the woman subject that has appeared intermittently in de Kooning's work since he introduced it in the early 1950s. In a decade dominated by earthworks, curtained natural scenery, conceptual art, and various manifestos of anti-art, it is gratifying to find an "old master" evolving in the tempo of his own style—just as Edward Hopper did—and, for that matter, Matisse, Claude Monet, Frans Hals, Titian, and Botticelli. All these "old masters" in their literally old age remained true to themselves. Excitement about the latest novelties—particularly rife and even destructive today—could not touch them.

246

247

Sterling and Francine Clark Art Institute

Location: South Street
Hours: Tues.-Sun. 10-5, throughout the year, and 10-5 on Memorial Day, Labor Day, and Columbus Day; closed New Year's Day, Thanksgiving, and Christmas
Admission: Free

Open to the public since 1955, the institute houses the impressive art collection formed by Mr. and Mrs. Robert Sterling Clark. Born in New York City in 1877, the grandson of a partner of Isaac Singer, inventor of the Singer sewing machine, Mr. Clark graduated from Yale in 1899 as an engineer and entered the army, serving in the Philippines and in China during the Boxer Rebellion. After leading a scientific expedition into the remote areas of northern China, he settled in Paris in 1912 and began acquiring works of art.

Collecting was an interest that ran in the family, and both Sterling and his brother Stephen undertook art-buying sprees in Europe, some with the guidance of the American sculptor George Grey Barnard. Initially, Clark focused his attention on Old Masters, particularly Italian, Dutch, and Flemish artists. Then, in the 1920s and 1930s, encouraged by his French-born wife, he concentrated on French nineteenth-century painting, examples of which now dominate the collection. His interests did not extend to twentieth-century modern art.

Just before the Second World War, the Clarks, who had previously divided their residence between the United States and France, returned to New York and drew up plans to make their collection—nearly three hundred works (not counting drawings, prints, or the extensive collection of silver and porcelain)—available for educational purposes. In 1950, they selected Williamstown for its natural beauty and associated cultural advantages, and five years later dedicated their Neo-Classical building of white Vermont marble. In 1964, a service building was added behind the original edifice to house a regional conservation laboratory and the institute's workshop. A red granite building designed by Pietro Belluschi and the Architects Collaborative of Cambridge, Mass., to the south of the original complex, was opened to the public in 1973. The new structure provides exhibition galleries, offices, an auditorium, and an art library, as well as a locale for a two-year graduate program leading to an M.A. degree from Williams College.

Since the deaths of Mr. and Mrs. Clark (in 1956 and 1960 respectively), the institute has grown slowly with deliberate restraint. A dozen major painting acquisitions have been made by the trustees, from interest on the endowment, along with many additions to the drawings and print collections. The first purchase, made in 1962, secured for the museum its oldest work, a seven-part polyptych over 11 feet long: *Virgin and Child surrounded by Saints, Old Testament Prophets, and*

Angels.[248] This tempera panel painting is attributed to Ugolino da Siena, active from 1317 and one of the more distinguished followers of the great Trecento master Duccio, painter of the *Maestà* for the Siena Cathedral (MA 204).

Ugolino's altarpiece reflects the conventions of an earlier, hieratic tradition. The rigidity and frontality of the figures, the richly ornamented background of gold leaf, and the ensemble's overall iconic didacticism perpetuate aspects of late Byzantine style, modified by a suggestion of the linear rhythms of Gothic art. The work is in a good state of preservation; the materials used (cobalt, lapis lazuli, violet), bound to their support by the classic egg-yolk emulsion, have retained much of their original luster. In terms of quality, size, and completeness, the painting is matched in New England only by the five-panel altarpiece by Simone Martini in the Gardner Museum, Boston (MA 34).

Another devotional altarpiece, *The Madonna and Child with Four Angels*,[249] assigned on the basis of style to the Renaissance master Piero della Francesca (c. 1410–92), almost begs for comparison with the earlier Sienese example. Certain pictorial conventions have been adhered to: again, Mary and the Christ Child are the center of attention, but how differently the two artists have rendered them! Where Ugolino promotes ethereal/mystical sensations, Piero emphasizes physical presence (the qualities of weight, solidity, and mass) and intellectual clarity. The cessation of all movement, supported by Piero's blue-gray tonality into which even his reds are absorbed, projects an intense calm into the work. Swags stretch across two marble panels, one black with deep red veinings, the other the color of porphyry. The columns have some of the re-

248

249

silience of living figures, yet the figures themselves seem to vie with them in immobility. The artist's skillful handling of line and of soft light, blond and fresh, has enabled him to impart depth and form to every element of the composition. Contrast the four silent, full-modeled angels, standing firmly on the ground in a defined space, with the seraphs hovering restlessly in the spandrels of Ugolino's altarpiece. Working approximately 150 years later, Piero has imbued his design with an intense interest in the theoretical studies of perspective and geometry. His work is marked by deep understanding of the revolution in thought implicit in the Italian Renaissance.

No documents exist to uphold the panel's attribution to Piero, and it may not be entirely autographic. Moreover, while the picture seems to be complete in other respects, it may have been the central panel of a triptych. A shadow at bottom center, possibly cast by another column outside and to the left of the existing composition, supports this theory. An examination of the panel's edges might help solve the mystery, but this is not possible because the original poplar support was replaced by a composite panel in 1957.

Pietro Vannucci (1445–1523), called Perugino from the principal city of Umbria, was separated from Piero by a full generation. Though both were Umbrian by birth, Piero went to Florence for his training before returning to work in Arezzo and Urbino. These facts account for some of the differences evident in their work, but we may also assume a fundamental difference of temperament. Perugino was typically Umbrian in his gentleness. There is no hint of Piero's cool rigidity in the *Sepulcrum Christi* (inscribed with Perugino's name, but not otherwise documented as his work).²⁵⁰ What predominates is delicacy of sentiment and lusciousness of soft color. The iconography of this picture is unusual. Placed upright on a stone parapet or sepulcher cover and attended by young Nicodemus and the bearded Joseph of Arimathea, the dead Christ is the focus of attention. No ancillary figures complicate the scene; no outward movements distract the eye from the limp body. The subtle but engaging look of Nicodemus is enough to establish a psychological link with Joseph, and to invite the spectator to meditate on the

250

image of Christ as Redeemer. Thus, the sepulcher seems to become an altar with Christ offering the Eucharist. Quiet and contemplative, the privacy of the scene is accentuated by the placement of the figures close to the picture plane; its serenity is sustained by the artist's evocation of atmosphere more than by the rendering of sculptural form.

Such warm and suffused light and such softened contours and muted detail are salient aspects of Perugino's art, but here they somehow transcend the character of Perugino's known work (see page 381). Was his art ever so accomplished? We know that he was the chief master of Raphael (1483–1520). But what of the possible impact of a gifted pupil on his less-talented master? This phase in the careers of the two artists has been left in considerable shadow. The *Sepulcrum Christi* also clearly bears a close affinity to certain inventions of the Venetian Giovanni Bellini (c. 1430–1516)—the composition of the group, the quiet dignity of the figures, the soft modeling of the flesh, the poetic quality of the colors. Perugino is believed to have made a trip to Venice in 1494; some scholars list Venice as the actual provenance of the Clark painting. Could it represent Perugino's response to Bellini's types and forms? Surely, such mysteries add to the picture's allure.

Among the Flemish paintings here is the small *Portrait of Canon Gilles Joye*[251] by Hans Memling (c. 1430–94). It is only 15 inches high, including the engaged painted frame. Memling came from the Rhineland and studied in Brussels, perhaps with Roger van der Weyden. Settling in Bruges in 1466, he continued the tradition of Jan van Eyck to the end of the fifteenth century. One of the most admired portraitists of his day, his popularity was due to his ability to render physical likenesses and to capture something of the intellectual and spiritual character of his subjects. Though portrait panels like this were originally intended as covers or wings for small private altarpieces, during the second half of the fifteenth century the demand for portraits as independent works rapidly increased. It is likely that the portrait of Joye, an important prelate and musician at the court of Philip the Good, Duke of Burgundy, was commissioned for itself alone. The name of the sitter was established with the help of a small label discovered on the reverse of the panel, written in Latin and visible only with special photographic equipment. Though not contemporary with the portrait, the label and other related bits of information enabled scholars to trace the insigne

251

on the frame and the matching crest on one of the two rings on the canon's finger to make a positive identification.

If the impression of calm, cool piety in the Memling portrait is reinforced by the artist's highly controlled treatment of the painted surface, what a contrast this makes with the surface of our next painting! The *Portrait of a Man*,[252] traditionally called the Warrior, by Jean Honoré Fragonard (1732–1806), sparkles with the fast-moving rhythms associated with Rococo painting—and music. A strong and important work, 32 inches high, it is thought to be one of fourteen *têtes de fantaisie* completed c. 1764–69. A favorite of Louis XV and the French court, much in demand for his delightful vignettes of dalliance, his pastoral subjects, and his landscapes, Fragonard here proves himself capable of portraying powerful character. The high cheekbones, the angular face, the lips pursed pessimistically, the eyes gazing off into the distance, the hand extended to rest on the stone parapet, the flamboyant costume, the torso twisted arrogantly to one side—all these details would seem to indicate a specific person. Portrait or not, it is a masterpiece.

Color is of paramount importance here. Note how in the face, pure tones have been juxtaposed without transition, and how, when combined with Fragonard's virtuoso brushwork, a whole symphony of yellow, white, red, and orange is developed. Witness too the Hals-like square strokes that model the tip of the nose and the fingers—can one deny a premonition of what was still considered audacious in late nineteenth-century French painting?

The Clark Institute is fortunate in possessing a very fine example of the sort of English landscape painting that cast a spell on the French Impressionists during their formative years. Its full title is *Rockets and Blue Lights (Close at Hand) to Warn Steamboats of Shoal Waters*, and the artist is Joseph Mallord William Turner (1775–1851).[253] A late work of 1840, it stands in extreme contrast to his Dutch-inspired beginnings. Even at its size of 3 by 4 feet, it seems more daring than his enormous *Falls of the Rhine at Schaffhausen* of 1806, now in the Boston Museum of Fine Arts (MA 79). An artist of immense range, Turner often ran afoul of the arbiters of taste, producing works the nineteenth

252

253

century was not conditioned to accept or readily appreciate. Here his extraordinary imagination transforms a scene of storm-tossed ships into an abstraction of filmy shapes and glowing colors. Turner completed many such canvases, attempting to render in oil the same brilliance he achieved in watercolor. A contemporary, John Constable, described such works as "airy visions painted with tinted steam." Turner becomes virtually Expressionist in his vehemence of effect as he appeals straight to the viewer's sensibilities, setting them on edge.

Another picture whose composition and treatment point to the future is *Rouen Cathedral, the Facade in Sunlight*,[254] by Claude Monet (1840–1926). One of a series of twenty or more canvases completed between 1892 and 1894, it offers a view of the cathedral's west facade from a second-story shop window across the square. Notice the effects of cropping the motif at the top and both sides, and even at the bottom; witness the tensions that arise through the elimination of both sky and ground. Also, note the fusion of subject and art object, that is, the linkage between the complicated, shifting planes of the building's stone surface and its elaborate Gothic tracery and sculpture, and the thick layers of paint applied to the canvas. The paint itself collects light, reflects it, and casts small shadows.

The institute owns six other Monets, dating from five to thirty years earlier, all representative of the artist's Impressionist technique. But it is with the Rouen Cathedral series that Monet made his great breakthrough from Impressionist recording of visible nature to the transformation of objects into symbols of images of personal consciousness. To quote George Heard Hamilton, Director Emeritus of the institute, "Twenty moments represented by twenty views of Rouen are less views of the cathedral (one would have been sufficient for that), less even twenty moments in the going and coming of the light (which is an insignificant situation), than twenty episodes in Monet's private, perceptual life. They are twenty episodes in the history of his consciousness, and reveal a new psychic, rather than physical, reality."

Camille Pissarro's *River Oise near Pontoise*,[255] an early work of 1873, is charming in its simplicity and subtle in its combination of form and

255

254

atmosphere. Pissarro (1830–1903) was a much more traditional artist than Monet, his younger fellow Impressionist; yet under his brush the unromantic industrial outskirts of Paris become magical. This picture clearly reveals Pissarro's indebtedness to the landscapes of Corot, especially in the use of grays and gentle greens, in the relatively un-broken patches of color, and in the overall quiet modesty. The arrange-ment of small geometric units parallel to the picture plane, however, may herald the influence of Paul Cézanne, with whom Pissarro often painted at Pontoise in the 1870s.

Pierre August Renoir (1841–1919) began his career as a painter of porcelain in Limoges, a training that may have inclined him toward his light palette. He then studied with the Academician Gleyre in Paris. He exhibited in the Salon of 1864, but ten years later was among those organizing the rebellious first Impressionist exhibition. After trips to Algeria and Italy in 1881, his work began to diverge from that of his colleagues; his drawing became firmer and less spontaneous, his color more directed toward the creation of solid structure and form.

The institute is particularly rich in Renoirs, as the Clarks began to purchase his work while the artist was still unappreciated in Europe, and in one instance even before his death. From the thirty-seven paintings they collected we have selected a still life of onions on a table, painted in Naples in 1881. Though of small size, it manages to become the grand composition Renoir's later pearly-fleshed nudes merely aspire to. *Onions*[256] is a supreme example of the artist's gift as a colorist. All his joyous abandon, his subtlety in texture and movement, appear in this little masterpiece. Note how the pure reds and blues at the edge of the tablecloth are taken through myriad variations, even to form the dry, flaky skins of the vegetables. Such a work is a triumph of the human mind. As Walter Pater once said, the greatest painting aspires to music. Here the least promising of themes has become a symphonic tone poem. *Onions* was one of the first three Renoir purchases made by Mr. Clark and remained one of his favorites.

At one point Renoir, on being fitted with a new pair of glasses to correct his myopia, threw them to the floor and exclaimed: "Bon Dieu! Je vois comme Bouguereau!" Alas, the Academicians, notably William Adolphe Bouguereau (1825–1905), whom we next discuss, were the successful artists of their era, esteemed and at the height of their careers in the mid-to-late 1800s. Their Impressionist rivals, insisting on painting how and what they liked, were the butt of public scorn. Today the tables

256

are turned. Artists once admired are often later maligned, their work ironically eclipsed by what had been considered a sign of barbarism. The climate of opinion is changing again, but on the whole, previously valued Academic qualities are still scorned.

Representative Academic works obediently cater to pre-established theories of beauty, reality, composition, and color; their execution bears witness to endless training in the fields of historical research, anatomy, costume, and drawing from the nude. The original basis of the Academic system was sound; but for various reasons the program degenerated to a level of reducing painting to sterile repetition of formulae. With the onset of the twentieth century, it began to suffer a barrage of criticism, and works by the likes of Bouguereau, despite the fact that during the artists' lifetimes they were snapped up with enthusiasm, were dismissed as fit only for storage or barrooms—that is, until recent years.

No one genuinely interested in painting can deny admiration for such artists' technical aplomb. Their performance was truly staggering. Bouguereau was among the ablest practitioners of his craft; so clever, in fact, that his dexterity gained for him membership in what was dubbed "The School of the Invisible Brush-stroke." He had an avid interest in formal values. The composition of the Clark's notorious *Nymphs and Satyr*[257] (1873), nearly 9 feet high within its huge frame, is elaborately synthesized, all its elements tightly coordinated and yet stated with almost photographic precision. Color verges on the eerie as the whites of the flesh glimmer against the dark greenish shadows. It is hard indeed to accuse Bouguereau of having created something with merely the outer skin of art and none of its deeper qualities. Yet Pissarro, painting on the banks of the Oise in the same year, 1873, was light-years ahead of him artistically.

The Women of Amphissa[258] (1887) by Sir Lawrence Alma-Tadema (1836–1912) is another excellent example of the kind of large narrative pieces and scenes of exotic splendor or debauchery that were calculated both to satisfy the Academy's requirements and to titillate the bourgeois consumer. Drawing on Plutarch for his source material, Alma-Tadema painstakingly researched story and period detail to assure representational

257

authenticity. With all its Victorian histrionics, this work is a fetching depiction of the waking debauchees from Phocis encountering the kindness of the Amphissan women. The effects of light on marble and drapery are marvelous. Nevertheless, we have the jarring feeling that we are watching the artist's contemporaries posturing in togas. At the same time, we enjoy Alma-Tadema's joy in *painting*. Unlike Bouguereau, he did not hide his own process.

Winslow Homer (1836–1910) began his career in the heyday of huge landscape panoramas of the Hudson River School; while many of his contemporaries fled America for the Continent, searching for less "provincial" inspiration, he draw his material from the domestic American scene (CT 80). There is something astonishingly modern in Homer's work. Witness his *Sleigh Ride*,[259] a mysterious little picture of 1893 just over a foot high, similar in style to the great *West Wind* of 1891 at Andover (MA 18). Here we are aware of the artist's belief that lines, shapes, and colors can represent reality and at the same time convey meanings on their own. Homer's painting is wonderfully understated and reserved. His composition testifies to extremely careful planning; an effort to simplify, eliminate, and concentrate on large forms and movements is clear. There is an exquisite sense of balance—note how the diagonal of the snowbank forms a solid base for the entire design, how this playing-up of the great mound makes for a forceful statement about man, the elements, and nature. Unusual here is the accent on blues. The institute owns ten Homer oils (and many watercolors, too), but though *Sleigh Ride* is one of the few small ones, it is surely the most poetic of them all.

John Singer Sargent (1856–1925) was an international figure. He commuted constantly across the Atlantic, painting portraits of the rich

258

259

and influential in a manner reminiscent of Velázquez peppered with the brio of a Sir Thomas Lawrence (see CT 56). As much at home in Paris, London, or Florence as in Boston, Sargent, like many artists before him, harbored a weakness for the magic city of Venice. He was forever fascinated by its unique combination of water and architecture and its endless subtleties of light. The actual location of his gemlike *Venetian Interior*[260] is unknown; the dim hall could be the loggia of many a shabby Renaissance palazzo. A spear of light cuts in to warm the bleak dampness. In the foreground, girls gossip. It is a quiet, mundane scene; but the occasional red accents enliven an overall somberness. The sharply receding perspective lends the picture an evocative air of mystery. Sargent was only twenty-six when he painted it in 1882, but it is in his finest vein, without the showiness of *El Jaleo* (MA 51), of the same year.

We turn now to two of the institute's most outstanding portraits. Hilaire-Germain-Edgar Degas (1834–1917) was an artist of varied subjects. His motifs, drawn largely from urban life, included ballet dancers, women bathing, and racehorses; but it was as a portraitist that he reached his greatest heights. The sitter in *Portrait of a Man*[261] has not been identified, but the date of the painting is roughly 1881–85. The beauty of the work lies first of all in the drawing, as seen, for example, in the crisp linear accents about the eyes and at the neck. The girth of the figure and the forceful structure of the skull are established with a minimum of effort. The man's bulk is bolstered comfortably at the right, and as our eye travels to the left, the broadly curved forms gradually give way to angular ones. Especially remarkable is the painting of the hands. A subtle pink at the far left lends its echoes to the flesh tones and the background. Degas has not sought to flatter his subject; his aim was not to provide a pretty picture, but to render the truth as he saw it.

The institute is rich in Degas works: oils, drawings, pastels, and bronze casts made after his death from wax figures of dancers and horses, used by him in developing his compositions on these themes. In addition, there is his celebrated *Little Dancer, Age Fourteen*, 39 inches

260

261

high, of which there are several casts. We reproduce and discuss the one at the Shelburne Museum, Vermont (VT 23).

Henri de Toulouse-Lautrec's *Portrait of Dr. Jules-Emile Péan*[262] (1891) provides us with another occasion where the artist has turned in unexpected directions for his inspiration. Best known for his vivid portrayals of Parisian nightlife—for cabaret performers, dance hall habitués, nudes, ladies of the evening—Toulouse-Lautrec (1864–1901) has selected as his subject an outstanding Paris surgeon performing an operation (a resection of the maxilla). Péan, who scorned the usual clinical attire, is shown with a napkin tied about his neck. A versatile man, he was one of the founders of modern gynecological surgery, and he designed the arterial clamp being used in our picture. At the right an assistant administers ether. Painted on paperboard in oil mixed with turpentine, this apparent sketch projects enormous power. We find an almost Expressionist violence here, a totally new use of the broken colors of Impressionism; but these only accentuate the drawing, which closely resembles some of the most advanced work of Daumier. Note how a few flourishes suggest the existence of a background.

Like Vincent van Gogh, Toulouse-Lautrec went to Paris to study with the Impressionists, became their apt pupil, and then found his own artistic direction. Of his four splendid paintings in the institute, two are "early" (c. 1885)—but at sixteen he was already well launched—and two come from the final decade of his meteoric career. We may contrast the early half-length *Carmen* with *Jane Avril*, or *The Studio* with the Péan portrait just discussed. Within each pair the composition is almost identical, but the scale, the handling of the paint, and the controlling conception are vastly different.

The Clarks were avid collectors of master drawings, but until the publication of a superb two-volume catalogue, under the direction of Professor Havercamp-Begemann of Yale University (Yale University Press, 1964), the extent and quality of the collection were little known. Among the earlier examples, consider a page of *Sketches of Animals and Landscapes*[263] by Albrecht Dürer (1471–1528), in pen and ink

262

263

and colored washes. Six animals and two landscapes fill the sheet, vying for our attention. The identification of the landscapes is uncertain, but it is thought that Dürer drew the lynx, the chamois, the baboon, and the three lions at the zoological gardens in Brussels on a visit there in 1521. The grouping of the figures is unusual and would have resulted in a confusing page had not the artist anchored each image to its own ground plane and viewed each from different levels and distances. The crisp quality of Dürer's line also lends clarity. Its range is amazing: from the lion's rippling mane to the lynx's dagger-pointed ears.

In 1926, Mr. Clark purchased a superb drawing by Peter Paul Rubens (1577–1640), a brown ink-brush *Study of Thomas Howard, Earl of Arundel*,[264] for the portrait now in the Gardner Museum, Boston (MA 47). While its main purpose was apparently to fix the composition of the final oil, what strikes us is the spirited description of this eminent connoisseur and antiquarian. Working quickly from life, Rubens made summary use of his medium. A few strokes sufficed to outline costume and suggest surroundings; a slight turn of the body was enough to energize it. Our attention is riveted by the face, where the artist has detailed an imposing demeanor, accentuating the unruly curl of the mustache, the flare of the nostrils, and the penetrating stare. It is interesting to compare the Clark drawing with the finished portrait, where we see a more introverted man whose features and expression are less subjected to Rubens's modifications. Both versions almost certainly date from 1629, when Rubens was in London designing the Whitehall Palace ceiling (CT 52). According to the eminent Rubens scholar Professor Julius S. Held, the drawing is a rarity in the artist's oeuvre; such elaborate retouching in ink is most unusual.

Rubens exerted a strong influence on our next master draftsman, Antoine Watteau (1684–1721), especially in his facility for capturing gesture and attitude with the merest suggestion of line. In Watteau's *Studies of a Flutist and Two Women*,[265] quick delicate strokes, not long contours, build up the images of the flutist (dressed in what resembles the sixteenth-century costume of the Comédie Italienne) and two women. The profile of the older one is set against the three-quarter view of her lovely young companion. Such drawings combine two major themes in Watteau's art—modest femininity and music. We quickly recognize the

264

265

hand of the painter of the celebrated *fêtes galantes*, dreamworlds replete with the pleasures of the theater, music, dance, and a life of elegance. Watteau's extreme sensitivity to pose and his feeling for textures are everywhere in evidence in the Clark drawing. He used only red, black, and white chalks here, but the colorism he has created almost rivals that of a Degas pastel.

In *Hagar and Ishmael in the Wilderness*,[266] by Giovanni Battista Tiepolo (1696–1770), swift and bold pen lines are applied over an extremely summary chalk underdrawing and touched lightly with dark and paler brown wash. All these magical marks combine with large areas of blank paper to strike a sensitive balance between the suggestion and the full realization of form. Tiepolo manages to introduce here some of the delicate luminosity and airy perspectives of his great ceiling decorations and allegorical compositions (see MA 75). This sketch has not been connected with any known painting, but the theme is a favorite one in Tiepolo's vast oeuvre.

Our last selection, *Study for "La Source,"*[267] in black-and-white chalk on blue-gray paper, is by Pierre Paul Prud'hon (1758–1823). While it may seem related to those Academic nineteenth-century paintings we have already discussed, it truly reflects the tenets espoused by the academies before their takeover by the bourgeoisie. We sense here that Prud'hon has achieved much more than a faithful copy of a female nude. The purpose of the study may have been a preparation for an official commission involving a monumental column with allegorical figures of the rivers Rhine, Po, Nile, and Danube at its foot. The nude is appropriately statuesque. Prud'hon's expert use of his medium, with the blue-gray paper becoming the middle value of the modeling from light to dark, imparts a softness to the figure, reminiscent of Correggio. The result is a suggestion of not-so-innocent sensuality.

An introduction to the Clark Art Institute should not conclude without mention of its very distinguished collection of silver. Spanning nearly five centuries, it includes examples by many world-renowned metalsmiths, with English artisans predominating. Paul de Lamerie (1688–1751) heads the list. Apparently, the Clarks were as fond of his work as they were of Renoir's.

266   267

Williams College Museum of Art

Location: Opposite the college chapel on Main St. (Route 2)
Hours: Academic year, Mon.-Fri. 9-5, Sat., Sun. 1-5; summer, 1-5 daily; closed legal and college holidays
Admission: Free

The museum was founded in 1926 by Karl E. Weston, first chairman of the Williams College department of art. On his initiative Lawrence Hall, the former college library, was renovated for its new function, and classrooms and additional gallery space were provided in a new rear wing. The original building, designed in 1846 by Thomas Tefft of Providence, is a brick octagon containing on its upper floor a handsome Ionic rotunda in Greek Revival style. This was the gift, at a cost of nine thousand dollars, of Amos Lawrence, Boston manufacturer, founder of Lawrence, Mass., and a major benefactor of the college through his great friendship with President Mark Hopkins. His full-length portrait, in Paisley dressing gown, was delivered to the college in 1846. Painted by Chester Harding (1792–1866), it is an exact replica of the portrait now in the National Gallery, Washington—although the unlikely possibility exists that the Williams version came first.

Wings along the Main Street front were added in 1890, and in 1938 an addition on the west side provided two large galleries, the Edwin Howland Blashfield Room (the gift of his heirs along with examples of the artist's work) and the George Alfred Cluett Room (the gift of an alumnus-collector of Spanish painting and furniture). Plans for extensive further additions and renovations are well advanced as of this writing.

Like other college museums, Williams's is an indispensable asset to instruction in art history and the practice of art. During the college year there are frequently changing temporary exhibitions. The permanent collection, including some one thousand prints and a growing corpus of photographs by outstanding masters, is being developed to provide a broad coverage of world art in original examples. Since the impressive holdings of the Clark Art Institute are for the most part limited to European and American art and to the period 1300–1900, the college's collections of Ancient, medieval, contemporary, and non-Western art provide an important complement to them.

Sculpture is especially well represented in the Williams museum. In addition to the examples discussed below there are Greek and Roman terra-cottas, bronzes, and small marbles (primarily the gift of the family of Charles B. Bolles-Rogers); important examples of Romanesque and Gothic stone sculpture and silversmith work; a life-size fifteenth-century Italian *Madonna* in polychromed wood; Baroque and Rococo bronzes and wood sculpture; nineteenth-century bronzes by Barye (see VT 1), Meunier, Rodin (head of the *Naked Balzac*, RI 23), and Saint-Gaudens (small replica of *The Puritan* at Springfield [MA 209]); and twentieth-century examples by Bourdelle, Maillol, Duchamp-Villon, David Smith, Ferber, and Rickey. A selection from the museum's non-Western sculpture is discussed below.

Among the first works of art given to the college are two large Assyrian reliefs from the Palace of Ashurnazirpal II, near Nineveh. These were shipped by camelback in the 1850s to a Mediterranean port and thence by sea to Boston—and thence across the state of Massachusetts long before the construction of the Hoosac Tunnel. They were the gift of a missionary alumnus of the college, the Reverend Dwight W. Marsh, who wrote of his hopes that "students who look upon the relics of the past may think wisely of time & be led to take a deeper interest in the efforts to rescue the degraded from the beastliness of their present life. . . . May they remember that God is older than the ages— that the glorious future of America is not eternity." The reliefs are similar to those received at the same time by other New England colleges; our discussion of them will be found in the entry for Amherst College (MA I).

The primary examples of Greek and Roman marble sculpture at Williams are a *Hellenistic Head*,**268** presumably of Zeus, dating from about 50 B.C., and a headless Roman male, clad in toga, tunic, ankle gear, and boots, probably from the first century A.D. The bearded Greek head, probably originating from the Syro-Phoenician coast, reflects the style and workmanship characteristic of a very late phase of Hellenistic art. The deep undercutting and fluidity of forms of such examples have been called Baroque because of their similarity to the works of seventeenth-century sculptors like Bernini (see MA 121). Indeed, it is possible that there was some recutting about the mouth in Bernini's own time.

268

Two more heads, an ancient *Roman Mosaic*[269] and a *Byzantine Fresco*,[270] provide an unusual opportunity to contrast Western and Near Eastern traditions of representation. The mosaic, probably of an enemy warrior from the North (note his blond hair), is executed in a manner strongly influenced by the illusionist tendencies of Roman painting. Its relatively late date of c. A.D. 300 is suggested by the rather large stones with which it is composed (Pompeiian mosaic tesserae are extremely small). The image is strongly sculptural in effect: the three-quarters pose and the modulations of shadow seem to mold space behind the head. The diagonal tilt, the flying hair, the set of the eyes, and the curve of the mouth all suggest action, and thereby the sense of a moment in time. The concern for physical mass, for the pull of gravity, and for the organic resilience of the human figure is evident—nearly a thousand years after its inception in ancient Greece.

The Byzantine fresco fragment, which includes a small portion of the Saint's halo at the right, comes from a church in Jerusalem and may date from as late as the 1640s. Here an austere frontality rules, held fast by the perpendicular axis. There is a small amount of modeling by shading, but thick dark outlines—all in the same plane—dominate. Shadows under the eyes are stark flat triangles, and the whites are perfect circles. Such simplification of forms accounts for the work's special appeal to twentieth-century taste. (Three other heads from the same source are in America: two in the Museum of Fine Arts, Boston, and one in the California Palace of the Legion of Honor, San Francisco.)

On a basis of quality, the fifteenth-century Franco-Flemish alabaster figure of *St. John Evangelist*[271] is surely one of the museum's finest treasures. Brownish-warm in tone, elegant in shape, fluid in cascades of soft drapery, the Saint projects an intense spirituality as he gazes up-

269

270

271

ward. The throat with its prominent Adam's apple framed by a *V* of straining muscles is remarkably expressive; in profile, the sequence from chest to chin develops a powerful rhythm. From the rear, all is columnar grace and peace save for the hunched shoulders and the turn of the head. While the sculptor was not unaware of classical understanding of organic anatomy as retrieved from antiquity by the Italian Renaissance, he clearly thought in terms of a limited frontal view. The rear view, however beautiful, may never have been intended to be seen; the figure probably formed part of a Crucifixion assemblage placed against a back plane of stone. For a contrast in sculptural intention, note in the draped Roman statue, mentioned above, how the folds wind around to the front, making the figure an organic whole. A large group of alabaster sculptures, generally similar in style to our *St. John Evangelist* and found in museums around the Western world, is often assigned to an itinerant artist known as the Rimini Master because of a Crucifixion altar originating in that Italian town and now in the sculpture museum of Frankfurt-am-Main. Since this altar is missing its required St. John, some scholars have suggested that our figure actually belonged to it. Experts who have seen the original in the Williams Museum, however, agree that its quality is much superior. Thus the hypersensitive Master of the Williams College *St. John Evangelist* still lacks a more definitive name. His style is clearly not Italianate; analogous works suggest an origin in the lower Rhenish region of France or Flanders, and a date c. 1430. Comparison with the Busch-Reisinger Museum's Austrian *Madonna and Child on a Crescent Moon* (MA 99), also c. 1430, indicates that our sculptor was more attuned to the influence of the Italian Renaissance.

Williams's representation of Florentine and Roman Renaissance art cannot match that of the Clark Art Institute, but two prints of exceptional importance offer a most useful complement: the great engraving of *The Entombment* by Andrea Mantegna (strongly influenced by Donatello's sculpture at Padua and subsequently influencing both Raphael and Rembrandt), and Ugo da Carpi's chiaroscuro woodcut of *Diogenes* (after a lost drawing by Parmigianino inspired by the art of Michelangelo).

A *Millefleurs Tapestry* measuring about 8 by 7 feet, replete with falcons, rabbits, a lion, a stag, and a unicorn, appears to be the work of Flemish craftsmen working in the Loire Valley area. Its date of c. 1510–25 reminds us that in the "Gothick North" the incursions of the Italian Renaissance were both gradual and sporadic.

The gift of George Alfred Cluett included fine paintings and furniture from Spain and Spanish-owned Naples. Further acquisitions have resulted in the museum's owning the leading collection of Spanish art before Goya in New England outside the major cities.

Francisco Pacheco, the master and father-in-law of Velázquez, proves himself a true Spaniard with his portrait, signed and dated 1626, of an unidentified *Knight of the Order of Santiago*.[272] Adjectives that come to mind to describe its Spanish character include austere, precise, reserved, astringent, and above all dignified. Much of this flavor passed on to the young Velázquez, as seen in his *Portrait of Luis de Góngora*, in the Boston Museum of Fine Arts (MA 72). Note how Pacheco has focused attention on the knight's face by the accent of the white collar, and on his bleak gaze through a calculated emphasis on his eyeglasses.

Though no document supports a traditional attribution to Juan de Valdés Leal (1622–90), a chief painter at Seville during Spain's Golden Age, the large *Annunciation*,[273] an oil nearly 6 feet high, reflects his masterly blend of the Baroque action of Rubens and Bernini with the Venetian technique of Titian and Tintoretto. It is not often in New England that we can experience so completely the spirit of the Baroque as here through the dark colors, dramatic lighting, plunging diagonals, and energetic action of this picture.

Two other Baroque painters in the museum's collection, both active in Naples and both influenced by Caravaggio (see CT 12), offer an opportunity to contrast differing cultural heritages: Jusepe de Ribera (1591–1652) and Massimo Stanzione (1585–1656). Archrivals and almost exact contemporaries, Ribera (*The Executioner*) came from Spain, worked for the local viceroys, and was twice visited by Velázquez, while the Italian Stanzione (*St. John Evangelist Exorcising a Demon from the Cup*) trained in Rome under the strong influence of the Carracci and Guido Reni. We find tautly restrained violence in the former, operatic sentiment in the latter.

Our final selection from the Spanish pictures is an impressive *Still Life*[274] of c. 1626 measuring 32½ by 50½ inches. It is signed by a leading master of this genre, Juan van der Hamen y León (1591–1631). Born of Flemish parents in Madrid, he spent his life there and became a painter at the court as well as a member of the palace bodyguard. Although he resented being praised only for his still lifes, they were, and continue to be, in great demand. Flemish still lifes (such as Frans

272

273

274

Snyders's at Amherst College, MA 6) are earthier and more festive than Spanish ones, which tend to be somber in tone and, despite their intense realism, as abstract in form as Picasso's of 1908/09. Van der Hamen lit his compositions theatrically from the left side into a black depth. Those of the early 1620s have a less cohesive arrangement than the later ones, such as the Williams example. Here much of the weight is shifted to one side with the balance redressed by placing the elements on large gray plinths. All of them cast a spell of silence.

Through the bequest of Charles M. Davenport, of Boston, the museum acquired an extensive collection of Early American furniture and British and American portraits. Other acquisitions make it possible to compare in fine examples of almost the same year the Englishness of Thomas Gainsborough (*Robert Butcher*, variant in the Prado) with the Colonial stamp of John Singleton Copley (*Reverend Samuel Cooper*, c. 1770, earlier variant in the Emerson House, Concord), and to compare Copley with the itinerant Connecticut painter William Jennys (*Colonel Benjamin Simonds* of Williamstown, signed and dated 1796—see the discussion of this artist in the sections on the Connecticut Historical Society at Hartford and the Lyman Allyn Museum at New London, CT 87). Reynolds, Romney, Raeburn, and Gilbert Stuart are also well represented.

Nineteenth-century paintings seen here include Kensett's *View of Lake George*, two watercolors by Homer, one from the key year 1880 (see ME 31), an Eakins portrait of the music critic *John Neil Fort*, several landscapes by George Inness, fool-the-eye still lifes by Harnett and Peto, a huge *Niagara Falls* by William Morris Hunt, and an 1877 *Pontoise, on the Banks of the Oise*, by Camille Pissarro (see MA 255). Among twentieth-century American watercolorists, the museum boasts three by Maurice Prendergast, four by John Marin, and six by Charles Demuth.

Off York Island, Maine[275] is a powerful and explosive work of Marin's maturity (1922). A certain viscosity pervades it, suggesting an intention to carry the liquid medium into the more symphonic effects of oil painting. This example stands in greatest contrast to Colby College's *Brooklyn Bridge*, of 1912 (ME 38).

"John Marin and I drew our inspiration from the same source, French Modernism. He brought his up in buckets and spilt much along the way. I dipped mine out with a teaspoon, but I never spilled a drop."

275

That this oft-quoted statement was actually made by Charles Demuth
(1883–1935) has been questioned; but authentic or not, it is apposite.
It has the stamp of Demuth's own art: crisp, elegant, cool. His variant
of Cubism, developed from study in Paris in the crucial years 1912–14,
departed widely from the somber tone of the formal discipline invented
by Picasso and Braque. The museum's six watercolors range in date
from 1914 to Demuth's last years. *Trees and Barns, Bermuda*[276] (1917)
marks the artist at the height of his powers, and is radically different
from the loose fluid handling of the medium that typified the preceding
years. Note the precision of the finely penciled contours, over which
the thin washes of watercolor were laid, then touched with blotting
paper to absorb the moisture and to produce Demuth's special delicacy of
texture in a fragile tracery.

Cubist vocabulary is also evident in Lyonel Feininger's oil painting
Mill in Autumn[277] (1932). Feininger's style evolved during visits to
Paris between 1906 and 1911 from exposure to emergent Cubism, which
he tempered with the Orphist color of Robert Delaunay and the angularities of Italian Futurist painting. Connections with the tradition of
German Romantic landscape painting have also been proposed. In *Mill
in Autumn*, the accent is less upon forms or motifs than upon a subtle,
poetic, very personal depiction of a season. Rich browns, ashen whites,
and muted bluish greens pervade the work, lending it a melancholy
grace accentuated by the rhythmic sweep of the mill vanes.

Mill in Autumn came to the museum in 1977 with the bequest of a
large number of American paintings, drawings, and sculptures from
Lawrence H. Bloedel, whose collection was divided equally between
Williams College and the Whitney Museum of American Art, New
York. Another masterwork in the Bloedel bequest is *Morning in a
City*,[278] by Edward Hopper (1882–1967). Signed in 1944 and measuring 4 by 5 feet, it has been widely exhibited in the United States as
well as at the Ninth Bienal at São Paolo, Brazil; and it is generally
acknowledged as one of Hopper's major paintings. Here we find his
poetic realism expressed through a remarkable economy of statement.
His detached view of a woman facing another day captures the loneliness

276

277

of the person in a city of anonymous millions; and it imparts much of the artist's own vision of the American environment. Plain and nude, the woman stands solid and silent in a cramped bare room. The black windows opposite reveal no inhabitant. Stark planes, sunlight cutting into the room to mold shapes with strong color value—everything is calculated to transform the facts of routine existence into something universal.

Modern art is well represented in the museum, not only by the work of sculptors already mentioned, but by drawings and prints and by the paintings of such leading figures as de Chirico, Léger, Miró, Tanguy, and Matta, and by a series of boxes and collages by Joseph Cornell, the gift of his sister, Mrs. John A. Benton. One of the finest examples of post–Second World War Abstract Expressionism is *Black and White*,[279] a collage and oil by Franz Kline (1910–62). Concentrated on a sheet of paper less than a foot high, this work of c. 1958 can stand comparison with the artist's best large canvases (see MA 162). *Black and White* projects a sense of vast scale and an almost brutal power. Note the force of the black diagonals, the drag and sputter of paint from a dry brush, the range of textures in the sparingly applied collage of papers—torn edges, a sparkle from grains of sand—and the unexpected touches of color that energize the whole surface.

As in Kline's collage, much of the appeal of *Valor*,[280] an elegant sculpture by the Japanese Masayuki Nagare (born 1923) hinges on the

278

279

280

artist's sensitivity to his chosen medium. Carefully polishing Swedish
black granite to a high sheen, leaving only a few areas roughly chiseled
—as if eroded—Nagare created surface contrasts that manage to invest
the piece with a living presence. The unfinished look also injects an
element of tension in this age of machine tooling and plastics. The date
is 1967. At the base a human face is suggested clearly enough to
transform the major element above into a black headdress like those
worn by Japanese heroes of long ago (see MA 96). Our first impression
of this element is also relevant: that it suggests the blade of a ritual
sword. As in the work of Isamu Noguchi (see ME 45), the influence
of Brancusi (see CT 68) is strong here.

The collection of Oriental art, while small, has distinguished examples
of Indian sculpture, Moghul painting, a superb Buddha head in stone
from the T'ang dynasty (on indefinite loan from the Clark Art Institute), and a rare gilt-bronze *Seated Vairocana* (the central principle
of later Buddhist cosmology) from the Yüan dynasty (1279–1368) of
the Mongol Kingdom. This piece, only a foot high, is another example
—with Kline's collage—of majestic power achieved in a small compass.
The Williams bronze makes an interesting comparison with the colossal
Japanese Sun Buddha at Providence (RI 28). It was shown at Cleveland and at Asia House, New York, in the exhibition "Chinese Art
under the Mongols" (Cleveland: Cleveland Museum of Art, 1968,
number 13 of the catalogue).

Perhaps the finest of the museum's Far Eastern works is the sandstone
Female Divinity[281] from Koh-Ker, Cambodia, early tenth century, some
three centuries before the celebrated sculptures of Angkor Wat. Three
feet high, the headless figure is wonderfully restrained and simplified,
as in the subtlest columnar draped figures of early Archaic Greece. It
differs strikingly from Indian images, with their full sensuous forms,
deeply convex surfaces, and often provocative postures (see MA 90).
In the same way it contrasts with the work of Gaston Lachaise (1882–
1935), who was inspired by the lush female images of prehistory and
by Indian temple sculpture as well. The museum's bronze *Torso*,[282]

281

282

from the Bloedel bequest, is a relatively early work derived from Lachaise's first life-size female figure, *Elevation* (a cast in the Whitney Museum, New York). There is nothing titillating or lascivious here, only an earthy fervor steeped in the exaggerations and distortions of the art of bygone ages. Observe the flowing rhythms evident throughout, the upward lift that starts from the knees, whether from front or back view, and the solidity of the modeling. One's first impression that the woman is fat is quickly dispelled; on the contrary, she is abundant. The breasts are full but firm, the buttocks narrow and spare. How powerful are the empty shapes between each upper arm and swelling hip!

For further information on works in the museum, see my *Handbook to the Collection*, published by Williams College in 1978, with over seventy discussed and illustrated.

In addition to the Clark Art Institute and the Williams College Museum of Art, Williamstown is blessed with the leading collection of rare books and manuscripts in any *college* in the nation. The Chapin collection is housed in Stetson Hall, once the college library and now a branch of the new Sawyer Library. The manuscripts range from Egyptian papyri to illuminated medieval and Renaissance volumes. The collection of incunabula is extensive, and it includes a fifteenth-century block book and the complete woodcut *Apocalypse* by Albrecht Dürer. There is also the complete *Book of Job*, as engraved by William Blake. Modern typography and book illustration are well represented through recent gifts. As in most libraries of this kind, Piranesi is in abundance, but not all of them have Audubon's elephant portfolios, or the great series of reproductions of Holbein drawings at Windsor Castle.

American Antiquarian Society

Location: 185 Salisbury Street
Hours: Mon.-Fri. 9-5, except on legal holidays
Admission: Free. Ⓗ

Founded in 1812 by Isaiah Thomas, this was the first national historical society to be established in the United States. It owns the largest collection of printed materials relating to American history and culture up to the year 1877. This cutoff date also applies to its art collections, which include some ten thousand prints, thirty-five thousand book plates, a few very impressive pieces of furniture, and—within the purview of this book—over 150 oil portraits and miniatures. An illustrated brochure published by the society in 1970 on the portraits and furniture, written by two experts, Louissa Dresser and Wendell Garrett, is highly recommended. Visitors interested in early American music may wish to know that the society also owns sixty-five thousand examples of sheet music.

The *Portrait of Hannah Bush*,[283] signed "M'Kay" and dated 1791, measuring 36 by 30 inches, will not soon be forgotten. While the portrait of her husband, John, likewise signed and dated, has no such monumental construction to fill the top of the composition, it is equally intense. Little is known about M'Kay or MacKay (for *both* versions appear in signatures on the husband's portrait). The only other surviving work of this rugged artist is a portrait (signed "MacKay" and dated 1791—it would be hazardous to call that his vintage year) in the Garbisch collection at the National Gallery, Washington. All three portraits were presumably painted in New York, where John Bush had moved from Worcester at an early age, to become a broker. There, a certain John M'Kay, "painter and glazier, 10 Warren" appears in the city directory for 1795; but this M'Kay is not necessarily the painter of the Bush portraits. The meticulous detail and sharp observation seen in Hannah's portrait are so much in the tradition of the anonymous Freake

283

portraits in the Worcester Art Museum (MA 303) that it is hard to believe a gap of some 120 years separates them. Like Mrs. Freake, Hannah Bush manages to emerge as a personality from the multiple details that encase her. Despite such attractions as her vast white bonnet with its bows and loops and its clawlike termination, and the long journey of the black ribbon that holds a miniature of her husband, her emergence is something of a triumph. The whole picture is a symphony of salmon reds, pinks, and grays. As to Hannah's age, in Early American portraiture one soon gets used to surprises, forgetting that life was hard: she was twenty-six. When her portrait was shown at the Metropolitan Museum of Art in 1939 ("Life in America," number 44 of the catalogue), it was accompanied by the following verses, published in *The Universal Magazine* in 1768—not entirely appropriate, but surely worth reproducing:

> When he views your tresses thin
> Tortured by some French *friseur*,
> Horsehair, hemp and wool within
> Garnished with a di'mond skewer,
>
> When he scents the mingled steam
> Which your plaster'd heads are rich in,
> Lard and meal and clouted cream,
> Can he love a walking-kitchen?

The stern *Portrait of Isaiah Thomas*[284] was painted in 1818 by Ethan Allen Greenwood (1779–1856). It was bequeathed by Thomas himself, who not only founded the society but was its first president, from 1812 to his death in 1831. The portrait, in oil on wood panel 32 by 26 inches, shows him at the age of sixty-nine. Printer, publisher, and bookseller, Isaiah Thomas played an important role in the American Revolution. In its early stages he made his newspaper, the *Massachusetts Spy*, the voice of the Whig party. Couriers of the Committee on Correspondence distributed it from Quebec to Savannah. Just before the battles of Lexington and Concord he managed to move his press from Boston to Worcester—and the Antiquarian Society still preserves it. His desire to keep a record of the Revolution for posterity led to his founding of the society. His portrait is in the tradition of Gilbert Stuart's *Thomas Jefferson* (ME 13), with the obligatory column and red curtain, but the

284

sharp delineation of the strong features has a more incisive American flavor.

Among other portraits are examples by Thomas Smith (see MA 304), *Peter Pelham* (the master of Copley), Copley himself, and Winthrop Chandler.

The present building, dating from 1909, is by Winslow, Bigelow, Wadsworth and (Richard Clipston) Sturgis of Boston, with a 1972 addition by Shepley, Bulfinch, Richardson, and Abbot. (How the great Boston names perpetuate themselves!). The spacious Antiquarian Hall, with its surrounding balcony, is a handsome setting for the varied historical and artistic exhibits.

The John Woodman Higgins Armory

Location: 100 Barber Ave. (off Route 12, north of the city, east of the north end of Indian Lake)
Hours: Tues.-Fri. 9-4, Sat. 10-3, Sun. 1-5; closed national holidays
Admission: Charged. Ⓗ

This museum of metal craftsmanship opened to the public in 1931. It was founded by John Woodman Higgins, chairman of the Worcester Pressed Steel Company, who served as its president from 1910 to 1950. Chartered as a nonprofit educational institution, it is devoted to the history of the world's steel industry from its origins in the Bronze and Iron ages to modern times. The building itself is of open steel and glass construction.

Its collection of medieval armor has earned the museum worldwide fame. The exhibits also contain armor of all periods, and, more generally, fine metalwork from earliest times. In addition, there are a library, an armorer's workshop, a display of stained glass contemporary with the great age of armor making, and a number of paintings and tapestries with related subjects. One of the paintings, *The Forge of Vulcan*, is by Jan Brueghel (1568–1625), one of the sons of Pieter Brueghel the Elder (see M E 8).

The magnificent array of suits of armor occupies a hall of Gothic style hung with appropriate banners and weapons.[285] An armored dog guards the central passage. Throughout, the emphasis naturally falls on functional beauty. While any beautiful object may be said to serve a function —to refresh the spirit and to stimulate the imagination—there is no necessary conflict between such an intention and that of serving a more practical end. Anyone who has visited Carcassonne or a modern warship will have already discovered this truth.

One of the rarest and most beautifully fashioned suits of armor in the

285

collection is of Nuremberg make, about 1520. It is of the type associated with the Emperor Maximilian I. The flutings, or corrugations, add to the strength of the armor without adding to its weight. At the time this was a very practical consideration, because as firearms improved, armor had to become heavier. Carried at several points of the body, the weight is well distributed. The lance rest appears by the right arm. The back plate, gauntlets, and elbows are stamped with the mark of the Nuremberg guild. The suit is etched with birds and rustic persons in contemporary costume. The process of etching designs on armor led to printmaking, first from an iron plate, and later from a copper one. Albrecht Dürer of Nuremberg, one of the first etchers, made a few prints from iron plates early in the sixteenth century.

Maximilian was a great exponent of the joust. While this suit was designed primarily for such a purpose, it could also be used in unmounted battle. The square toes were much better for walking than the long pointed ones of earlier Gothic suits.

Worcester Art Museum

Location: 55 Salisbury Street. Parking nearby

Telephone: (617) 752-4678

Hours: Tues.-Sat. 10-5, Sun. 2-5; closed July 4, Thanksgiving, Christmas, and New Year's Day

Admission: Charged, except Wed. Ⓗ but phone ahead

The Worcester Art Museum has long enjoyed the reputation of being one of the finest small museums in America. The visitor will soon discover, however, that "small" is a relative term, for the Worcester Museum is small only in comparison to the great metropolitan treasure houses. After the Boston Museum of Fine Arts, its position as the second largest art museum in New England is challenged only by those of Hartford, Providence, and of Harvard and Yale universities. The Gardner Museum in Boston has a greater concentration of masterpieces, but its range is much more limited.

Founded by Stephen Salisbury III in 1896, the museum opened its original building two years later. Major additions were constructed in 1921, 1933, and 1970. The latest of these includes facilities for the museum's professional art school and studio areas for art classes for all ages. The collections span fifty centuries of world art, and works in all media. The museum issues a bulletin and an illustrated handbook is available.

From the many fine examples of ancient art at Worcester exhibited on the ground floor to the right of the Salisbury Street entrance I have selected two limestone figures, a life-size *Female Torso*[286] of the Egyptian Fifth Dynasty, c. 2440 B.C., and a foot-high *Male Statuette*[287] of the early dynastic period of Sumerian civilization (3000–2500 B.C.).

287

286

The latter was found at Khafaje, northeast of Baghdad, by an expedition from the University of Pennsylvania. The two make an interesting comparison, particularly when we realize that they may have been carved —in the very round numbers of ancient history—at about the same time. Both are "Archaic" in their rigid frontality and their minimal undercutting. But here the similarity ends, and one quickly learns that general terms like "Archaic" can be very misleading. In the company of the dwarflike Sumerian deity, the Egyptian torso looks almost Greek in the push of the forms through the sheath of clothing, and in the subtle transitions of modeling. It must be pointed out, however, that if the head and feet were not missing the whole effect of the statue would be more rigid than it is now. Furthermore, the Egyptian carver was less bound by convention in representing the female figure than the male, that is, when he represented, as here, a person of high station. (Compare the Boston group, MA 53; the Worcester figure undoubtedly belonged to a similar one.) To give the face of his statuette a more striking expression, the Sumerian artist carved the eyeballs separately and fixed them into the sockets. One is missing.

These two figures should also be compared with a small (6-inch) marble fertility figure from the Cycladic Islands, dating from c. 2000 B.C. We have discussed this aboriginal Greek art in the large (4-foot) example at Boston (MA 56), which is much more boyish in form than Worcester's and more svelte in execution. Such figures, almost on tiptoe with knees slightly bent and arms tightly clasped, convey a feeling of resilience that brings the stone to life, however schematic the anatomy. The Egyptian and Sumerian examples cannot match them in vitality.

From the field of ancient Classical art, a wine container and a gravestone of a warrior have been selected. Because of its quality, preservation, and large size, this painted clay *Amphora*[288] is an outstanding example of Greek ceramic art. The frieze represents Leto mounting a chariot, with her children Apollo and Artemis. At the right is Hermes with his winged sandals, herald of the gods. On the other side is a standard image of Dionysus flanked by Maenads and Satyrs. By its style this vase can be dated in the late sixth century B.C. Like the first two selections, it may be called Archaic. A similar insistence on profile and frontal views leaves the picture surface unbroken by movement into depth. Space is suggested merely by overlapping areas, as at the base.

288

The artist, known as the Rycroft Painter, was particularly skilled in representing the anatomy of humans and horses. The process used here is called black-figure because the lacquer is applied flat within the silhouettes, while interior lines are incised with a stylus to expose the red clay beneath. (See the discussion in the entry for Bowdoin College, M E 1–3.)

Except for temple sculpture and grave reliefs, original marble sculpture from fifth-century Greece is rare. Most freestanding figures are copies made in Hellenistic or Roman times. The life-size *Gravestone of a Warrior*,[289] despite its evident damages, is therefore a precious possession. That its quality is of a high order may be seen by comparing it with a much coarser stele fragment in the same gallery, representing an old man. The Warrior could almost be placed beside the metope sculptures of the Parthenon, and is of slightly later date (420–410 B.C.). It is carved from the same Pentelic marble. The position of the figure approximates that of the famous *Spear Bearer* (known only in debased copies) by Polykleitos. The modeling of the exposed shoulder is especially vigorous, and the circular curve of the shield closes the easy upward swing of the limbs from the base at our left. Note how the modeling guides our eye around and across the torso, breaking up any sense of Archaic frontality and achieving a new sense of classic ease and repose.

Another much-damaged fragment from a fifth-century grave stele, a *Woman with a Jewel Box*, combines the columnar severity of drapery and the sense of human anatomy with much of the success of the Erechtheum Maidens on the Athenian Acropolis. In this figure the marble has a lovely reddish cast, resulting from its iron content.

The bronze *Bust of a Lady of the Antonine Period*,[290] 2 feet high, is an unusually refined example of Roman portraiture of the second century A.D., but without the energy of the *Bust of Elagabalus*, from the next century, at Boston (M A 60). Said to have been found in Anatolia, in Roman Asia Minor, it may represent a person of such high

289

290

station as one of the daughters of Marcus Aurelius. For such an image
of high society normal Roman realism is here softened. An extreme contrast is provided by Worcester's scowling and bloated figure of a man,
recumbent atop his clay cinerary urn, an Etruscan work of the second
century B.C. Such unflattering observation passed on to the Roman
artists of the Republic and continued into the Empire, despite a counter-
trend to imitate the high nobility of Greek art (see MA 232 and CT
63).

We skip some 350 years to consider the huge *Floor Mosaic from An-
tioch*291 (about A.D. 500), in the entrance court, a prize from an expedition sponsored in part by the Worcester Museum. Here the illusionism of earlier Roman mosaic (MA 269) has broken down into isolated
fragments of pink and greenish stones set against a flat light ground.
The forms of Byzantine art are already at hand, though as yet the intention is purely secular. This "carpet" style has practical advantages:
we may approach the mosaic from any direction, and we do not seem
to be stepping into a hole. Note how the pomegranate trees, set at
diagonals in the four corners, give structure to the composition.

The large bronze *Buckle*,292 engraved and silvered (7 by 3¼ inches),
is characteristic of the art of the Merovingians, who ruled France before the time of Charlemagne. It dates from the seventh century. Although such objects are rare today, they were produced in quantity for
the luxury trade. This example was found near Toulouse, in southern
France. The patterned and dotted ornament on the shaft is curiously
similar to that on the seventeenth-century African plaque from Benin,
in the Peabody Museum, Cambridge (MA 143)—indicating, of course,
no connection or influence, but the universal language of certain forms
of art.

As for the nomadic peoples who swept over Europe at the fall of the
Roman Empire, their art should caution us about calling them "barbarians," and even about using the term "Dark Ages" except in a very
relative sense. Art history is full of terms that originated in opprobrium
to express one culture's opinion of its superiority over another. For the
Greeks the Persians were also barbarians; the Italian Renaissance, look-

291

292

ing back to Classical Antiquity, regarded the intervening centuries as
a lowly midway station between two pinnacles of enlightenment; Gothic,
Baroque, Impressionist, Fauvist, and Cubist all were originally terms
signifying inferiority; while "primitive," as we have suggested before,
is best left to denote merely "early." However that may be, the art of
the barbarian invaders, seen in a very fine belated example in Worcester's
Merovingian buckle, passed on as a formative influence to the Irish
metalworkers and manuscript illuminators, and to Spain.

Outside the Metropolitan Museum of Art and the Cloisters in New
York and Harvard's Fogg Museum, Romanesque figure sculpture is by
no means plentiful in the United States. Worcester has a superb polychromed wood *Virgin and Child*,[293] 3 feet high, of the late twelfth
century from Autun, Burgundy, one of the greatest centers of Romanesque stone sculpture. As she appears in the photograph, the Autun
Virgin seems precariously unbalanced, not entirely because part of the
throne is missing. This fact serves to demonstrate how completely the
carver thought of his image in frontal terms, though one must admit
that the head expresses a wonderful roundness through the soft modeling of the cheeks.

Nearby, a gallery off the entrance court was remodeled in 1932 to
contain an entire Romanesque chapter house reconstructed after its removal from the former Benedictine priory of LeBas-Neuil, near Poitiers
in west central France. Dating like the Autun *Virgin* from the later
twelfth century, it shows the intrusion of the new Gothic method of
ribbed vault construction in an otherwise pure example of Romanesque
building.

The ivory relief (height 8 inches) of the *Virgin and Child*[294] is a
supreme example of the elegance and sophistication that marked Paris
of the fourteenth century. If it was not made there, we can be certain
that the craftsman was a close student of the fashions of Paris, where a
whole industry of ivory carving developed at this time. We may be
shocked to learn that this ivory was once gilded, though probably with

293

294

discretion. Today we enjoy the beauty of its texture, aged to the tone of natural wood. For a comparison to other ages, one must go to Praxiteles (see MA 59), to Leonardo da Vinci, and to Chinese sculpture of the Sung dynasty (MA 93). It would be difficult to find a better illustration of the change in European culture that occurred from about 1175 to 1325 than in a comparison between the wood Virgin and this exquisite Gothic masterpiece.

Similar elegance in fourteenth-century Italian panel painting, which was probably influenced by such portable Parisian art as the ivory just discussed, is seen in the art of Simone Martini of Siena (see MA 34) and in Worcester's 30-by-18-inch panel of *St. Agnes* with her symbolic Lamb of Purity, painted by a gifted follower. As courtly life grew more and more elaborate toward 1400 (after recovery, that is, from the ravages of the Black Plague of 1348), an art of almost unparalleled delicacy and grace became its natural expression. The ingredients of the style were Parisian and Sienese—their early union marked by the appearance of Simone Martini at the court of the Popes-in-exile at Avignon—plus an admixture of Flemish realism.

We see the end result in Worcester's superb little *Madonna of Humility in a Rose Garden*,[295] attributed safely to the Veronese painter Stefano da Verona (c. 1374–1438 or later). In this so-called International Gothic Style, which spread from Spain to Hungary, languid reverse curves, brilliant high-keyed color, boneless figures, buttery surfaces, and a tapestrylike profusion of ornament make up an enchanted world. The date of Stefano's painting is toward the middle of the fifteenth century, when the style was rapidly falling victim to the Florentine Renaissance, and had done so in centers more progressive than Verona. Renaissance Madonnas, like those of Masaccio and Donatello, are full-bodied humans enthroned in high majesty.

One can argue *ad nauseam* whether such late fifteenth-century Northern Madonnas as Worcester's superb example by the anonymous Master of the St. Ursula Legend[296] are "Renaissance" or "late Gothic." There are excellent claims for both sides of the controversy. Clearly the International Gothic Style is here only a distant memory and the knowledge

295

296

of anatomy owes much to the Florentines. Yet the space is ambiguous, lacking the measured depth of Renaissance perspective, and the drapery develops wayward rhythms independent of the forms beneath. The Virgin's sweetness is not worldly, but filled with medieval piety. This master, who owed much to Roger van der Weyden (see MA 66) and Dieric Bouts (see MA 100), seems to have worked mainly at Bruges, but appears to have had connections with Cologne as well. His name comes from an altarpiece at Bruges. In this painting the pale blue crown-bearing angels are set against a cinnamon ground and the cloth behind the Virgin is a deep yellow-green with violet edging. The Child holds an apple; he is thus the Second Adam, marking a new beginning for a sinful world.

The Miracle of St. Sylvester,[297] by Pesellino (c. 1422–57), whose real name was Francesco di Stefano, is a fully developed example of Florentine Renaissance art, albeit in relatively informal vein. Painted in tempera (the powdered colors were mixed with egg yolk) on a panel 12 by 31 inches, it formed (with two other panels now in the Doria Pamphili collection in Rome) the predella-base of an altarpiece. The sainted Pope, kneeling in prayer, brings a bull to life in the enthroned presence of the Emperor Constantine and his mother, St. Helena. Other witnesses to this proof of the power of the Christian God are representatives of pagan and Jewish religions. Above the slowly rising bull, the Jewish magician who had caused its death acknowledges his own defeat. The figures are methodically placed in a converging space laid out on the Florentine system of one-point perspective, invented in or about 1425, reputedly by the architect Filippo Brunelleschi. Pesellino once collaborated with the better-known Fra Filippo Lippi, and seems to have been greatly influenced by him. As the dress shown here is contemporary and Pesellino had a sharp eye, his paintings are an important source for the study of mid-fifteenth-century Florentine costume.

The Discovery of Honey by Bacchus,[298] a tempera panel 32 by 51 inches painted by the Florentine Piero di Cosimo (c. 1462– after 1515), takes us into a world of playful fantasy. Here the artist, described by

297

298

Vasari as a mad genius, has taken the story from Ovid. Bacchus stands
at the right, nude and very self-satisfied, beside a richly dressed Ariadne.
Beyond them a boisterous Silenus rides in on his donkey. A motley crew
of satyrs and humans bang on pots and kettles to make the bees settle
in a hollow tree, which looks strangely like a standing bear. Even the
landscape seems to oscillate between the everyday reality of the hill town
at the left and the almost sinister fantasy of the rock formations at the
right. Another fine work by Piero di Cosimo, *The Discovery of Wine*,
in Harvard's Fogg Art Museum, makes a pair with this one, commissioned for the house of Giovanni Vespucci in Florence. Still another,
at the Wadsworth Atheneum in Hartford, perhaps representing *Hylas
and the Nymphs*, is one of a group of six scenes of primitive man—as
imagined by an unfettered spirit.

It is hard to believe that the great Flemish tapestry of *The Last
Judgment*, which hangs in the entrance court, was made at about the
same time as Piero di Cosimo's painting. Such was the force of medieval
tradition in the European North, particularly in the decorative arts. Our
discussion of the tapestry art, however, is centered on another magnificent example at Manchester, N.H. (NH 19).

Portrait of a Man,[299] painted about 1555 by the Bergamask master
Giovanni Battista Moroni (active 1546/7–78), brings us to mid-cen-
tury Mannerist art as seen in the bronze sculpture of Benvenuto Cellini
(MA 42). In this large canvas, 3 feet high, the nervous contours flow
with great confidence, while the abstraction of the design is sealed at
the corner by a plain rectangular window frame. Note the clever coun-
terplay of minor diagonals in collar and cuffs, edged in coral. Degas
would have admired such a design had he known it. He too found delight in small diagonal projections—the point of an umbrella, a cigar
at a saucy angle, the brim of a top hat—just as Moroni found it in the
end of a sword and its scabbard.

We pass by a fine Bernardo Strozzi (see CT 14), the *Calling of
Matthew*, and an adequate early Rembrandt, *St. Bartholomew*, to consider two paintings by lesser Dutch masters of the seventeenth century
among many fine examples from this school owned at Worcester. Pieter
Saenredam (1597–1665), who specialized in church interiors, is seen
in the superb *St. Bavo Church, Haarlem*,[300] an oil on oak panel 28 by

299

300

22 inches, completed in 1660. Like Vermeer of Delft (MA 50), who was born thirty-five years later, Saenredam worked so slowly and painstakingly that scarcely fifty works are known by his (or by Vermeer's) hand. These masters, whom we may think of as progenitors of the twentieth-century Piet Mondrian (see CT 85), are at the opposite pole from prolific and rapid painters like Frans Hals and Rembrandt. Everything depends in their work on exact adjustments and balances. Less concerned with the play of light on surfaces than Vermeer, Saenredam in his austere compositions came closer than anything before Mondrian to approximating that ideal of orderliness which we associate with Dutch life—Hals, Rembrandt, and Vincent van Gogh to the contrary notwithstanding.

Gerrit Heda (active 1640–67), like his father Willem Claesz Heda, specialized in still-life painting at Haarlem. Worcester has a fine example[301] by Gerrit, an oil 31 by 25 inches, in which glassware, silver, pewter, and cloth are rendered with refinement and precision. Although such painting lies behind the art of Chardin (see MA 216) and the American William M. Harnett (see MA 220)—both discussed at the Springfield Museum of Fine Arts—Chardin arranged his forms more compactly and employed a fatter, more succulent medium, while Harnett insisted on such microscopic detail as to invite inspection rather than contemplation. Unlike Harnett, however, Heda does not crowd his canvas. There is space to breathe in, and room to savor the wonderful shapes of his glasses, as well as the subtle tones of olive, olive green, nut brown, and dark tan.

In Spanish painting at Worcester, Ribera, Alonso Cano, and Murillo are well represented, but the *Repentant Magdalene*[302] by El Greco (1541–1614) is so fine that, in its different way, it rivals Boston's *Fray Felix Paravicino* (MA 71). Blue is the dominant color of the Magdalen —a blue that reappears in Picasso's emaciated figures of the first years of the twentieth century; whereas Paravicino is seen in ashen grays, deep reds, and with skin tones like old parchment. The Magdalen's symbols, a skull and an ointment vase, exist in an unearthly light. The whole picture has a glow that requires an adjective that all writers use—no

301

302

other will do—phosphorescent. It was painted about 1577–80, not long after El Greco arrived in Toledo and some thirty years before the Paravicino portrait.

A happy outcome for the 1963 purchase of a freshly and vigorously painted *Head of a Girl,* attributed to Peter Paul Rubens, followed doubts about its authorship. It is now accepted as a superb example of Rubens's earthier assistant and pupil, Jacob Jordaens (1599–1678), from about 1615–20. Far better a fine Jordaens (who is otherwise not well represented in New England) than a not-quite Rubens!

Acquisition in 1963, after a long-term loan, of the portraits of Mr. and Mrs. John Freake gave Worcester the finest known examples of American painting in the 1670s. There are advantages to considering them now, in their seventeenth-century context, rather than as the beginning of a new line of development. We shall concentrate on the *Elizabeth Freake and Baby Mary*[303] because the portrait of the husband gave the anonymous artist less opportunity to show his mettle. In the absence of any evidence to demonstrate that such art evolved from prior work in the American settlements, we are forced to suppose that the Freake Painter was born in England and that he had some impression of provincial English painting of around 1620 and even of outmoded Elizabethan work. Obviously, the elegant imagery of Sir Anthony Van Dyck (1599–1641), court painter to Charles I, was no part of his experience. Yet the dimly seen red curtain echoes Baroque tradition even if nothing else does so. A date of c. 1674 is proposed from the fact that the marriage of the Freakes, in Boston, took place in 1661, and that Mary was the youngest of their eight children. If our painter inherited his passionate obsession with ornamental detail from English sources, it is still true that his sharp eye set a standard for realism that was to become the most basic characteristic of American painting until modern times. Miniature in appearance through its microscopic scale, the picture nevertheless measures 43 by 37 inches. Its airless rigidity (as later seen in Harnett, MA 220) by no means precludes sensitivity in two-dimensional design. Any doubt you may have on this score should be quickly dispelled by turning the illustration upside down and observing the interlocked rhythms.

303

It is generally agreed that the *Self-Portrait*[304] by Thomas Smith, a mariner who came to America around the middle of the century, is the earliest painting done in New England by a known painter. The naval battle, seen in the same position as landscape views in early Flemish portraits, involved English and Dutch forces, as the flags tell us, but it has not been identified. The annals of Harvard University's Corporation tell us that one Thomas Smith was paid four guineas in 1680 "for drawing Dr. Ames effigies." The Worcester portrait is usually dated c. 1690; that it is a self-portrait is demonstrated not only by the naval reference but also by the skull and the poem below it—in part, the poem reads, "Why why should I the World be minding / therein a World of Evils Finding. / Then Farewell World . . ." Other works by Captain Smith include the *Portrait of Captain George Curwin*, c. 1680, at the Essex Institute, Salem. Smith's bulky forms, including a more massive version of the Baroque curtain than in the Freake portrait, suggest a Dutch rather than an English origin, or at least that sort of Dutch painting brought to England in the early seventeenth century by such artists as Daniel Mytens, favored by James I and Prince Charles before the arrival of Van Dyck.

It is not often that we can compare artists of major importance in works of first quality in a museum of Worcester's relatively moderate size. In the field of British painting of the eighteenth century, however, the *Portrait of William James*[305] by William Hogarth (1697–1764) and the *Portrait of the Artist's Daughters*[306] by Thomas Gains-

304

305

306

borough (1727–88) give us such an opportunity. Furthermore, they allow us to compare England's two most original painters of the Century of the Enlightenment. Both were influenced by Rococo trends in French art. Hogarth limited the connection to a method of painting, while insisting on the virtues of middle-class English life. Gainsborough, equally chary of the boudoir overtones of the Louis XV style, created an image of diaphanous elegance that approached the earlier effects of Watteau (see MA 265). Indeed, Watteau and Gainsborough at his best may be called the most lyrical poets of eighteenth-century art.

William James, whose subject served as High Sheriff of Kent, characterizes the substantial country squire whom we meet in the pages of Henry Fielding. Hogarth painted him in 1744 at the age of forty. Undercutting the easy flattery that marred much of the portraiture of the day, Hogarth stressed his subject's moral integrity despite a good-humored suggestion of self-importance. The companion portrait of his wife, Elizabeth, is competent, but more standard fare. At a measurement of 30 by 25 inches they are of what was called "cabinet size," as are the general run of portraits of lesser personages in British and American art of the time. The internal painted oval frame is also standard.

When Gainsborough painted his daughters, about 1770, he was well established at the fashionable resort of Bath. Note the moist sparkle of highlights in the eye of the standing girl, and along the drawing instrument held by her older sister. The cool tones of their white and blue dresses suit the mood of quiet reverie. Hogarth, on the contrary, used bright colors in his forthright statement. For a double portrait the cabinet-size format was not appropriate, and Gainsborough has given us a full-dress performance on a canvas measuring 50 by 40 inches. Mary and Margaret, here aged about twenty-two and eighteen, were among his favorite subjects. Much has happened to him since the early 1750s, when he painted *Girl Seated in a Park*, already discussed at Yale (CT 54). Now silvery and fluid, his art has a languidness that approaches sadness. Attenuated forms—the statue, Mary's left hand—are especially close to Watteau, as are the complex rhythms and textures of the drapery. Even the bow that ties the picture-album in Margaret's lap seems to droop in sympathy with these frail creatures. Still faintly visible at the left is the original position of the older sister, facing in the opposite direction. Gainsborough's revised composition is surely a great improvement.

By the 1770s Gainsborough was independent enough to indulge his passion for landscape painting, for which there was little demand on the English market. Worcester owns a superb large example, 58 by 63 inches, of slightly earlier date, c. 1765. Later ones are more vaporous and the tones move away from browns and greens toward low-keyed lavenders.

Nineteenth-century painting and sculpture in Europe is not Worcester's strongest field, but two examples of highest quality demand inclusion here. *The Brooding Woman*,[307] painted in 1891 in Tahiti by Paul Gauguin (1848–1903), is unusually sculptural in the work of this master of flat decoration. (Compare the large picture in Boston's Museum of Fine Arts, MA 86.) Gauguin tended to oscillate between these poles, occasionally combining them, as here, in a wonderful synthesis.

The apricot, blue-violet, and yellow-green tones of this painting implied a voyage of discovery into uncharted seas of color. The sculptural aspect of Gauguin's art derived from two sources: his study of Far Eastern and primitive sculptures in the Paris museums and a deep appreciation of the art of Cézanne, by whom the Worcester Museum owns a superb oil sketch for the central figure in the *Card Players* (in the Barnes Foundation, Merion, Pa.). For a brilliant study of Gauguin's often bizarre responses to primitive and exotic arts, and his preparation in Paris and Brittany for the Tahitian adventure, I strongly recommend an essay in Robert Goldwater, *Primitivism in Modern Art* (revised edition, New York: Vintage Books, 1967, pages 63ff.).

Auguste Rodin (1840–1917) was a contemporary of the Impressionists—Claude Monet was born in the same year and Renoir a year later —and while it is easy to find connections between their fluid surfaces and Rodin's ever-fluctuating effects of light and shade, to call him an Impressionist sculptor would be an egregious error. It is helpful to remember that Rodin was only eight years older than Paul Gauguin, who, trained by Pissarro in Impressionist technique, quickly veered off to his own exotic version of the newly emerging Symbolism. Rodin avoided the exotic, but he carried Symbolism to the level of Michelangelesque Expressionism. Stated with fewer "isms," this means that Rodin has much more in common with Daumier (see MA 80) before him and later with Edward Munch (see CT 29) and Wilhelm Lehmbruck (see MA 240) than with his own contemporaries. It was with Daumier alone, however, that he shared a passion for the grandeur of Michelangelo.

Head of Sorrow: Portrait of Eleanora Duse[308] is in many ways a summation of Rodin's career. The double title is appropriate (but not always given), for the head had emerged by 1882 on two figures for the *Gates of Hell*, a gigantic undertaking that spanned most of Rodin's working years. In simplified form it is seen there as the head of the *Prodigal Son* (the whole figure is remarkably prophetic of Lehmbruck's art) and of Paolo in the group of *Paolo and Francesca*. Toward the end of his life Rodin planned to use the head in a monument to Joan of Arc for New York City, but the project was never carried out. In 1905, how-

307

308

ever, he reworked it into a portrait of the great Italian actress Eleanora Duse. Thus he combined the sublime universal—human anguish—with the particular, much as in Michelangelo's Medici Tomb effigies. As we have seen more than once in these pages, the continuity of an image, ever evolving, is one mark of genius. We think of Leonardo da Vinci's *Mona Lisa*, whose face appeared years before he met her and continued, androgynously, ever afterward, or of Cézanne's Mont-Ste-Victoire. Illuminating discussion of this and other facets of Rodin's art will be found in Albert Elsen, *Rodin* (New York: Museum of Modern Art, 1963).

American painting at Worcester starts out with the Freake portraits and Thomas Smith's self-portrait, already discussed. We pass over many superb eighteenth- and nineteenth-century examples only because the artists concerned have been studied in other museums. Do not miss, however, John Singleton Copley's *Portrait of John Bours*, c. 1761, with its brilliant sheen and elegant pose; or Ralph Earl's *William Carpenter*, 1779, a twelve-year-old in a bright red suit, painted in England not long after Yale's *Roger Sherman* (CT 75); or Gilbert Stuart's virtuoso oil sketch of *Mrs. Perez Morton*, c. 1802; or John F. Kensett's *Conway Valley, N.H.*, 1854; or Thomas Eakins's oil study for the head of *Dr. Gross* (the *Gross Clinic*, in Philadelphia, 1875, is his masterpiece); or Marsden Hartley's *Wave*, 1940, perhaps *his* masterpiece, at least among the later works.

Although the oil painting of John Singer Sargent (1856–1925) has been discussed on several occasions, to omit his brilliant watercolors would be unfortunate. Worcester owns one of the most spectacular, *Muddy Alligators*,[309] signed and dated 1917. Painted in Florida, it is unsurpassed in sheer virtuosity in this medium. Note how Sargent utilizes the white of the paper to achieve his sparkling effect. The alligators may be muddy, but Sargent's color certainly is not.

Worcester's collection of modern art is not large, but it contains good examples of oils by Kandinsky, Rouault, and Kline, and an impressive cast bronze by the Italian Arnaldo Pomodoro (born 1926). A sphere entitled *Rotante dal Foro Centrale* (1966), 7 feet in diameter, interrupts the perfection of a geometric form by signs of erosion and decay, as in the cylindrical *Ruota* at Ridgefield (CT 96), of five years earlier.

Pre-Columbian art at the museum is spectacular, especially as it is shown in a special modern gallery. Our single example, while only a sample of these riches, is only a bit over 4 inches high. Nevertheless, the

309

veined onyx *Pendant in the Form of a Mask*,[310] of classic Teotihuacán style, A.D. c. 500–700, rivals the grandeur of Old Kingdom Egyptian sculpture and that of the T'ang dynasty of China, which we now consider.

Worcester's Far Eastern section is also distinguished. Among its Chinese objects the over life-size *Head of the Buddha*,[311] carved in gray limestone, is considered one of the great examples of T'ang sculpture anywhere in the world. It came from the famous caves at Lung Mên. The reader may wish to review the discussion of Chinese art at the Boston Museum of Fine Arts and at the Fogg in Cambridge in order to clarify the position of this head as a masterwork of the "Classic" phase of Chinese culture. Comparison with the contemporary painted head from Tun-huang at the Fogg Museum (MA 136) will show how strong a connection existed between sculpture and painting during this period (A.D. 618–906).

In the Sung dynasty (960–1280) Chinese art became freer and less austere. Sculpture seems to have followed painting in striving for movement and more complex light and shade. The delightful little green bronze *Incense Burner*,[312] perhaps representing Lao-tzu, the founder of Taoism, on a water buffalo, perfectly exemplifies these trends. A most dangerous beast, the buffalo is tamed by the philosopher's exalted detachment from the unruly aspects of nature.

We conclude our long, but much too brief, survey of this outstanding museum with a small masterpiece, only 10 inches high, a Persian manu-

310

311

312

script illumination of the fifteenth century representing a *Giraffe with Its Keeper*.[313] It comes from a history of Tamerlane (1307–1404) and seems to have been executed at the beginning of the century. The strange beast was presented by the Sultan of Egypt to the ruler of Persia. The lavender background against a sky of gold sets the scene in hilly country. Such art became a major source of inspiration to Matisse, early in our century, and thus it lies behind the modern liberation of color as flat tone. It also became, more immediately, the basis for the manuscript art of Moslem India, of which we have discussed a fine example at the Fogg Museum (MA 138).

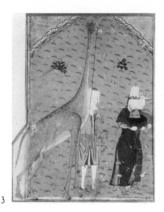

313

Index

Numbers refer to pages, not illustrations. In longer entries only the first page is indicated.

The Art Museums of New England

was designed by Jean LeGwin and set in linotype Garamond, a face designed by Claude Garamond, who died in 1561. Garamond lived and worked at a time when black-letter fonts were in course of being superseded in France by types based on the Renaissance hands we now call roman and italic. He derived his inspiration from the Aldine old face, and the influence of his work dominated European typefounding for the succeeding two centuries. Many punches cut by other hands were subsequently ascribed to him, including the historical prototypes of many of the revivals bearing his name at the present time. The roman is based on fonts recorded as Garamond's work in specimens issued in Germany between 1592 and 1702, and its italics derives from originals ascribed to Robert Granjon of Lyons in the same specimens. Both series were the work of R. Hunter Middleton, and were issued in 1930.

THE ART MUSEUMS OF NEW ENGLAND was composed by Lamb's Printing Company, Clinton, Massachusetts and printed on Monadnock's Greenfield Opaque. Halliday Lithograph, West Hanover, Massachusetts was the printer and binder.